HOME AND AWAY

Also by Karl Ove Knausgaard

A Time to Every Purpose Under Heaven
A Death in the Family: My Struggle Book 1
A Man in Love: My Struggle Book 2
Boyhood Island: My Struggle Book 3
Dancing in the Dark: My Struggle Book 4
Some Rain Must Fall: My Struggle Book 5

HOME AND AWAY

WRITING THE BEAUTIFUL GAME

KARL OVE KNAUSGAARD
AND FREDRIK EKELUND

Translated from the Norwegian by Don Bartlett and Seán Kinsella

ALFRED A. KNOPF CANADA

PUBLISHED BY ALFRED A. KNOPF CANADA

www.penguinrandomhouse.ca

Alfred A. Knopf Canada and colophon are registered trademarks.

This edition is a slight abridgement of the original Norwegian edition. The authors would like to thank Cathrine Sandnes for her work in abridging the text.

Library and Archives Canada Cataloguing in Publication

Hjemme-borte. English
Home and away : writing the beautiful game / Karl Ove Knausgård and Fredrik Ekelund ; translated by Don Bartlett and Seán Kinsella.

Translation of: Hjemme-borte.
Issued in print and electronic formats.

ISBN 978-0-345-81075-5
eBook ISBN 978-0-345-81077-9

1. Knausgård, Karl Ove, 1968– —Correspondence. 2. Ekelund, Fredrik, 1953–. —Correspondence. 3. Soccer in literature. I. Knausgård, Karl Ove, 1968–. Correspondence. Selections. English. II. Ekelund, Fredrik, 1953–. Correspondence. Selections. English. III. Title.

PT8951.21.N38Z4813 2017   839.82'374   C2016-905534-5

Cover image: © Image Source/Getty Images

Printed and bound in the United States of America

10 9 8 7 6 5 4 3 2 1

Penguin
Random House
KNOPF CANADA

HOME AND AWAY

Limhamn, 10 June

Dear Karl Ove,

Let me start off with a memory I have from 19 November 1983. I was in Paris devoting myself to my studies, living at the Cité Universitaire, writing for the now-defunct daily paper *Arbetet* and working on a dissertation about a French author I had discovered the year before, Georges Navel. This was a happy time in my life. In August of the same year I found out that my first novel *Malmö Dockers, Report!* had been accepted by Bonnier, and I was still on a high knowing I'm was to be what I'd dreamed of being for a long time: a writer. My days were spent attending the Collège de France listening to Michel Foucault and Emmanuel Le Roy Ladurie, or sneaking in to the École Normale and listening to Jacques Derrida. To sit at the feet of Foucault and Derrida only served to intensify the intellectual high I was living on at the time.

November 19 was the day before my thirty-second birthday. I was sitting in a student restaurant on the Boulevard Saint-Michel when a man with the stern, sad features of a South American Indian sat down across from me. We fell into conversation. It turned out he was Mexican and worked as a chemist on the nearby rue d'Assas. I'd been planning a small dinner party at my student bedsit to celebrate my birthday the following day, and on a whim I invited along Juan, as he was called. We became friends, began to socialise, and after a while I learned that he'd moved to Paris with an American woman with whom he had a child. He

1

settled down in the city, but after some time, he'd realised he was a homosexual, got divorced and was now living with a French man. One day we got around to talking about Octavio Paz. I expressed my admiration for the Mexican poet and informed my new friend that I wished to learn Spanish so as to be able to read Paz in the original, and I wondered if we, Juan and I, could read Paz together. And that's what happened. On a park bench in the Luxembourg Gardens. He read aloud to me. I repeated after him and savoured phrases like El laberinto de la soledad and A cinco años de Tlatelollo and the word soledad was so beautiful, I thought, it was worth learning a whole new language for that alone.

And that was how the door to Latin America opened for me.

The park bench in the Luxembourg Gardens allowed me – if you can say that every language is a house – to clamber into the Spanish house. The strange thing is I've always felt so at home there, as though Spanish had been waiting for me, or in me. There's an airiness, it's a language of beautiful sonorous vowel sounds and through it I ended up in Portuguese – NB: the Brazilian variant – also beautiful, but more difficult to pronounce, harder to comprehend and much more consonantal, without the same buoyancy.

So I'm off again. Latin America for, I think, about the twentieth time. On my first trip, in 1985, when I was flying to Chile, we had a stopover in Recife and on descending the aircraft steps I knelt down and kissed the ground. An intuitive act, a homage to the footballing heroes of my childhood, Pelé and Garrincha. I don't do it any more, kiss the ground that is, but I feel a powerful yearning, and mentally have already been there for some time.

Best wishes,
Fredrik

Glemmingebro, 11 June

Dear Fredrik,

At about the time you got off the plane in Rio de Janeiro I was at a parents' get-together for my eldest daughter's class, on the beach a few kilometres from here, where we first barbecued some sausages we had brought along, then played rounders: the third class against parents, with the shadows lengthening under the light of the setting sun. My plan was to write to you after the children had gone to bed, at around nine, but I was in the US just a few days ago and I still have jet lag; at half past eight I fell asleep fully clothed, with all the kids around me, and didn't wake up until half past one at night, surrounded by silence. Plan B was to write this morning. I had organised a nanny, as the Swedes call them here now, to come and take care of our four-month-old daughter while I was writing. Anne – that's our youngest daughter's name – is usually cheery and happy and never causes any trouble – she goes to sleep at half past eight and wakes up at six or half past – but today of all days, when I had to find time to write, she was screaming like a banshee. The nanny couldn't handle her, so I had to do it, calm her down first, then feed her and change her nappies – and when I handed her over, what happened? Another fit, she screamed so much her face went puce and tears rolled. I took over again, and when she was calm the nanny put her in the buggy. They are still out walking, in the summer drizzle. And I am writing at last.

From the letter you wrote yesterday I have drawn the obvious conclusion: you are a romantic. At least your writing felt romantic to me. Studies in Paris with Foucault and Derrida, meeting young South Americans – it reminds me of what Paris was for Latin American writers, especially Cortázar, who was exiled there for many years and who wrote some of the most fantastic stories I have ever read. Your words awaken a longing in me to be there and a sense that it is too late, I have missed the bus, all of the buses. But you were there. And your first book was accepted – that is also romantic, the young author in Paris. I, on the other hand, am a Protestant deep into my bones. I am the kind to deny myself things, to tell myself no, and if I like to read about wild, exuberant, extrovert, high-spirited lifestyles around the world, where energy is of the human variety, not material or financial, this is not a world I can inhabit, I can barely stand it, I turn away, long to be alone, I don't know how to relate to all this generosity and warmth.

Why am I writing this?

You have guessed correctly. Brazil is not for me. Nor is Brazilian life, which, granted, I have never experienced and only know through descriptions. Nor Brazilian football. During the 2002 World Cup in Korea and Japan, when Germany met Brazil, I supported Germany. I have never done that before and will probably never do so again. But it was the lesser of two evils. I watched the match with my brother, at a bar in Stockholm, and when Brazil scored he leaned forward and pointedly clapped in front of me, as if to say, you are so wrong, don't you see?

Not supporting Brazil, distancing myself from Brazilian football, is a bit like saying I prefer ugly to beautiful women. If I can choose I always pick the ugliest girl. Or, to take another example, and not one which will immediately be interpreted as sexist – it is like saying I prefer reading bad books to good ones.

It hasn't always been like this. When I was young I wanted to .

venture out into the world, I wanted to see, smell, hear and taste everything. I wanted life. I had visions of travelling down through Europe, doing odd jobs on the way, being abroad for many years while I wrote the Great Novel. I wanted to meet people, have adventures, fall in love, get drunk and affirm life. It didn't happen, I never went, instead I stayed in Bergen – never Paris, like you, nor South America – and set out on a slow, life-denying process, which has culminated here in a tiny rural village in Sweden, where I live, hardly meeting anyone and with no social life whatsoever (yesterday, at the parents' get-together, I didn't talk to anyone). I barely ever drink, and I eat very little, I am not interested in food at all. I have a constant guilty conscience because I work too little – it is not good to do nothing at all, just loaf around.

Thus your letter, which is all about youth and life, evokes strong yearnings in me. But I have missed the bus, and in the football World Cup, which starts tomorrow, I have strong sympathies for two teams, as always: Argentina and Italy. Both are traditionally cynical teams, as you know, which in their best years were always extremely well organised defensively and played on their opponents' weaknesses rather than their own strengths. They possess extreme qualities, but there is something about their never using them in an excessive manner, about their never doing anything beautiful for the sake of beauty, only if there is some outcome. And the fact that they can do so, but hold back, appeals to something deep inside me.

The first televised images I can remember are from the summer of 1978, the World Cup in Argentina. The sea of spectators in the stands, the confetti-strewn grass pitch, Ricardo Villa, Osvaldo Ardiles, Mario Kempes. I knew nothing about the political situation, of course, I was nine years old, but I was spellbound. Argentina, both the country and the team, represented an adventure for me. Later the adventure grew because I read Borges, I read Cortázar – and I am reading Cesar Aira now – and I read the exiled Polish author Witold Gombrowicz. (His diaries are brilliant, they were written in Argentina, and when he goes to Paris at the end, to the Old World, it is as though his diaries die, they lose all their vitality, all their power – did they come from his exile in Buenos Aires?) There is a lot of romanticism in this, but it is a different kind from the romanticism I see in you and your letter – for the simple reason that the Brazil you affirm is a physical entity in your life; you have been to Brazil countless times, you have friends there, and you have intimate knowledge of the culture – you know the language, you have translated Brazilian literature into Swedish – and you play football like a Brazilian. That above all else! For you Brazil is life lived, it is alive. Argentina for me? I have never been there, it is no more than a dream, fantasies, anchored nowhere else but in the books I have read. It is the opposite of lived, the opposite of alive, it is non-life, which in its extreme form is life-denying – and that was why the working title of my last novel, which came to be called *Min Kamp*, was for a long time *Argentina*.

Tomorrow the World Cup starts. I am happy. I remember all the world championships from 1978, what I was doing, how I was living, who I was and the world in which the contests existed. But I have always watched them on TV, never in reality, and I would like to continue doing this – so that is the basis for this book, isn't it? Life versus death, yes versus no, Brazil versus Argentina.

All the best,
Karl Ove

Rua Assunção 174, Botafogo, Rio, 11 June

Dear Karl Ove,

I've landed now. It's so dreamlike, this world of airports and planes. The sense of alienation in the departure halls, everyone transformed into mere bodies, like large lumps of meat in suits and dresses. And almost everybody with such closed faces. How did it become the norm to take your seat before a transatlantic flight without so much as a hello to your closest fellow passengers?

On the plane I read Rubens Figueiredo, an author from Rio who writes fantastic short stories set in surreal jungle landscapes. Afterwards I anaesthetised myself with a whisky, followed by three glasses of red wine and a sleeping pill. Woke up refreshed and then, only then – after ten hours this is – did I speak to the woman sitting next to me, a lady in her forties from Rio. One word, Karl Ove, a little knock on an unfamiliar door, and then the world opens up. I avoid this type of contact all too often but I do love it. She worked as a beautician, had her own salon in Rio and had just been to Moscow and Vienna with two colleagues. Suddenly she's showing me photos of her son, a twenty-year-old young pro at Cagliari. Then she went on to describe herself as a flamenguista doente (a fanatical Flamengo supporter) and laughed, and when I said I was going to stay in Botafogo she suggested I share a taxi with her friend Patricia, which I did, and thus ended up engaged in intense conversation with another beauty-salon proprietor as our taxi sped through the Rio morning, through the bleak, poor, northern part of the city, wet and grey under heavy rainclouds, on a motorway where balas perdidas (stray bullets) are never far from your mind on account of the two gangs with territory on either side of the road, who are at constant war with one another, and it's said that people in passing cars have been hit by bullets. Innocent people die this way every year in Rio: sleeping at home, making love in a luxury hotel, mothers on their way to kindergarten or taxi drivers just doing their job.

That thought is never far from my mind here: sudden death.

They dropped me off by a rusty iron gate at Rua Assunção 174, where my bleary-eyed host – it was seven in the morning when I arrived – was there to welcome me. His name is Afonso Machado, a musician by trade, a guitarist who's played with many of the greats, including Chico Buarque and Elza Soares. I have my own room in Afonso's old house, which is enclosed by the jungle, a rock face, other houses and some blocks of flats.

Now I'm ensconced in my own world: a little library, TV, CD player, my own books and a printer. What bliss it is, come what may, to create your own world and workspace. That's where I'm writing to you from, and looking out of the open window I can see a patch of sky, two high-rises and every ten minutes an internal flight coming in to land. This is also historic ground in the footballing sense, because only a few hundred metres from where I am sitting is Fluminense's old stadium, with its chateau-like facade, and it was on this pitch that Brazil became South American champions for the first time in 1919, with a goal in extra time by Arthur Friedenreich, the Afro-Brazilian who wanted to be white.

I hit it off with Afonso right away, he has a twinkle in his eye, a ready smile on his lips, a warm charm coupled with, like so many people here, a Rio-ish, listless, casual quality, not ironic nor affected but quite natural. He laid on breakfast, and after a few minutes we ended up where you usually end up here, in the world of football. He is Botafogo. That's what they say. You are your team, you aren't content with merely supporting them. And it wasn't long before we were talking about Garrincha, Botafogo's best player ever. I told him about the film Lasse Westman and I made about Garrincha's Swedish son, Ulf Lindberg. Afonso told me that he'd toured with Elza Soares, who'd been in a tempestuous relationship with Garrincha for many years, and about her voice, about how incredible he thought it was, and still is. And then he told me, between mouthfuls, that his father used to take him to the Maracanã Stadium when he was a little boy to see Botafogo, and that he'd been there that day in 1962 when Botafogo beat Flamengo 3–0 in front of 160,000 spectators, in the final of the Rio State Championship, possibly Garrincha's best game ever, certainly on a par with the one in the group stages in 1958 between Brazil and the Soviet Union in Ullevi.

Yes, it's true what you wrote, that at a certain age we're extremely receptive to new impressions and they never leave us. The first World Cup to seep into your pores was in 1978, hence your love for Argentina. My first World Cup was in 1970, when Pelé was at the height of his career and Brazil, according to many, had the best national team that has ever existed. But, and this is an important but, I shy away from your dichotomisation, your either-or, having to be one thing or the other when often we realise – or at least I do! – we are both. When I was twelve, England won the World Cup with players like Bobby Charlton, Bobby Moore, Nobby Stiles and Alan Ball. Players I would take to my heart, not least Moore, whom I thought so manly and handsome and therefore – or so I imagined at the time – also skilful. I loved the total football of the Dutch: Cruyff and Neeskens were emissaries from a new world. I have a mental index of great German football players I admire (Seeler, Beckenbauer, Netzer, Rummenigge, Littbarski and Hässler, for example) and I also liked the Argentinian team that won in 1978, especially Kempes, that force of nature, and the way he raced forward through the blizzard of confetti, no one able to stop him, and Maradona, Karl Ove, oh my God! There's no other football player – with the exception of Garrincha – I've revered more than el pibe de oro. One of the highpoints in my life was meeting him in Florence in 1990, after that game in the last sixteen between Argentina and Brazil, which he effectively sealed with that miraculous dribble from midfield before releasing the ball to Caniggia. I was sitting in the front row at the post-match press conference, completely in thrall: the intelligent eyes, the quick replies and the modesty he displayed towards their crushed opponents. As the press conference ends, he gets to his feet, and then, suddenly, I hear myself say, Diego, por favor! Whereupon he, who was so abhorred and traduced in Italy, turns, walks over and signs his autograph in the notepad I'm holding out. And at the same instant the two-hundred-strong crowd of sports journalists all undergo the same transformation as me: they revert to being little boys and storm the podium, allowing me to sneak away with my precious, later to be framed, prize. By all means, let's keep some sort of football debate alive, but then surely Brazil–Italy or Brazil–England/Germany are better suited as opposite poles, and the match in Barcelona in 1982 (Italy–Brazil, 3–2) must certainly have embodied this contrast between 'the Brazilian style of play' (whatever that may be) and 'the Italian' (whatever that is).

Tonight I'm having dinner with Afonso somewhere here in Botafogo, and that brings to mind what you wrote about food, drink and women, and I can't help but experience a tinge of sadness when I think about it since it's so at odds with how I perceive these things: I love food and drink, and sometimes feel, at a heaving table in the company of good friends, or at a steakhouse like Porcão here in Rio (all you can eat for a set price), that I'm not human, I want to become one with what I eat, an internal rapture takes hold of me (at home Marianne and the kids are in the habit of pointing out that I make a sort of low humming sound to myself when I'm in that state), which is also the case with wine, beer and spirits, I keep trying to go further and further, into something else, something greater – something Dionysian? And what you wrote about women, I don't understand that either. Or rather I understand, but for me it's the opposite. When a beautiful woman enters the room I feel an electric current pass through me, it happens often and it isn't Jorge Amado's desire to bed all the women in the world, but some sort of beauty worship, the fleeting joy at being privileged enough to partake in the mystery of beauty. Since that kind of thing was already taboo, in the Protestant sense, then in the Maoist (read: hyper-Protestant) 1970s I could sometimes find myself, on impulse, fighting all manifestations of Eros within, wanting to be castrated and transformed into an utterly asexual and enlightened being in which all human activity was reduced to reasoning and dialectics. God help us!

I'm signing off for the day. Copacabana is next on the list. Hopefully a game of beach football with old friends, but a dip in the ocean at the very least, followed by one, or maybe two, caipirinha(s).

Best wishes,
Fredrik

Dear Fredrik,

I have been interested in football for as long as I can remember. Some of my very first memories are about football, I was perhaps five years old, or six, and we played in the fields near where we lived, sometimes there would be throngs of kids, sometimes only two or three, but it was one activity we did which filled us with joy: a ball, a pitch and two jackets as a goal. Oh, the shouts that rang out through the evening air, the ball, heavy and slippery or dry and light with the bladder showing between the leather laces, the constant excitement, and the disappointment when the first boys began to go home and the teams had to be shuffled, perhaps only two against two until that no longer worked, either because it was too dark or the last diehards had slunk off home. Autumn in the rain, winter in the snow, spring in the mud, summer in the heat: football, football, football. On the tarmac outside the house, on the gently sloping meadow, on the plateau behind the mountain, down towards the sea, on the field of hard-trampled earth in the forest. I remember once a tournament was organised, anyone could sign up a team and all of us living in the same road did. That excitement. We cycled a few kilometres to get there, and we had team kit (T-shirts all more or less the same colour), and we played on a proper pitch against a proper team. It is one of the strongest childhood memories I have, that day. I think, if I am honest with myself and view the various stages of my life democratically, with equal rights to each, that day, when we scraped together a team and played the whole tournament, is one of the greatest times of my life. I was in goal, I wanted to be a keeper then, I could only hurl myself to one side, to the left, but when I was seven and began to play team football (for the juniors in Trauma – a name all my mother's psychiatric nurse colleagues laughed at when they saw it on the back of our track suits), there was already a keeper and I played out of goal. We trained twice a week, I remember, and we had a match every week in the season. Not only that, we played at home in the evenings, and in every single break at school. The team I played for had five or six talented players, we used to win our games by large margins, often double figures, and I think we won the league every year I was in the team – which means until we moved, when I was thirteen. We took part in the Norway Cup in the summers, reaching the last sixteen one year, where we met Tromsø, and all their players were a head taller than us. I played in midfield and was not one of the better footballers, even though I longed to be and could spend hours and hours banging a ball against an enormous wall during those endless, lazy, boring summer days, or sneak onto a grass pitch with a friend and take penalties for hours on end, but that was never the real point, that wasn't why I played football, it was because it was always, without fail, fun. It was never boring. It was always exciting. And perhaps, I think now, everything else lost importance, that was the point, you did something together, everyone was in on it, no one was excluded, and you disappeared inside yourself. Playing football was like being somewhere, it was like your own world inside a world, with its own rules, where I was happy. Yes, for Christ's sake, that was what it was all about: happiness. Being somewhere else apart from inside yourself. This continued right up to the age of sixteen. Then I began to have other ideas about myself, and not being good at football suddenly got in the way, I was listening to British post-punk, music was immeasurably important, and I could only have justified continuing to play if I was really good, then it would have been possible to continue with dignity, but I wasn't, and I stopped. At the same time I started drinking and found something similar in alcohol: a world inside a world where other rules applied and where you could disappear from yourself. But I didn't stop watching football. My teams were IK Start in Norway, Liverpool in England and, every fourth year, in the World Cup, as I said, Italy and Argentina.

At that time, in the 70s, football wasn't as commercial as it is now, it wasn't as big, it wasn't something everyone did or followed. In my class there were perhaps five boys who got involved. There was hardly any football on TV – there was the pools match every Saturday, from the English First Division, and then there was the FA Cup in May, a big day, and then the two finals of the European Cup and the Cup Winners' Cup, also in May. In addition, there were the Norwegian international games. I grew up in a football family. My paternal grandfather, who lived in Kristiansand, cycled to the stadium every other Sunday and watched IK Start's home matches. I remember the excitement, the street down from our house was full of fans as kick-off approached, and again when the whistle had blown for full time, and you could always tell how the game had gone by Grandad's face. He used to talk disparagingly about the team, they were bad, but that was mostly a way of speaking because the next Sunday, there he was, on his bike, presumably hope sprang eternal. We were there because my dad used to watch the home games as well, and in time my brother and I joined him. Going to football matches was one of the few things my brother and I did with our father, and it was one of the few things we did as a family with many others. I still get shivers down my spine when I hear the roar from a stadium. IK Start won the league for the first time in 1978, I suppose I must have seen some of the games, but don't remember any. However, I do remember my dad driving into Kristiansand in midweek once, it must have been the year after, in 1979, because they were playing Eintracht Frankfurt in the UEFA Cup. This was a big experience for my father, a German team in Kristiansand Stadium. We went to several away games, I remember only a few of them, sitting in the car almost all morning, sitting in the opponents' stadium for two hours, then the long trip home, in the darkness. I recall a match against Mjøndalen, or the brown shirts as they were called, rather inappropriately. In 1980 I was at Kristiansand Stadium when Start won the league for the second time and we invaded the pitch. Afterwards I stood cheering the team from beneath the changing room, they came out and threw their shirts down, I grabbed one, Svein Mathisen's, but a grown man tore it out of my hands. Oh, the names of these players, they bring back a whole world: Svein Mathisen, Helge Skuseth, Reidar Flaa, Trond Petersen, Roy Amundsen, Steinar Aase. I read football magazines, I read all the sports pages in the papers after games, I watched all the televised football there was. The fact that there wasn't much was probably part of the joy. Seeing the likes of AC Milan or Real Madrid or Bayern München was such a rarity that it felt like a gift, a moment of grace. In a world where everything really did revolve around football the World Cup was truly exceptional. Matches every day, many of them with players I had only read about. The first World Cup I was big enough to take in ... was that 1982? France then, with Roucheteau on the wing, the classic long-haired mazy winger, do you remember him, Fredrik? The match against Germany. I still maintain it is the best game I have ever seen. I grieved for days afterwards; in fact, 'grief' is the only word that covers, to any satisfactory degree, the emotions I felt.

And isn't it incredible that the same World Cup also had Zico and Socrates for Brazil, and Paulo Rossi for Italy? For me there are three separate realities which I keep, each in their own compartment, in the weft of my memories. The matches, they are there, but also the whole world I watched them from. In 1998 I remember Argentina v. England and my first novel coming out, but also, somehow partitioned off from everything else, Brazil v. Norway, the penalty kick in the final minutes which I couldn't watch, my brother's strangulated voice on the phone afterwards because we had beaten Brazil to take the second qualifying place. I saw the game in Molde, and in the streets afterwards everyone was hugging everyone else, friends and strangers alike. The 2002 World Cup, when Italy were robbed by the referee, I watched the game in Stockholm, in an Italian coffee bar and was more in love than I had ever been – it was the time matches were broadcast in the morning. We lay in bed watching football. Sweden v. Argentina, then the game when Sweden were knocked out, after Anders Svensson turned past a defender in the box and shot against the post. The 2006 World Cup, we had two children then and the final with them in a Bergen hotel room, outside it was dark, lightning flashed, I seem to remember, and Zidane, whose every move was a joy to behold, he has to be one of the greatest European players ever, headbutted Materazzi. And then Spain in the last World Cup, which we saw here, we had rented a house, went swimming in the morning, were shown round houses afterwards – and at length we bought this house! – in the evening we saw two games. It was a perfect summer, as all World Cup summers are.

Thank you for your letter. I didn't get it until late in the day and read it in bed before going to sleep, with a slight blush on the cheeks because it deals with reality while mine didn't. I wrote about theories, which I examined closely and caricatured, and actually I was quite happy with my efforts, I reached the point where everything hung between life and death, yes and no, all or nothing. Your letter kindly corrected this, not by making a comment but being an example of something else – to wit, complexity. This often happens to me, I write something which sounds good enough, only to realise, after an hour to several years later, that it is never like that, never so simple, never one thing or the other. This is actually a question of distance and is a fundamental literary issue, I think: writing establishes a distance to what you are writing, and distance simplifies. Form simplifies even further. If you consider literature an autonomous entity it is no problem, then it has no responsibility for what it represents. If, however, you want to write about life, simplification is a great danger, which you must constantly guard against. You do that by going as close as you can to where all the broad sweeps, all the higher-level generalisations, no longer apply and are nowhere apparent. For me, the way I see it, this is the task of literature. Not necessarily in the form of realism and description of reality, but as a stubborn, tireless insistence on, and search for, the disintegration of the structure of that which we know. In life things look different, there it is almost the opposite, simplification and generalisation are necessary, they constitute the framework for the everyday and for life with others, the absence of which would make everything chaotic and confusing. This is abstract, I know, just an idea I have had, maybe even an idée fixe, but it is based on experience, and of a quite specific kind: Linda, my wife, is bipolar and during those periods in her life when the inherent mood swings are not held in check it is as though her personality is in flux, from down, where everything is mute and silent, immovable and impossible, to up, where everything is open, movable, possible, life-affirming, and all the levels imaginable between the extremes. So life at home has been about seeking stability, rules, fixed repeatable patterns – routines have been a way through the chaos and confusion, and this has worked well, we are fine, all of us. But a person you know so well, the way you can only know someone you have lived with for many years, suddenly changing, being in flux, makes me wonder what personality really is, what character really is. I am used to regarding it as something fixed, a core, unchanging. With some variation of course – we all know a man or a woman who gets a new lease of life and starts doing different, previously alien, things – yet is still recognisable and relatively together. On reflection, there is not much I don't know about my friends, most I have a clear picture of – he is like this, she is like that – and it is within this simplification I socialise with them. The distance such generalisations create is necessary for social life to function. That is why we almost never lay bare our souls, and if it happens – as it does now and then, there is always someone who cannot stay within reasonable limits – it is unpleasant, unbearable, a burden to us, and then it is a relief to get away. In literature it is the opposite: there it is precisely the breaches we look for, both as a writer and a reader. There it is the disintegration that is important. It is as though it is a pragmatic truth which we live by, and thus an essential truth which perhaps we know, perhaps we don't, but which we seldom deal with. It appears in crises, when someone dies, when someone is born, when someone falls in love, when all the rules, all the limits are lifted in one fell swoop.

I hope you're well over there, Fredrik – live a little for me too!

All the best,
Karl Ove

Botafogo, 12 June

Dear Karl Ove,

I have a sharp image of you in my mind's eye from a few years back, when I guess you would have been in the middle of working on the third or fourth book in your series. I was in my car on Skolgatan, waiting for a couple of musicians I was taking to a performance we were giving. I was parked by Pizza Siciliana when you came along. It was bucketing down, I had the windscreen wipers on, and there, in the rain, with a tight grip on the stroller and with that serious, focused gaze you have, you looked like the captain of a ship in a storm with children hanging from and holding on to every corner of the stroller, and right now, as I set these words down, I see this image again – OK, so you had only collected the children from kindergarten but still – this steely determination of yours to stride onward, with life, with the kids, love, Linda and your writing, this is your forte. No one can stop you. Nothing can stop you. And then you disappeared down the street, like a phantasm washed away by the rain.

'Lay bare our souls'? Yes, it's strange. We socialise, live and toil side by side: companions, lovers, colleagues, childhood friends and yet we know so infinitesimally little about each other and so seldom see each other. Truly look into one another's eyes. And we're so fearful whenever it happens. I've attempted to change this over the years and now try to look into other people's faces, make a conscious effort to meet their gaze to see what is going on, but also because I desire reality, intensity, life, which is probably something to do with the fact that I'm getting older and was, as you know, sixty last autumn, and I want everything to be real, tangible. I don't want to squander the time I have left on sleepwalking through conversations, sleepwalking through life, and that's also why I'm irritated when people yawn and I'm annoyed by people who don't want to do anything with their lives, or leave dinner parties or social occasions early. I'm aware, Karl Ove, this must seem like a kind of hysterical overreaction, and perhaps it is a symptom of despair. I can accept that and believe it might be due to my surviving prostate cancer eight years ago. After the operation was over, and when it became clear that I would still be capable of an erection, I promised myself that from then on I would strive for everything to have meaning and intensity, there would be no relapse into a somnambulant life.

Now, I'm not going to claim that this has been the case, but the ambition is still there, and perhaps that is what you're referring to when you use the term bon vivant. Yes, I want everything to taste. And yesterday something occurred that's tied into that. After finishing my letter to you, I walked to the metro station and took the train to Cantagalo, a stop in Copacabana, and when I emerged up on Rua Barata Ribeiro I felt a tingle in my chest, a sensation of being present, a feeling of happiness. You're here, now! Right at this instant you're here, in the middle of this throng, in the middle of this reality, and the bars are packed and the traffic is thundering by, and there, at the end of the street, off in the distance like a blue fleck: the Atlantic.

It was at this moment I truly landed here, but my excitement wasn't because of the World Cup but with being in Rio and Brazil, the joy of being in a place which, more and more, I do not understand. Every time I comment on 'Brazil', I feel as though what I'm talking about slips through my hands, like a bar of soap, an eel, something which doesn't allow itself to be captured, and in the course of a conversation with a friend here, Lennart Palméus, a former seaman who now owns a seaside hotel, I told him that no matter how much I read about Brazil, or how often I am here, it still feels as though I will never quite understand. A smile flitted across his weather-beaten features and he laughed, this man who has lived here for thirty years and has four children with a Brazilian woman, and he said, 'Fredrik, that's exactly what it's like for me too!' What would you put that down to? Give me France, Italy, Germany, Argentina or any number of other countries and I feel I can understand, give some kind of rationale, but it's not possible with Brazil, and the reason for this, as far as I can make out, is Africa. I know too little about Africa and African religion and culture, because Brazil is Africa, Portugal, France, Holland and diverse indigenous Indian cultures in one heady brew, so-called syncretism. In our European world we are almost always either/or, here they are often one thing as well as the other.

So I made my way towards 'the fleck', the ocean, down to the beach and past the bars filled with supporters from across the globe. After which I dived into the waves. I took in the view of container ships on the line of the horizon, the Sugarloaf, the high-rises along the beachfront, and then jogged along the shore and followed up with some stretching exercises, before taking the few nervous steps over to the pitches at Posto 4, where a game was well under way.

I stand on the sideline, following with interest, and then comes the question. You want to play? And when I answer, Sim, quero jogar (Yes, I want to play) I'm greeted by a broad smile from o ladrão (the thief) as he's called. I've played with these guys quite a number of times over the years, but new faces pop up all the time, although I always recognise a good few of them, two in particular. (They play every day at 5 p.m., every day, Karl Ove! All year round.) These two are frighteningly good and exhibit almost total ball control in the deep sand (beach football is difficult, you need to get the ball up and hit it while it's in the air, playing the ball on the sand requires a real delicacy of touch, but these two are experts). I'm fascinated by one of them, and could watch him for hours. He has a rather stern demeanour, never laughs and spits abuse nearly the whole time (Porra! Filho da puta!) as though impelled by an innate compulsion or a genetic disorder (and if a 'refereeing decision' goes against him his behaviour regresses to the infantile, and he bawls and screams until he gets his way) but what a shot he has! Oh my God! In a fraction of a second he'll flick the ball up into the air and volley it over the sand like a comet. This world, the grass-roots game, is more real and filled with joy for me than the World Cup. That's how it's always been. That magic feeling of having the ball at your feet has always been greater than the experience of the spectator, but I'd be lying if I said that I haven't been deeply passionate when occupying the role of a fan as well. First and foremost at Malmö Stadium, but also, from time to time, when the national side is involved. There are other teams that stir my blood too, and it's interesting you should bring up two matches that have left an impression on me as well, France–West Germany in 1982 and Sweden–Senegal in 2002.

It still hurts me to think of the French game. I watched it in a café in Arles. I was working as a coach driver in France for a group of twenty-two photographers who were at a festival there. None of them was interested in football so I saw it on my own. The previous year I'd sunk into a prolonged depression, but now everything had turned around. I had gone from one extreme to the other and was head over heels in love with a French woman who had been my teacher in Lund. She was in Paris and I was heading there afterwards. My mind was as much filled with her, the things she said, her face, her beauty, as with that unbelievable game of football, which of course became a parody of all we are wont to perceive as 'French' and 'German', elegance against efficiency, and if it had just been the Germans winning, then you could have reconciled yourself to the result. It's healthy for o jogo bonito (the beautiful game) to be taken down a peg or two now and again, but the brutality of Schumacher's assault on Battiston was criminal. Not only should he have been sent off, he should have been sentenced to six months or more in prison, a serious sanction.

Based on the result of that game, I've devised a little theory: there are two parallel World Cup histories, an objective one (set in statistics and results) and a football lover's parallel truth of the World Cup, and in this coexistent world, which is also the world of the memory, it is France, with Platini, Tigana, Giresse & Co. who are the winners, the ones we remember. The same goes for 1954, the 'actual' winners that time were the Hungarian team with Puskas at the forefront. Or in 1974, Holland with Cruyff and Neeskens, who won our hearts . . . two verbal moods confront each other here. The subjunctive (the world as it might be) and the indicative (the world as it is), and as we know, Germany are very good at indicative football.

The other match you mention has also left its mark on me, perhaps to an even greater extent since Sweden were involved. The quarter-final against Senegal in 2002. I'd been sitting in the Swedish Television World Cup studio the previous evening with, among others, the former manager of the Norwegian team, Drillo, and had returned to my hotel for the night. The match against Senegal was due to be played early in the morning. I was woken at dawn by screaming from the street below: Fuck off, you coked-up cow! I presumed it was some desperate Östermalm schoolkid breaking up with his girlfriend. The words cut through the morning air and lingered like an echo in me throughout the game, which I watched from my hotel bed. A somnambulant Lagerbäck didn't have the guts to bring on Zlatan early in the game, and, well, the rest we know. That's the way footballing memories stay with us, mingled with everything else, and sometimes the period around a World Cup can be a time marker, a bit like pop music, which we associate with all kinds of events in our own lives.

It's getting close now. It's 1:14 p.m., the Brazil–Croatia match starts at 5 p.m. here, and in the background I can hear a few car horns blaring. I'm going to watch it on the big screen at Copacabana. What is a World Cup really? One big theatre of dreams, and it's these moments, prior to the first kick-off, which loom largest. When all the supporters' dreams are still alive and intact. The Brazilians, the Argentinians, the Germans and the Italians, for example, dream of gold, just like the Iranians, the Australians, the Cameroonians and Swiss dream of getting beyond the group stage. It is beautiful. The party is still alive. Everyone has arrived. The table is laid. No one has been forced to go home yet, and that first melancholic sense of decay – the withering of the first flowers – and of the end being close, the reality of loss, of defeat, has yet to set in. There is after all – this is my fourth World Cup – a strong feeling of melancholy around the tournament too, an emptiness even, that creeps up on you after the group stages, not to mention when the semi-finals are getting close. Then there are only four happy people left at the table while all the others have left the party.

Best wishes,
Fredrik

Glemmingebro, 13 June

Dear Fredrik,

It has started. The very special sound that TVs make on summer evenings when it is warm and dark outside, the constant cheering, the excited commentators; you can watch or not, but it will still define the time, frame the moment, in a historic way even while it is ongoing: Summer 2014.

I supported Croatia yesterday. I have always liked the team, the footballing country which has produced so many technically gifted players yet has also had an ugly side to its play, an element of brutality in its game, which has always crossed the line. Yesterday they didn't, there were a couple of scything tackles, one by Corluka particularly caught my eye, but all teams do that nowadays. No, it was the velocity of their game that was so remarkable. Modric runs like the wind, he has something all his own, everything he does is propelled by forward motion, not a defensive thought enters his head. The ball has to be won, the ball has to go forward and it has to be at speed. I had the feeling they were playing to the limits of their abilities, giving everything they had, beyond this there was nothing. Even when they took the lead after eleven minutes and were clearly the better team, I didn't think they would win, they have a different kind of composure in Brazil, the frenetic, almost manic play that Croatia offered was slowly ground down, or so it felt, by a team that is solid above all else but also has a greater repertoire. I watched Gustavo and Paulinho in particular. Paulinho had a bad game, he was almost totally uninvolved – I don't really know what he can do because when I've seen him play at Tottenham he has cut a pale, marginal figure – while Gustavo was brilliant, he did everything right and allowed the team to relax. Totally unspectacular, totally uncomplicated, but impeccable, stable, composed. Even if Oscar was good yesterday and pulled off some sensational dribbles, tightly marked by three men, whom unbelievably he ran past, and even if Neymar showed flashes of brilliance, there is still something about this team that doesn't allow me to believe they can go the whole way. They have a pair of excellent midfield stoppers, but the backs, Alves and Marcelo, are not the strongest defensively, Alves especially was easy to get past yesterday. They have a good defensive midfield, but Neymar, Oscar, Hulk and Fred, are they really good enough to take them to the final? Just think who Argentina have got in the same positions – Di María, Higuaín, Messi and Agüero . . .

I supported Croatia but realised early on they wouldn't do it, and then I fell asleep! I couldn't keep my eyes open. It was half past ten, the children were up, but even though I had been looking forward to this game for several months and even though I really tried, constantly changing position and forcing myself to concentrate, I went out like a light around the thirtieth minute. I woke up with five minutes left. I saw the goals in the round-up after the game, semi-delirious, and went to bed, once again in a quiet, darkened house. I'm beginning to wonder if I have narcolepsy . . . But it is just jet lag, and on top of that I must be extremely tired. I have been on the road promoting my book for three weeks, and nothing taxes the soul like that – and it is my soul that is tired, that wants to sleep.

Yesterday I was woken by Anne at half past four, she was babbling away in her cot beside me. I heated some milk and gave it to her, then I went to the kitchen and living room and tidied them while she lay happily in bed – we've got a home help who comes once a week, and for her I feel things mustn't be in too much of a mess. At half past six I woke the other children, it was their last day of school and relatively easy to see them off. First Heidi and John, whose school is a few hundred metres from here, I take our stupid dog with me and Anne in the buggy – afterwards I walk with Vanja, who catches the bus half an hour later. Once that was behind me I did some more tidying, sterilised the bottles and mixed some milk which the nanny would use – I hired her for a couple of days so that I would have time to write this – and when she and the home help came, I slipped in here, into the little shed I use as a study, and worked for a few hours. How does that make me feel? Having two women work for me? Yes, doesn't it create solidarity with the working class, Fredrik? At half past one I collected Linda from Ystad Station, she has been in Helsingborg for two days, we did some shopping, and then she looked after Anne while I played drums for an hour – more about why later perhaps – until the children came home. We had lunch, Linda cooked some fish, and then we went to school, first there was social mingling, which conveniently enough we missed, then there was the end-of-term ceremony in the church. It took three hours in total. There might be the odd grandparent who loves their grandchildren so much and considers it such fun to see them in church that they don't begrudge the time, but ninety per cent of the parents had that jumpy, restless look you normally see in animals at the zoo. Fortunately Anne began to scream, so I was able to leave, put her in the buggy and push her round the cemetery for the last hour or so while smoking a cigarette, studying headstones and musing on the transience of life.

This morning Linda took Anne, so I slept until half past six, had breakfast and came here, where I watched the last hour of

Brazil v. Croatia on the net. I knew the result, but not how unfair it was – by which I mean, Brazil deserved to win, no doubt about that, but the second goal was, as everyone has been saying, a good old-fashioned classic blunder by the ref. Fred dived, Fred got a penalty, Neymar put the ball just past the goalie, and Brazil were given a dream start.

With the spectators cheering every time Neymar touches the ball, doesn't that suggest this is a fair-weather crowd? People who don't know a whole lot about football but idolise a star? That was the feeling I had. Yet, what an impact when the music stopped during the last verse of the national anthem and only the stadium choir, the sixty-thousand-plus voices, sang. The Swedish commentators said the hairs were standing up on the backs of their necks, but that is just because both sport and Brazil are exceptions, places where Swedishness doesn't count, because normally, my Swedish friend in Brazil, such happy nationalist singing is something Swedes are unable or unwilling to understand. I know that after thirteen years as a Norwegian in this hypocritical monarchy.

In the break yesterday the TV showed a series about former Brazilian heroes, which I saw today. It was the turn of Socrates. Then I remembered that it was also in 1982 that Brazil was exceptional, with Zico, Socrates and Eder, among others.

So much nostalgia, so much yearning for what is lost for ever. All while we are in the midst of our lives, which is all we have and which in all probability is no worse than what we had once and long for again.

Isn't it strange? In twenty years' time a whole generation of people in their thirties will hark back to this summer, the one around us right now, and the TV pictures we are watching now will be filled with their own special aura and mystique.

Now they are only TV images.

One of my favourite books is Stefan Zweig's *The World of Yesterday*, in which he depicts his upbringing in the Austro-Hungarian monarchy at the turn of the century in the, for us, old and alien world that disappeared with the First World War. He describes how youth was not the ideal it is now, but middle age – all young men tried to appear old, they grew stomachs, beards, wore spectacles and carried walking sticks. He also describes how at school they were obsessed by art, by music, especially Mahler and by poetry, Rilke was the great poet, in more or less the same way that we were obsessed by pop music. But the most interesting part is his description of the time just before war broke out. No one knows what awaits them, there has been peace for so long, and the wars there have been have all been limited, enacted between soldiers, not involving the civilian population. The summer is hot, and there is a profundity to it, something eternal, I imagine, and a fullness and laziness. The approaching war, of which, however, no one knows or can guess the full extent, is desired only because it brings change, something will happen. It is exciting and it is romantic. Their notions are of a world exclusively to do with buying and selling, enjoyment and pleasure, peace and calm, and suddenly a chance appears for action, to show heroic courage, to win honour. But I don't want to go there, my point is simple: we never know what can happen, everything can be rent asunder from one day to the next. On a personal level, of course, for it happens, someone we love dies or leaves us, but also on a collective level. When the conflict between Ukraine and Russia came to a head earlier this spring and Putin annexed the Crimea on the basis that Russians lived there, I was reminded, like everyone else, of Germany's annexations in the 1930s, which were justified with the same arguments. At the time I met an American journalist who was working for *The Times*, and she told me about the plight of Jews in an eastern European country,

I think it was Hungary, where they were being openly harassed and many of them had emigrated. The threshold for what you can say about Jews is lower. Their question is when do we know when the limit has been reached, when do we have to get out? What all the Jews in 1930s Germany shared, and other Germans too for that matter, was an ignorance of what was going to happen. One such German Jew was Victor Klemperer, I have mentioned him earlier, but I will do so again, because it is striking how he tries to interpret everything in the best possible sense, from the way life used to be.

One thing is sure: if the same horror were to return, it wouldn't return in the same form. It will appear as something we don't know and won't be able to anticipate. That is why the present is innocent, there is always something naïve and ignorant about it. When those who are ten or fifteen years old now are filled with nostalgia for this summer, which the television images from Brazil anchor in us, they will also know something we don't: how things went. What happened afterwards.

That is as terrible a thought as it is fantastic. The nation state collapses, it happens slowly, but that is what happens. What does it open up? What world will we live in twenty years from now?

When I was in New York recently I had lunch with some other writers. There was Zadie Smith and her husband Nick Laird, the Northern Irish author, and Katie Kitamura and her husband Hari Kunzru. Zadie is British, her mother is Jamaican and her father English, Katie is American with Japanese parents, Hari is a British-born Pakistani. They talked about how they planned to bring up their children. They talked about expressions thrown up by American racism compared with British. This wasn't theory, this was practice, something they knew from their own experience. In Great Britain something has happened over the last couple of years, the threshold for what you can say has been lowered, and UKIP, which is like the Swedish Democrats, has grown exponentially. I was in Hay, in Wales, before New York, staying at a private hotel, and the owner who welcomed me started talking about immigration after only two minutes, completely unbidden. That wouldn't have happened five years ago.

I think this is what you wrote about, Fredrik, about what happens when you look someone in the eye. It happens in both the beholder and the beheld.

What do you do when you don't look people in the eye?

You defend yourself.

Against what?

Well, against life, of course.

It is so damned hard to live.

Nothing of what you've written so far has given me greater pleasure than what you said about life having to be real, genuine, alive, intense and how you have started looking into people's eyes in a different way from before. I know exactly what you mean. Something opening, not closing. You want to keep the world open. You want to appreciate what is in it. Because you know you don't have long left. Then it is over. Then it is no more and there never will be anything more. It is only now, and it is now or never.

Nevertheless, I look down. I hide.

I don't initiate conversation with people on planes, I hardly even talk with my neighbours, and if I do it is with the intention of getting away, which of course they notice because it is reflected in your body language.

In Sweden coming from the working class is a term of honour, nothing is better for a writer here than being able to say, 'I'm working class,' even if no one actually knows any more what this means or implies. Not much money, poor working conditions, hard graft, few opportunities – what's good about that? Where has the association come from? The association is in the language, it is only there that it is great to be working class. And as we know, the better your education, the healthier and more active your lifestyle, the less TV you watch, the better you eat, the longer you live. Class, that is the privileged versus the non-privileged. Those on the inside versus those on the outside. Those who can express themselves and their values versus those who can't. I don't know if you read Jonas Thente's article in *Dagens Nyheter* about hatred on the net. How can it be, he says, that middle-aged white men can hate women and immigrants so much and express their sentiments anonymously? He left the answer there, in short, these people are on the outside. They have no voice, their opinions don't count, and if an opinion is heard, it is looked down on. The working classes are also looked down on. I know you have written about this specific topic, the old working-class culture, which still exists but which has also subsumed hatred against women and immigrants and is perhaps no more than an expression of powerlessness. Of not being valued. Social exclusion, utenforskap, as they say in Sweden – another positive term here! For me, all this is connected: 1914, 1933, 2014. Crises, changes, displacement, new hostility, new collectivism, uncertainty. What is right, what is wrong? History will judge, but it hasn't been written yet. Now it is open.

Football belongs here too, for what else is football but an opium of the people? It is an anaesthetic, an escape, fiction. But it is also the opposite. Football creates contact; we can talk about it with anyone. Neighbours and fellow airline passengers as well. It is something we have in common, a frame of reference. The game in itself is perhaps meaningless, something to help pass the time (or as my friend Geir usually says, something to help pass your life), but what isn't meaningless when it comes down to it? What you get from a World Cup is joy, excitement, fascination, togetherness. And that is not bad.

And finally a minor amendment: when I wrote that I didn't like beautiful women, I didn't mean that literally, it was more the analogy with Brazil I had in mind, not liking Brazil is the same as not liking beautiful women. Food is not my thing, nor drinking, but when it comes to women and their beauty and attractions I am on your side! Actually I wish I wasn't because it creates constant problems, the dizzying divide between what one would like to do and what one can do. Yes, you know. There are some who say you shouldn't think like this, there are even some who say they don't think like this, but they are lying, I'm convinced of that. All the men I know constantly think about women, every day from the age of six until they are ninety-six. This isn't sexism, it is being human.

All the best,
Karl Ove

Botafogo, 13 June

Dear Karl Ove,

Such a great letter from you today, a real pleasure to read. I've just finished it now, and it twists and turns in so many directions and raises so many interesting questions that I don't quite know which thread to take up. This is of course liberating but also gives rise to a mild feeling of panic, which is merely heightened by the banal fact that I'm suffering from a hangover. And that the world is swaying to and fro for me here as I sit.

So, what happened last night?

First I took a long walk through Botafogo, discovered streets where I had never set foot, street corners I never knew existed, before eventually making it to the long tunnel connecting Botafogo with Copacabana as I headed for the big screen to watch the match. But just before I entered the tunnel, where the noise of the cars drowns out every other sound, the highlight of my day took place: along came a pirate on stilts, probably about three metres up in the air, appearing pretty drunk and swaying back and forth in the middle of the traffic, looking for all the world like Johnny Depp in *Pirates of the Caribbean* and on top of everything playing the trumpet. Everyone witnessing the scene smiles and laughs, no doubt wondering who this lunatic lurching perilously along in the middle of the busy road is. No one has a clue. I entertain the thought that he's taken it upon himself to open the World Cup. In any case he cuts a very baroque figure, very

'Brazil'. A term like magic realism has no meaning here, other than in the opposite sense perhaps: Swedish 1970s realism could pass for magic here, while realism, as a concept, includes things like a pirate on stilts materialising in the middle of a busy roadway, before disappearing and leaving you to wonder if you were dreaming.

At Copacabana I join a long queue on the beach, and the expectation in the air is almost palpable. People congregate in their thousands and many are heading to the same place as me: the FIFA Fan Fest, a fenced area with free admission. That's where I watch the game, in a sea of Brazilians and supporters from other countries, but the atmosphere is never really electric. In São Paulo, where the match is being played, it looks different, and I can't help noticing an awful lot of well-to-do people among the supporters. This isn't the people's World Cup, Karl Ove. It belongs to FIFA and the affluent elite. Ordinary people can't afford to attend the games. I'm going to see Bosnia–Argentina on Sunday at the Maracanã. The price of a ticket? £200! That's ludicrous. With regard to the actual game, the faces of Thiago Silva, Neymar and Hulk during the national anthem made an impression on me. The tremendous tension evident in their expressions. How they fought back their own tears and the external pressure of 190 million fans who expect only one thing: a World Cup trophy. I'm struck by the thought that it ought not to be possible to play football after experiencing such a maelstrom of emotions, and that brings me to a question that's been bugging me since last summer, and that fantastic game in the Confederations Cup against Spain, the reigning world champions, which this young Brazilian team won 3–0: are they mentally tough enough to withstand the pressure? I think Felipe Scolari made a mistake in not naming Kaká or Ronaldinho in his squad, not that they should have made the starting eleven but for the experience they have of previous tournaments. I think their omission is a mistake that will prove costly.

As for the match itself, I'm afraid my insights may disappoint you: I'm no analyst. I love football but am no good at explaining what's happening on the field and the neologisms they employ (zoning, cutting down space, pressing high, sitting back, etc.) make me break out in a rash. Yes, I think Brazil can go all the way after having seen Neymar yesterday, because everything is going to start with him and revolve around him, he's yet another in a long line of exceptional players who have worn the number 10 shirt for Brazil, his ability to read the game, his speed in possession, dribbling ability of course, but first and foremost how he strikes the ball. And the size of him. If you were to see someone with his slight build sauntering along the main street in Glemmingebro one sunny day you'd probably think, 'For God's sake, eat something. Don't they feed you at home?' And that brings us on to one of football's 'mysteries': how can small, skinny boys stike a ball so hard? The secret is musicality, at least that's how I see it, all great players are musical, have rhythm in their blood, and in Neymar's case it's about a large number of muscles harmonising in one single concentrated motion. Once the match got under way, Brazil regained their composure and you had the feeling that sooner or later they'd manage to prise open the Croatian tin of sardines; however the way it happened was nothing short of scandalous. There were no grounds for a penalty, not in my book, as well as which the Croatian equaliser shouldn't have been disallowed, there was nothing wrong with the contact made on César when he fumbled the ball. You could tell the crowd felt the same. People here aren't idiots. They love their football and the national team, but they want o jogo bonito, attacking football and victories won fairly, not by cheating. The celebrations were therefore somewhat subdued when Neymar slotted away the penalty, but resounding cheers rang out when Oscar put the result beyond doubt with his goal to make it 3–1. Croatia played a fantastic game (I agree with what you said, they played at their very best) in classic Croatian style, not the prettiest at times, but with a tactical composure sprinkled with some dazzling, individual performances. Modric! Brazil, in spite of the scandalous penalty decision, deserved the victory and played some great football at times, but also revealed their weaknesses: a poor keeper, some shaky defending and a Hulk who's really not up to it. Oscar and Neymar showed occasional flashes of brilliance. Midfield passable.

As I leave the FIFA zone on Copacabana, there are no horns sounding, no scenes of jubilation or of people spontaneously embracing. The general mood is one of weariness, as at the end of a day's work. No evidence of any real exuberance is to be seen, and I don't feel too exuberant myself. The bus ride back to Botafogo is quiet, as if a sense of slight embarrassment about the penalty still hangs in the air, and from the open windows snatches of chatter from family gatherings outside on the street can be heard, but no parties, no fireworks. The World Cup is under way. Brazil have won their opening game, but it is a quiet Rio with a full moon over Copacabana that dominates my image of the day. And the pirate, of course.

Later I went out in Lapa, the bohemian area of central Rio, a part of town that hasn't changed much in a hundred years. It boasts a great number of bars, both upmarket and cheap, in ramshackle houses and on the streets. People even set up 'bars' on the pavement where the prices are lower still. Lapa is synonymous with intellectual and artistic life in Rio. It was already the place to meet back in the 1920s and 1930s when Brazilian modernism was in its infancy. I love Lapa. And it was there I consumed a fair few beers and caipirinhas last night. Mostly at Bar Waldemar, where I met my friend Lennart and his wife, Nete. It's his local, carefully chosen due to its location midway along the street as opposed to on a corner. According to Lennart, you need to stay clear of bars on street corners, as they offer thieves two escape routes. The place was small, just a hole in the wall really, with some plastic chairs, two or three tables, also plastic, on the pavement outside, and an odd, sullen bar owner, Waldemar Junior, who serves beer and caipirinhas with supreme indifference, not even the merest hint of a smile – nada!

Lennart is a hard man. A tough guy. The kind who's gone into the favelas and given gang leaders a piece of his mind. He's been all over, in every port in the world. He has dabbled, as he puts it, in around twenty languages and despises the ruling classes no matter where in the world they may turn up, and during the course of our conversation – he's a bit like an old squeeze box, the kind you have to crank up – he often gestures disdainfully towards the south, in the direction of Ipanema, Copacabana, Botafogo, Barra, the parts of town where the wealthy and middle class live, and his signature refrain is that the 'ruling-class left' suppresses the 'working-class right' through language, work – on every front in fact – and if he was Dante he would have placed leftists from Ipanema in the seventh circle, along with sodomites and the rest.

As Waldemar brings the umpteenth round to our table I decide to try to alter that indifferent expression of his, see if I can conjure the merest little crack: 'Are you Waldemar?'

'No, I'm Waldemar Junior.'

His face is completely impassive. Has he suffered some great loss, some heartache, I wonder, and decide to give it another go, and knock a ball in from the other side: 'And the match, a disgrace with the penalty, wasn't it?'

He stops for a moment, two beer bottles in his hands, looks at me, not smiling as I'd hoped, but with careworn, bar-owner eyes and says, 'It's all fixed. Haven't you realised that? FIFA have rigged the whole thing from start to finish.'

I'm speechless. As I allow what he's said to sink in I have a peculiar thought: could it be true? Imagine if what he, Waldemar Junior, is saying is true, but before I have time to reply he's turned away and disappeared back through the hole in the wall, to take his place behind a crowded counter where he can be alone at a reassuring distance from all irksome fellow human beings, and then, right at that moment, the dancing begins.

The music is turned up and a buxom middle-aged woman in Brazilian yellow begins dancing with a man of similar age with an enormous pot belly, and it's incredibly beautiful, they glide around on the pavement tightly entwined, as though one body, in a slow rotation on its own axis, and I grow quiet, wanting only to watch, and am filled with such warmth that everything else dissolves in the face of this beautiful couple dancing in the Lapa night. A transvestite at the next table catches my eye. He/she is wearing glitter on his/her cheeks, and is a woman in every respect apart from a slightly rough complexion that gives the game away. When Lennart gets to his feet and leaves, swaying across Rua Mem de Sá, Cleo, as he/she is called, and I strike up a conversation and I ask, 'Are you a transvestite?'

'No.'

'What do you mean no? You must be?'

'No, I'm not. I'm a transformista.'

'Transformista? What's that?'

'I'm a man like you, but I like getting dressed up from time to time.'

'But surely that makes you a transvestite?'

'No. They want that identity all the time, twenty-four hours a day. I don't. I only do it when I feel like it.'

Then we part. I leave the bar and it feels as though I've learned something new. Transformista. I've never heard of that before. And isn't that what we want, to find out something new, to learn new things, all the time, Karl Ove?

Best wishes,
Fredrik

Botafogo, 14 June

Dear Karl Ove,

No letter from you today, which makes me think straight away of
your house, your beautiful garden, Linda, the children, the steril-
isation of baby bottles and suchlike, and the daily chores piling
up to put a temporary stop to your writing.

Yesterday was, as I'm sure you understand, a day to catch up
on things, and I spent it in my room for the most part, writing,
drinking water, reconstructing and imposing some order on my
thoughts and the things around me: my writing pad, notes,
clothes. I slept late and, at around half past four, I finished my
letter to you. After that I was considering a snooze, but when I
switched on the TV Holland v. Spain was just about to begin. I
thought, I'll give it a try, so I half-follow it and . . . well, what can
you say? An outstanding game from start to finish. Quite simply
a historic football match. Never before have the reigning world
champions been so outplayed in a World Cup, but the game itself
remains a mystery to me. Spain played brilliantly in the first
half. Iniesta, possibly the best footballer in the world, was just
about as good as he can be. Then utter collapse, the Spanish gal-
leon dashed on the rocks, not dissimilar to the game between
Denmark and, oddly enough, Spain, in Mexico in 1986, and as I
sit there wondering what on earth has happened to safe,
one-touch passing Spain, van Persie scores that incredible diving
header. Spain equalise right before half-time but so what?

I've never seen anything like it at this level. Holland played magnificently, were magic in the second half, and it felt like the World Cup began there and then. If the Dutch have set the tone this tournament should go down as one of the best. Van Persie, Robben, Sneijder & Co. – a fantastic combination of ugly play (which you want), physical football (for part of the second half the Spaniards looked like a youth team), imagination and frightening efficiency. Sleep was out of the question for me. It may rate as one of the best World Cup matches I've seen. And that brings me to the emotional aspect. I suffered along with Spain, with Busquets' Spain, with Iniesta, Xavi, Piqué and all those who gave us the tiki-taka style of play, who changed the history of football by the introduction of something new and who now, it feels, will be toppled from their throne by a different type of football, more efficient and physical. Xavi's bearing (doesn't that sound like the title of an intriguing poetry collection?) close to the final whistle had me almost in tears. That was down to the fact that I like those Spanish players, as people, first and foremost Iniesta, he has a humble, down-to-earth quality that makes him endearing and is such a blessed contrast to all the decorative tattoos in the world of football right now.

As for Holland? I don't like them, Karl Ove, and this takes us onto an odd aspect of football. It fosters, and nourishes, turbid feelings deep within us, curious aversions and empathies, peculiar irrational sentiments which oppose any attempt at intellectual analysis. Robben, for example, is precisely my type of player, he has fantastic technique as well as being a superb finisher, the kind I've always been partial to and always will be. But I don't like the look of him, his cold, clinical style, the absence of a smile when he scores, his constant lip. And I don't like Sneijder either, despite his amazing ability. I don't like the tough-guy look of many of the other tattooed clowns, who flirt with that whole gangster-chic aesthetic I abhor, wherever in the world it might appear. You see what I mean? Listen to my primitive attitudes. It's crazy! This is just one of the reasons I could never work as a football commentator, unsavoury sentiments like that have no place in serious football analysis.

I missed Mexico v. Cameroon, but saw Chile v. Australia in a nearby bar, Boteco Esquina de Botafogo, which was packed with fans from different countries, mostly happy Chileans, as well as devastated Spaniards, their heads bowed, resting almost, on tables behind a sea of empty beer bottles. I show another side to myself in this bar, somewhat more appealing than the aforementioned irrational antipathies. I leap up from my seat in celebration when Chile make it 1–0 and then 2–0, and delight in Alexis Sánchez's audacious dribbling and ice-cold finishing. The Chilean victory was fully deserved and the only realistic outcome. Australia were downright poor and a real disappointment. I think they may as well start packing their bags. I've tipped Chile as one of my outsiders, along with Belgium, and I still think they could make it to the semi-finals, despite a naivety to their play that had me slightly worried at times.

In a few hours I'm meeting up with my friend Claudio Aragão. He is the author of over fifteen books but has never been able to make a living from his writing. We're going to play football with friends of his in Duque de Caxias. But first I need to buy a new pair of football boots and today's newspapers. It's nine in the morning here now and still unbelievably quiet. Hope everything is well in Glemmingebro!

Warsaw, 14 June

Dear Fredrik,

Now I am in Warsaw, at one of the few old hotels in town, the Warszawa Grand. But it is not that old; as you know, the whole town was flattened during the Second World War, in theory there was nothing left, so almost everything here is from after 1945. The streets are incredibly wide and straight and long, and the houses are monumental blocks, Stalin-style. I love it. The interpreter told us on the way here that before the war Warsaw was like Paris. Beautiful old buildings, narrow streets and alleys, a town that hadn't been planned, that just grew over the centuries, in other words, a town for people. This town lying around me, stretching out into the distance, is the opposite. Here the system came first, people second. I don't quite know why I love it, I think it has a lot to do with the Cold War, the romance of those days, when all the countries in eastern Europe were inaccessible, closed off, secret, and where they believed in something quite different, and built and lived in a utopia. Whatever is different has an enormous pull on me. Now there are advertising posters absolutely everywhere, much more than in the towns at home, but still the impression the city gives, after having been here for three hours, I have to add, is alien and fascinating. Here there is no chance of you meeting a pirate on stilts in the street, I can vouch for that. Here people are lost among the buildings, nobody can shine brighter than them.

I got up at half past five today, showered, had a cigarette and a coffee, packed the little I was going to carry with me and drove to Kastrup. Usually I take the train, but they are on strike now, so an hour later I was sitting in my car in the middle of Öresund Bridge; it is always a wonderful sight, Copenhagen lies straight ahead, under black clouds, through which the planes rise from the airport. The sea, the boats, the tall high-rises, the sky, the cars, the planes. The wind turbines, the towers on the bridges. I don't normally consider such urban areas beautiful, but this one is a mass of movement, and seeing the planes makes me feel I am in the future, I have a sense of the future, and chills run down my spine.

On the plane I sat in business class, the only person to do so. The air hostess closed the curtain, so I was on my own at the front and was served food and drink. It felt uncomfortable, but that wasn't my fault, my agent had insisted on it. There is not a lot of money in Polish publishing, but agents don't care about that. So there I sat, feeling stupid and thinking about you, your life in Rio de Janeiro during these days. At the airport I was met by the interpreter, who spoke perfect Norwegian, and two men from the marketing department. We took a taxi to the Polish broadcasting headquarters. It was fantastic, an enormous brick building from the 1950s which, according to what they told me, had originally been planned as a prison. The entrance hall had pillars and floor tiles, and apart from the guard no one was there. The corridors on the higher floors were long, windowless and Kafka-esque. I have been on both Norwegian and Swedish radio, and those buildings also have a certain eastern-European feel, but this was the Real Thing. In the control room they had an ancient tape recorder, probably to remind them of bygone days – when I worked on student radio in the early 90s they were still in use – and even the studio was 70s style. The people working there were also different types from those I am used to, a large woman in her sixties burst in, looking more like a 70s housewife as regards her dress sense, and the technician in the control room was the same age, with a grey moustache that made him look like some kind of engineer – in other words, as though they had never had anything to do with pop culture of any variety. The technicians I usually meet look like they grew up with Nirvana and Metallica, and as though what they do is actually a sort of hobby, while the journalists often resemble businessmen or -women, unless they follow the arty convention. They make a professional impression. These people seem professional in a completely different way, they give off an air of competence but not a sense that they have any aspirations towards anything else or that their job is more than just a job. I don't know how to explain it. But in the 70s in Norway people caught the bus or drove to work with the same kind of bag, in which they had their packed lunch and a Thermos, and they'd always had the job they had, that was who they were. A bit like the people I met today.

After the interview we drove here to the hotel, where I have an hour before I take part in a literature festival and am interviewed on stage.

Thanks for your letter yesterday, Fredrik. It was lively and intense, like everything you have written on your travels. Once again I felt hot cheeks of shame because when you describe your world it is as if you are correcting mine: THIS is what it is about. Not stupid interpretations of war and the working classes – which in fact I know nothing about and have only a theoretical stance on – but you walk the streets on journeys of discovery, sit in bars and drink with friends, discuss, take an interest in what is going on right here, right now.

And then there was the football. Why do I try to analyse the matches I watch? I never do that normally. That is never what it is about. I watch football the way I read books: I get involved. I have no idea what is going on or why. It is the same with Dostoevsky, and it is the same with Dortmund and Donn (a lower-division team from Kristiansand).

After writing a letter and sending it to you yesterday I drove my eldest daughter to Malmö, where she was going to stay with a friend until Monday. We chatted the whole way. She is obsessed by the *Titanic* at the moment, the real event and the film, and she can easily talk about it for an hour at a time. I showed her a You-Tube clip of the *Hindenburg* disaster once, but it didn't hold her attention because, as she said, it happened so quickly! The *Titanic* tragedy unfolds slowly, the suffering is drawn out, and that is what she is after, I think. I asked her if she had heard of the Twin Towers, the World Trade Center, 9/11, the two planes that flew into the skyscrapers, but she hadn't. Can you imagine! It has only just happened! But she wasn't born then, they don't learn things like this at school, so where would she have picked it up?

She didn't want to hear that either.

I like driving places with the children, that is where we talk most, in the car, and I like the fact that I talk differently to each of them, I almost become a different person because they are so different. I also like the countryside we drive through, the county of Skåne, most of all the region where we live, the Österlen plains, where agriculture is alive and food is actually produced, the billowing wheat fields, right now green and stretching like a sea between farms, which are islands of roofs and trees, and then the churches – from Glemminge you can see four steeples from the low hill, and when I stand there scanning the horizon it strikes me that the view is the same as it was a hundred years ago: fields, churches, houses, hills, sea.

And in spring, when the rape is flowering, I have never seen such a yellow. It is magical.

In the autumn when I pick up the children from school it is

pitch black on both sides of the road, the tractors are still out in the fields with their lights on, like boats, and a sense of elation can explode in me. Or when it rains, everything is wet, the colours are brown, ochre, yellowish-white, the sky is greyish-black and heavy, and a bird of prey swoops down through the air. Then too: wild joy.

Yesterday was a typical June day, sunny and hot, enormous cloud formations over the horizon to the east. The clouds there are different from those where I lived before, much more dramatic and spectacular. I've told Vanja that so many times, look at the clouds, I say, she doesn't even glance up. They're just clouds, Dad, she says.

After I had dropped her off and driven back home, the hour it takes from Malmö to Glemmingebro, I watched the second half of Cameroon v. Mexico (I heard the first on the car radio), and when it was over I drove Heidi up to Geir's because he has a son in her class and they are friends. She is staying there until Sunday – as I will be away for two days I have arranged for all the children to stay with friends. The new nanny has been hired for Saturday and Sunday. You have to feel reassured; you must have all possibilities covered.

I had to stop writing to go to the literary event. It is over now, I am absolutely exhausted, but I have half an hour before they take me out to eat, so I thought I would write some more. In fact, I fell asleep in front of the football yesterday as well. I might have missed ten minutes of the Cameroon v. Mexico match. That has never happened before. It is strange that it is happening now, when my job is actually to watch all the matches and write about them. But Mexico had something, pace, technique, lovely passing movements, while Cameroon couldn't keep up and will probably soon be packing their bags. I must admit, I thought most about their muscles, they wore extremely tight-fitting shirts, and the rain was coming down like stair rods, so I felt I had to explain to Heidi, who was sitting and watching with me, why I didn't look like them.

The World Cup has lots of games like this, slightly indifferent, which you watch anyway because there is something about spotting things early on in the tournament, the feeling that you have discovered a great player, for example, who becomes 'mine', or a team for that matter. I was like that with Russia in one European Championship, the one before last, when Spain won for the first time. I followed Spain and Russia and wanted them to win.

I watched the Spain–Holland game from the sofa yesterday with Linda and John. John was wearing his Spain shirt, which was a coincidence because he had put it on just that morning without knowing anything about the match. I bought it for him two years ago. After just five minutes I said to Linda that Spain were going to win, you could see they were much better than Holland. They weren't dominant, but they had an easy superiority about them, I thought. Silva, Iniesta and Xavi, perhaps it was just that I know what they are capable of that did it, but I don't think so, they looked good and were also suddenly delivering long, raking passes, I had hardly ever seen them do that in the last eight years. When the penalty came I thought that was it, game over. Then came Silva's great chance, he was through on his own and tried to chip the keeper. They had control, they had chances, Holland had nothing. And then came the absolutely unbelievable cross from what-was-his-name, Blind? One of the new Dutch players. And van Persie's sublime header. It is one of the most beautiful moments I have seen. The pass must have been a good forty metres, and van Persie timed it perfectly, dived forward and not only met the ball but steered it over Casillas into the goal. It was more beautiful than Zlatan's bicycle kick against England, or at least in the same class, because there were two inspired elements, the cross and the header, and not just one, like Zlatan's crazy shot. Last year I was in Amsterdam, launching a book, and asked the publishing house if there were any Ajax matches I could see. There weren't, but there was an international against Lithuania, I seem to remember, which I went to see. Van Persie was playing, and he didn't do a great deal, but I still couldn't keep my eyes off him because everything he did, trapping the ball, running, passing, had class written all over it, as though he was incapable of doing anything that was not perfect. For some reason, it is not as easy to see on TV. Something to do with the picture making them seem like cardboard cut-outs, non-human, where even the most fantastic ball control becomes run of the mill, while live, in reality, you see that these bodies are in fact men, you can relate them to their own bodies, everything is slower than on TV, and the limits are clear. Against this background I saw that van Persie and his elegance, sureness of touch, made him stand out from all the others on the pitch. Robben was there, he had a bad night, the whole team did, so the real value was van Persie. Nevertheless, he isn't a player I like. He is hard to like, isn't he. Why is that? He is good, elegant, he can pull off amazing feats, like yesterday. But still he is not like Pirlo, because everyone loves Pirlo, don't they. Is it his aura? Arrogance? Pride? Lack of humility?

I hesitate to say this, but after the interval, with the game at 1–1 and at a pivotal point between two of the World Cup's best teams, I nodded off. Again! What is this? Have I got football narcolepsy in the four weeks I am supposed to be writing about it? It is a disaster. Suddenly I woke up and the score was 3–1 to Holland. How was that possible? Everything was different. Spain had no aggression, no desire, they seemed paralysed. And Holland, they just stormed forward, they did as they wanted, 4–1, 5–1, and it could easily have been seven or eight, they squandered fantastic opportunities in the dying minutes. It can't have been about formations, nor tactics, nor quality – there are very few midfields better than Spain's, with Xavi, Alonso and Iniesta – but it was as though – and actually it had been like this from the very beginning – Spain were devoid of aggression, devoid of the constant pressure they had always built up when they lost the ball – which they hardly ever did – in other words, what they lacked was desire, the insight that desire was the top, top priority. What an unbelievable force they were two, four, six years ago. I particularly remember the Germany game, was it the World Cup in South Africa? Germany, such a wonderful team, had absolutely no chance. It was as though Spain was in a different league from everyone else, they were simply unbeatable. The few times Germany got the ball they were overwhelmed. A swarm of Spaniards buzzed around them. None of that was apparent yesterday.

On the screen I am watching Costa Rica, and they seem to be the equal of Uruguay. Amazingly fast tempo in this game. And Chile won 3–0 against Australia earlier today, I see.

There, they scored!

1–1.

Suárez will be on within the next five minutes, I guess.

Mexico were good, Costa Rica are good, Chile are good. Then we have Brazil, Uruguay and Argentina.

A lot will have to happen for this not to be the South Americans' World Cup.

2–1 to Costa Rica!

A good half an hour left.

Where is Suárez?

There were perhaps a hundred people at the interview today. I was asked very different questions from in other countries, this time there were a lot about my father and the father figure, and about death. The questions were asked in Polish, and I answered in Norwegian, which the interpreter then translated. After an hour there were questions from the floor. That is always the best part because it is so unconnected with theory and so unpredictable, people really do ask about anything under the sun. Much of what they say is about identification and the bizarreness of that, because those of them whose youth was in the 1980s spent it behind the Iron Curtain, in a communist country, and the differences were so enormous you would have thought it impossible for them to identify with anything I had written. They had stood in long queues of about a hundred metres to get hold of everyday commodities such as sugar, there were hardly any shops, there was no pop music, literature was censored, criticism was out of the question, yet they find, from what I gathered, that a childhood spent in Norway, outside Kristiansand, with the Western cultural frame of reference, is similar to their own and reminds them of it. I usually say that being sixteen in Norway is the same as in France, Argentina or Angola, but I don't believe it is, not really. Where you are, Fredrik, what you can see there, everyday life with its own distinctive features and experiences, surely that marks people in quite definite ways, doesn't it? Perhaps this is all tied up with class; those who read books more often than not belong to the middle classes, or the cultural middle class, and it is their experiences which are the same everywhere?

The autumn we moved to Glemmingebro I had an unpleasant experience. I was driving Heidi to a friend's house . . .

3–1 to Costa Rica!

What a surprise.

. . . well, it was autumn and dark, and the road was so narrow that I blocked it completely when I parked. I accompanied Heidi in, was gone perhaps five minutes, and on my return there was a car in front of mine, blocking my exit. It was there because the driver hadn't been able to drive past. There was a house further down, where the road ended, and I walked to it. A dog charged to the gate and barked aggressively. The house was a hovel. I rang the bell. No one opened up. I knocked. No one opened up. I walked back to the car, got in and waited. Nothing happened. Back to the house. Rang, knocked and shouted hello! In the end a man came out. He had a ravaged appearance and was just as aggressive as his dog. He shouted abuse at me. Eventually he came out and reversed his car so that I could get past. It was extremely unpleasant; I was upset for several days. It was then I realised I lived in a bubble, surrounded by polite, well-meaning, literary-minded, politically orientated, sensible, sane middle-class people who all have the same values, read the same books, watch the same TV series, think the same thoughts and behave in the same ways. This ravaged, aggressive man stood outside all that. The universality readers of my books talk about had no validity for him.

This shook me because it was the first time I realised that what I call reality is a bubble in which what is valid is valid for me and those like me.

This is banal, and I don't know why I am writing it, but as I said, I am a little drunk, very tired and beyond self-criticism.

Red card!

Such a dirty tackle. Uruguay, another classic dirty team.

And then the match is over. 3–1 to Costa Rica.

Time for chat and analysis in the studio, in Polish.

Thomas Woztek has something to say in the Polish studio. Sounds like he knows what he is talking about.

Post-match clips. The speed of it all! This looks like it is going to be the championship of the counter-attack.

Karl Ove

Botafogo, 15 June

Dear Karl Ove,

I'd completely forgotten you were going to Poland! Liked your description of autumn in Österlen very much and how happy it made you, the tractors 'like boats' and what you said about being in the car with children, how you can chat while driving, get closer to them. Unfortunately, as they grow older you lose that contact, they do their own things, move off in different directions and everything drifts apart. Our five kids often sit on their own somewhere in the house, immersed in whatever is happening on the screen of a computer or a smartphone, only surfacing when we eat dinner together. But, and this is what your car image brought to mind, when they begin learning to drive and you ride along with them in the passenger seat, then oddly enough this closeness returns, the two of you sit together talking about traffic and road signs, but other topics inevitably come up. I do enjoy that, in spite of a simultaneous feeling of imminent departure, of them soon disappearing to get on with their own lives.

Afonso came home yesterday just as I was pressing Send on my letter to you. He'd stayed over at his girlfriend's. They each have their own place and live modern lives, the same as we do in Scandinavia. I like him and get the feeling he likes me too. We hadn't met previously, but everything is so straightforward with him, I don't feel any pressure to be over-friendly, chat or hang out all the time. He comes and goes, living an unobtrusive musician's existence. I like the smell of cigarettes wafting from the kitchen, where he sits smoking, his good-natured sense of humour and how he smiles when he says oi, oi, oi, an expression he picked up while touring with Swedish musicians in Sweden.

We sank down into deep armchairs in his living room, high white ceilings, white stone walls, dark oak furniture, and he, with a mixture of humility and pride, took out two big books he'd written about the musical history of Brazil. They were beautiful publications with a wealth of archival photographs, and after a while I asked to see his recording studio, so we made our way across the little backyard, which is only about five metres long, up some stone steps and, glancing above me, I could see a bright blue sky and vultures in the tops of some tall trees whose names I don't know, because the jungle – yes, Karl Ove, not park, not garden, but jungle – is so close to the city here, and thinking about that led me to start talking to Afonso about animals, the presence of the vultures above having no doubt pushed my thoughts in that direction, and he tells me what I don't want to hear, cobras are to be found here, and one time he came across one lying on a step outside the studio, and I detest snakes, there's nothing worse as far as I'm concerned, so I ask him, what do I do if I should find myself in a similar situation with a cobra, keep calm and call the fire brigade, replies Afonso with an amiable laugh. Afterwards he tells me that while on his way to the studio on another occasion he saw three big monkeys on the roof – each more than a metre high! – all glowering at him so intently he grew afraid, really afraid, and then they suddenly vanished back among the trees, back into the green of all that vegetation. And then he tells me about other animals, ones with strange Indian names, creatures as large as anteaters and badgers, but which are not anteaters and badgers, and that put me in mind of Clarice Lispector and her novel *The Passion According to G. H.*, which is a fantastic description of an encounter that takes place between a lonely woman and a cockroach in her apartment, a cockroach that grows to be the antithesis of a human being, and when I read it I shared the hatred and panic this woman experienced and displayed, and I wonder, as I make my way up the long path leading to Afonso's house, what I will do if I run into a creature I've never seen before, not a snake, not a monkey, not a dog, but an animal I can't even name?

I met Claudio this afternoon, the guy I was telling you about in my last letter, at Central do Brasil, the enormous bus station in Rio city centre. He's often serious, his demeanour downright sad-looking at times, and even in photos I've seen of him he is rarely smiling. He gives me a hearty handshake, but no more, no hug, which is the norm here. We subsequently board the bus that will take us to Duque de Caxias, a suburb with a million inhabitants – a million! – in the middle of the vast expanse of northern Rio, Zona Norte, the Rio of the workers, which is about as far from the Rio of the Sugarloaf and Copacabana as you could imagine. We chat the entire time, while outside endless rows of unpainted cinder-block houses fly by the windows of the bus, but I feel a distance of sorts, even though we've known one another for over a decade, not so much in his body language, more a melancholy absence on his part that's evident from time to time, a silence as though he's sinking into himself in some way.

You wrote a lot about the middle class in your last letter. I think much of what you said is true, about the conformity of taste in middle-class literature and the existence of a global middle class where *Min Kamp* can be adored whether the reader lives in Wellington, Beijing, Luanda or Buenos Aires. I've thought a great deal about class throughout my life, doctor's son that I am, promising golf talent that I was, class and the feeling of belonging, or of not belonging, what it takes for someone to be accepted into a group, what it takes to be excluded and when, occasionally, I think back to why I never succeeded at Malmö FF as a youth player, why I never managed to take the next step up, to the reserves and perhaps even break into the first team, I often think that class was what did for me, that tough working-man culture that dominated at Malmö FF in the early 1970s, with players like Puskas Ljungberg, Bosse Larsson and Krister Kristensson, types who epitomised the working class in Malmö, I didn't use the same language, was too sensitive, too shy and to a great extent too marked by my own bourgeois background to make an impression in the dressing room as well as on the pitch, a feeling of being outside, put simply, of not being the right way, speaking the right way.

On the subject of class, Claudio came to Rio from Ceará, a poor region of Brazil, when he was six years old at the beginning of the 1960s. His father got a job as a guard in Leme, a neighbourhood next to Copacabana. His mother was a housewife and Claudio has lived in the same part of Duque de Caxias for forty-six years, in a working-class area called Villa José. Dirty, potholed streets where you can see horses and carts pass by, large black pigs oinking along, small bars with plastic chairs outside, and then his little house, two small rooms, piles of books everywhere, untidy, testament to his bachelor lifestyle and of getting up at three o'clock every morning, catching the bus to travel the interminably long Avenida Brasil to make it to the restaurant in Lapa at four, where he opens up for the staff, works twelve hours, before making the long journey home again, always exhausted, only able to write at the weekends, even though that's what he loves most of all and longs to do.

Never able to get away, to break out of that low-wage world. A lousy four hundred or so pounds a month. My ticket to the match tomorrow costs, as I wrote, two hundred pounds. And when he tells me he can't make a living from writing, I say it's the same for me while simultaneously hearing how ridiculous I sound. After all, I've travelled here and am off to a World Cup match neither he nor his friends have any possibility of seeing, and it almost makes me ashamed of my Bosnia ticket. Class, Karl Ove. In Botafogo I'm at home, out here in this vast sprawl of cinder-block houses I'm away from home, and this isn't the world of the favelas, but of ordinary working-class Brazilians, respectable, hard-working bus drivers, truck drivers, oil platform workers, people who've taken early retirement, print workers, head waiters like Claudio, and when I say hello to his friends I recognise several of them but not all, and I'm O Freddy in their world, the guy who brought Garrincha's son here, the guy who brings small groups of foreigners here when I'm working as a guide for football-loving tourists, the guy . . . yes, who exactly am I in their eyes, in the world of Claudio and his friends?

It's impossible to know, and waiting in my immaculate Botafogo strip wearing my newly purchased football boots by the horrible, bumpy artificial pitch situated nicely in the shadow of high, terracotta-coloured mud walls, I feel like a well-turned-out little middle-class child and feel the membrane of foreignness that surrounds me: what the hell am I actually doing here? What are we going to talk about? And where is everyone, weren't we supposed to have a game? Then they saunter up, one after the other, sedate, slightly apathetic and very Brazilian. I begin to feel a little more at home, and soon Claudio is talking about Chico Buarque, the writer and musician (since I'd mentioned to him I was going to play football at Buarque's place, on his very own pitch in Recreio the following Monday), he's not only a musical genius, but also a great poet and unrivalled in Brazil in that regard, his writings are great poetry – a gift, Claudio says – Chico Buarque has the gift and it comes from something Claudio calls God.

I jog a little, do some stretches and am eager for us to get started. The bibs are handed out, I end up on the yellow team and suddenly everything changes. I'm a player on the yellow team. I'm here Freddy and there Freddy and play it Freddy! and push up Freddy! and like you wrote in your first letter, about playing for Trauma when you were a little boy, about being able to forget yourself, about what a blessing it is, well, it's a bit like that, I feel bigger somehow, grow in confidence, control the ball as though it were glued to my foot, execute a successful back-heel, suddenly enjoy being there, having the opportunity to join in and also enjoy the fact that in no time at all it turns so serious, they shout at one another, the tackles get tougher, people yell and others get the hump, and it's nearly always like this in Brazil, I don't know of any other place where a kickabout can turn so serious in such a short space of time, into a matter of life and death, a war on the pitch, but one fought by fair means and attractive play, at the same time as para brincar, é brincadeira! (it's just for fun, it's only a game!) is heard time and time again although no one pays any attention, and then I experience the fantastic understanding I've felt so many times on the football field, the almost telepathic communication with the 'Other', the player who spots you, the player who knows exactly what run you're going to make, the player who – without you ever having met or exchanged a word – knows exactly where you want the ball, and at the same moment you, or rather I, know where he wants it played back to him, and he's a talent, like you once were, and he's seventeen and you're sixty but that doesn't make a blind bit of difference, and suddenly he makes me sense this overwhelming belief, this certainty, which I recognise, having felt it so many times before, that within the next minute or two it's going to be nestling, the ball I mean, in the back of that bloody net and it happens now – because he hits a long ball the length of the pitch, over their entire defence, and it lands on my foot and one on one with the keeper I morph into the Clinical One and a minute later I return the favour and supply him with a similar ball, which he puts into an open goal, and the day is saved because I am something, Karl Ove, and that is a footballing animal, a monkey, irreparably destroyed by/in love with this game and the final scores of the four matches we play are 1–1, 1–1, 1–2 and 5–2(!), and we give each other the thumbs up, my seventeen-year-old fellow telepath and I.

After a shower back at Claudio's we meet some of the others again at their local bar. Claudio mingles, exchanges a word here and there, his expression serious almost the entire time. A pat on the back here, a tudo bem there, coming across as a coach of sorts for the whole neighbourhood, and his sincerity is a beautiful thing. I ask Claudio and Carlinho, one of his friends I like the best, to pick out Brazil's best-loved players of all time. They're in complete agreement as it turns out.

'Primeiro?'

'Garrincha.'

'Segundo?'

'Zico.'

'Terceiro?'

'Jair.'

'And Pelé?'

They both blink and look around as though searching for words. A man with a huge pot belly, coal-black skin, wearing a white cap, an oil platform worker who had played football earlier but had only been on the pitch briefly and whom the others jokingly refer to as dez segundos (ten seconds) for the entire evening, upon hearing my question breaks off from dancing in front of the TV and says, 'Pelé doesn't live here. He's not Brazilian. He lives where the money is. Lives abroad.' It's a harsh view, but it's not the first time I've heard it, or indeed seen it. During one of the demonstrations prior to the World Cup I noticed a placard that read: Pelé, traitor of the century!

Then Costa Rica score to make it 3–1. Unbelievable. Sensational and, as I perceive it in the quiet chaos where I find myself, well deserved, and now it's lambada time, and the discussions continue, Jeju, the bar owner, serves us more beer, more food, and as I make my way to the toilet a sentence flies through my head, a bird appearing on the inner horizon of my mind from out of nowhere, a people like this can never be broken. A people like this can never be broken? Just that. And what I think I want to say is that all this coração (heart), all this carinho (affection), all this everyday solidarity that is manifested in and around Claudio is evidence of extreme strength, it's the old Norse Hávamál, the humane message triumphing over man's predatory nature, and sometimes it strikes me that the modernity in which we now live, in Sweden and Norway for instance, some of this message has been lost despite so much else having been gained, we are completely free and have done away with poverty and all the other obstacles that have fettered mankind through the ages. Yet the price may have been higher than we think, a situation where that sense of collective happiness has been forfeited, and as I come out from the toilets the anticipated highlight of the evening, Italy versus England, is about to kick off.

A fresh round of beers. More sardines. We settle down in front of the TV, me, Carlinho, Claudio and several others. And now the negative side of being a football fan rears its ugly head again, Karl Ove. Everyone here is cheering on England, even me.

Everyone here detests the Italian style of play. And I suddenly feel warmth for Rooney's hard-bitten, Liverpudlian features, Gerrard's commanding gaze, Sturridge's darting runs, while at the same time I find my aversion to Gli Azzurri alarming (it all spews forth, my abhorrence for Mussolini, Berlusconi, the 'Ndrangheta, the Cosa Nostra, the Camorra, how the hell can we criticise tribal violence in the Middle East and not intervene in the worst in the world, the Italian clans. Oh these perfumed gravediggers of football! Oh these perennially elegant divers & dipsticks prancing back and forth over the pitch in their perpetual quest for yet another 1–0 victory), and as Italy go a goal up, the whole place, for the first time in the course of this strange night, goes completely quiet. Carlinho shakes his head. I let slip a shit, and the thought that you of all people, Karl Ove, you, no stranger to crunching tackles, can side with this team is INCOMPREHENSIBLE. Sturridge equalises and everyone celebrates. A fresh round of beer from Jeju. More sardines. There's justice in the world. As Balotelli makes it 2–1 the curtain falls. Life is unfair, and it's time for me to go home to my middle-class galaxy a few light years from here.

A big farewell. We line up for photos (one whole wall of the bar is plastered with pictures of their team, I feature in a few from previous visits, as does Garrincha's son, Ulf Lindberg). Finally, hugs and handshakes are exchanged. A beautiful thirty-something woman in cut-off jeans and an elegant blouse, who's been sitting on a plastic chair swaying to the music without following the football, comes over and says that I simply must stay. Somewhere, as she puts it. Claudio smiles, chuckles a little. My enigmatic friend smiles and laughs for the first time all evening! I decline the offer in a friendly but firm manner, I want to get home to write, process the vast barrage of impressions from the day and am moreover in a relationship, should there be ulterior motives. It was no doubt merely consideration. A gringo enjoying himself out alone in Zona Norte can land in trouble. The only member of our group who is clearly drunk offers me and Claudio a lift. He is Fluminense, has talked about nothing but samba and mulheres the whole evening, and as we get into his car I turn on that most fantastic of inventions, the GPS. He puts the vehicle in gear and drives, laughing, straight towards the lights of an oncoming car, swerves at the last second, misses four cyclists, whoops, then a bus out of nowhere, and he giggles the whole time and talks about the new alcohol legislation, a lei seca, and how if he was pulled over by the police he'd lose his licence, and I don't know why I don't get out of the car, well, actually I do. This is the Zona Norte, the enormous, flat expanse of northern Rio, and I don't stand a chance here on my own. I'm not even sure exactly where I am. I don't know how far I'd have to walk to find a bus or taxi to take me to my beloved picture-postcard Rio. So I place my life in the hands of this luna-tic and put my in trust in Claudio, and when we make it to the bus stop, Claudio has a few words with the driver, no doubt to ask him to look after me, Rio being almost an hour's drive away. Then I board the bus and it rumbles off towards the city centre along the interminable Avenida Brasil, and I doze, thinking that every morning at 4 a.m. my enigmatic friend Claudio sits and is shaken on this bus without shock absorbers, year in year out, without any hope of ever making a living as a full-time writer.

At Rodoviária I shift from bus to taxi and am as good as home. Walking up the long, dark path flanked by walls covered in vege-tation to Afonso's house, that big monkey comes to mind, I wonder if it's around, wonder how I would fare in a fight, then my mobile rings. It's Claudio.

'Opa, Freddy? Tudo bem?'

'Yes, everything's fine. Thanks for everything today. Talk soon.'

Consideration, Karl Ove. He was watching over me the whole way home.

Best wishes,
Fredrik

Warsaw, 15 June

Dear Fredrik,

It is morning, a few minutes after half past eight, I am sitting in the hotel room drinking coffee and smoking, soon I will be doing the interviews I have to do here, and they last right through till six in the evening. After that I will be catching the plane home, so today there won't be any time for football or writing. By the way, I checked the Norwegian reports of yesterday's matches in the papers and saw that Bolaños in the Costa Rican team is the same Bolaños who played for Start a few years ago! When I saw him on TV I thought, no, he can't be, a Start player can't be at the heart of a World Cup game against Uruguay, there must be lots of people called Bolaños in Costa Rica ... I had set the alarm clock for the England–Italy game, but I was too optimistic, I fell asleep almost immediately and woke up in a flash. What I saw was like in a dream, England attacking a score of 1–2, wave after wave, then I fell asleep again. Shame if England are knocked out, they seem better and more exciting than in many a championship, but I suppose they have to beat Uruguay and Costa Rica now to go any further, and that could be tricky.

I'll try and see the match on the net tomorrow, it feels as if the World Cup is passing me by, as if I'm relating to games in the same way I do to dreams, which I can only remember after an immense effort and actually don't begin to understand.

The interviews await. Looking forward to your letter!

All the best,
Karl Ove

Botafogo, 16 June

Dear Karl Ove,

Your letter today was a short one. Understandable, given how exhausting these endless promotional tours must be, you're probably worn out. But you only have yourself to blame. Never forget that. Your writing is simply too good, that's why you're in demand everywhere.

It's been a fantastic summer day here, even though the Brazilians maintain it's now 'winter'. A comical idea to a Swede, or a Norwegian, when that time of year means to us skiing, ice hockey and skating on glassy, frozen lakes. When we were little my father always used to take us to Lake Ekoln outside Uppsala, and later, after we'd moved to Malmö, to Fjällfotasjön near Svedala, if Dad sensed the slightest chance the temperature might creep below freezing. I went down to the beach at Ipanema after finishing my letter yesterday, rented a deckchair and basked in the heat. The water at Ipanema is better than at Copacabana, and the beach was filled with thousands of bathers, as far as the eye could see. A beautiful sight, only enhanced by the spectacular background visible in the heat haze of the twin peaks of the Dois Irmãos (Two Brothers) mountain, with the Vidigal and Rocinha favelas (the largest in South America) at its foot. I don't know if I've written this before, but I don't really care, so at the risk of repeating myself: Rio is exceptionally beautiful. Nature is responsible for the creation of this wonder, with its mountains, jungles, beaches and Guanabara Bay.

Cariocas, Rio locals, are beach people. This is where they gather, their meeting place, their café. Everything happens here. This is where they exercise, play, fall in love, spend time with their children, friends and relatives. It's a lifestyle completely at odds with the more puritanical way of life in São Paulo, where the world of work is very much at the heart of things. Hence the aversion so many people from São Paulo, paulistas, have to Rio and the city's inhabitants, whom they consider idlers. I'm firmly on the side of the idlers in this dispute, Karl Ove, and see no contradiction between work and pleasure, enjoyment and 'contributing to productivity and growth'.

Yesterday I went to see the only match that in all likelihood I will get to see live during the tournament: Bosnia v. Argentina at the Maracanã, which appeared before me like a beautiful, irradiant space station as I came up from the metro below. A sea of hermanos (brothers) in blue and white, their singing resounded all the way from the station to the stadium, where their colours dominated the crowd. I sat among the Bosnian supporters, since my ticket had been arranged through a Bosnian in Malmö. I didn't mind at all. You know what I think of Maradona. And you know how much I admire Argentinian football, but then there's the other stuff. Argentina is racially homogeneous; the Indians were completely wiped out. No blacks. Stefan Zweig would never have written a eulogy to Argentina.

For me, Bosnia is Malmö to a large extent, an attempt to bring together different people with diverse cultures and religions. Malmö is a miniature Sarajevo, a melting pot, and always has been. In that sense it's a pioneering city. Thus, it feels good to sit with the Bosnian contingent, and Damir, who's sitting beside me and informs me he's worked at the Statoil station in Caroli City in Malmö for twelve years, drapes a Bosnian scarf around my neck, which feels natural but also slightly odd of course.

I couldn't understand a word of what the people around me were saying. The game got off to a nightmare start with an own goal after one minute, and Damir looked crestfallen. His face was pale and he slumped in his seat. However, slowly but surely the Bosnians played their way back into the game, and as the Brazilian portion of the crowd, which was considerable, began cheering on the tiny Balkan nation (their motto being 'My enemy's enemy is my friend'), you could hear the Bosnian supporters rediscovering their voices and sense the players on the field grow in stature and confidence, and by half-time it felt like a pretty even game and – shortly after the restart – just as I was beginning to think the Bosnians deserved a goal, Messi, who'd been completely anonymous up to that point, struck. The secret to his genius is the same as Maradona's, a low centre of gravity, making it impossible for defenders to predict when he's going to change direction or stay with him when he does. Another feature of his play is that he hardly ever dummies, have you noticed that? And neither did Garrincha. He always went to the right, the only problem was the defenders never knew when, and Messi really only has one dummy, although it's the most unstoppable of all: his shot, and it's built on the same principle as Garrincha's, that the defender never knows when the shot he has flagged up will come. I thought the match was over there and then. But the Bosnians pulled a goal back and the final result of 2–1 seemed fair. Perhaps Bosnia even deserved a draw. Argentina were disappointing (the whole front page of today's *Lance*, the biggest sports paper here, ran the headline: Só isso? – Was that all?), plodding and uninspired. Bosnia were as expected, a competent team who with a bit of luck could reach the last sixteen, but no further. What sticks in my mind from the game? Messi's run and goal, and the Bosnian number 8, Pjanic.

Today I'm going to play football, with Afonso among others,

on Chico Buarque's pitch. I have a suspicion it'll be quite a contrast to the playing surface in Duque de Caxias and the game we had out there.

Best wishes,
Fredrik

PS Missed pretty much all of France v. Honduras and Switzerland v. Ecuador yesterday. Saw the goals afterwards but am in no position to offer a considered opinion of any kind. Other than that Benzema looked in form.

Warsaw, 15 June

Dear Fredrik,

Thanks for your letter! It comes from a different world, a total
contrast from Warsaw. Cobras, monkeys, football with Brazilian
pals, parties and more football and a woman who asks you to
stay when the evening is over. (In future, you don't need to
describe everything you experience, even though, of course, it is
fantastic if you do . . .) But what I like best in your descriptions is
the warmth between people. As for me, I'm here at Chopin Airport outside Warsaw, the game between Switzerland and Ecuador
is on the wall TV, 1–1, and the game is end-to-end stuff, great
chances for both teams, no defences to speak of. Is it just me or
have lots of the games been like that, played at extremely high
tempo, almost totally focused on counter-attack? Costa Rica
played like that, Mexico, Holland and now these two. I can't get
into the match, because it is being shown on a small screen in
the middle of a big café full of people and because I am so tired.
I have been doing interviews all day, seven in all, lasting eight
hours. I'm absolutely exhausted, not physically but mentally. I
might come back to this later, why what is happening to me and
my books is so agonising and soul-destroying, but right now I am
too tired to reflect on anything. Nevertheless, I have enjoyed
being here – architecture and history apart, which are everywhere, I have felt at home: something in the culture reminds me
of Norway, or how Norway was before I moved to Sweden nearly
fifteen years ago. I am talking about the culture with a small c,

what the great Polish writer Gombrowicz would have called forms, and about surfaces: I don't think I saw a well-dressed Pole during these two days, nor a well-designed room or furniture. This is how it was well into the 90s in Norway, before there was so much money that the appearance of objects took over from function – the difference between the Norway I left and the Norway I see when I go there now is immense and striking. I was reminded of it when I saw Warsaw. The behaviour is similar too, no one is interested in forms the way they are in Sweden, to a large extent most seems spontaneous. (But Poland isn't effusive and warm, the way you describe people, more melancholic, more reserved, which, something tells me, can probably explode into outpourings of friendliness and enthusiasm, given enough beers or a bottle of vodka on the table.) This becomes apparent at lunch in a restaurant, following the rules – serviette on your lap, meeting eyes as you toast and afterwards the finer detail I didn't know existed until I moved to Sweden – but this was completely missing during the meal yesterday, with three men from the marketing department, an English writer and a translator. We talked about drums, the marketing head, Marcin, who was in his thirties, had played in a band from his youth, first pop and rock, then jazz, and he still did. He asked me what drums I had and wrinkled his nose when I said Pearl. What colour? he asked. Red, I answered, and he wrinkled his nose again. The least you could have done, if you insisted on buying a Pearl kit, was to get a black one. He wanted a Ludwig, but it was too expensive. One of the others broke in to say that whenever he set out to buy himself a Ludwig drum kit he bought something for his daughters or the house instead. Recently it had been a coffee machine. Marcin threw up his arms and put on the Robert de Niro pinched face, drooping mouth, pleading eyes, whatcha gonna do? He told me about the Miles Davis test for drummers. They played a bit, then he left the room, had a smoke, and if the rhythm was the same when he returned the drummer was in. Miles Davis had rhythm in him all the time, Marcin said. He was a fantastic musician. Who do you like? Don't tell me: John Bonham! Am I right? I nodded and he laughed. And Stewart Copeland, I said. That caused Janos, who had three interests in life – books, jazz and craft beer – to nod in assent from the end of the table. Bonham played on a Ludwig kit, Marcin said. Copeland was an original, Janos said. And how many pop drummers are there? I don't know how au fait you are with the unsophisticated world of drums, Fredrik – I am not talking about jazz now, where drumming is an art form and drummers are artists, but about basic, simple pop and rock drumming. John Bonham was in Led Zeppelin and, like everyone in the band, a brilliant musician, and as they were a trio with a vocalist he played a dominant role in the music and their sound. They were an unbelievable live band. No bands, or very few – we are talking the 70s here – even came close to them. When John Bonham died in the early 80s they dissolved the band, there was no reason to carry on, without him they would have been quite, quite different. A couple of years ago they reunited for a concert, with John Bonham's son, Jason, on drums. He is good, but he copies his father on all the songs, down to the last detail, and it is obvious he isn't playing them naturally, they haven't arisen spontaneously, they have been carefully copied and stage-managed. It's incredible how much worse it is, and how sad it is, I am thinking of the son here, this was his big moment in life, playing with his father's band in front of a hundred thousand spectators. Stewart Copeland played the drums in the Police, a reggae-influenced pop punk trio who released five records, and Copeland's playing, for the genre, is extremely sophisticated and inventive and technically brilliant. Sting, who sang and played bass, used jazz drummers for his later solo records, and I have always thought that was the only place he could find the same quality. As for me, I bought a drum set with a friend at school and he taught me the basic beat. Boom boom chicka. Boom boom chicka, boom boom chicka. Keeping the beat was as much as I could manage. When I was in my early twenties I started a band with my brother, and he was the only reason I was in; the others were, musically, way beyond me. I sat there in rehearsal room after rehearsal room with my boom boom chicka, boom boom chicka and had more fun than I had ever had doing anything else. We played a few concerts in Bergen, we had a song on a CD collection and some of our demo songs were played on radio. We called ourselves Kafkatrakterne. Then Yngve moved from Bergen, and the band broke up, but I met another young man, by the name of Tore Renberg, who wanted to be a writer and had sung in many bands in Stavanger, his hometown. With two musicians from Kafkatrakterne, Hans Kristian Mjelva and Knut Olav Homlong, we formed a new band, called Lemen, which lasted only one year, we played a proper concert as well as a couple of gigs at parties. We broke up because Tore left us in the lurch, he had his first novel accepted and moved to Oslo to become a writer in earnest. This autumn he is bringing out a new novel, and that is why I play drums all alone in a Swedish village: first of all, he asked me if I wanted to interview him on stage, he was keen, also because I owe him, he did it twice for me when *Min Kamp 1* came out – and then he wondered if perhaps we could jam together. He had some pals, artists, who would play. I hesitated, well, yes, maybe, why not? Then the nutcase went and booked four of Norway's biggest stages. In Oslo we are going to play Sentrum Scene, and corresponding stages in Bergen, Trondheim and Stavanger. They seat a thousand spectators. We, a bunch of amateurs no one has heard of, twenty years after we last played together, are going to perform for a thousand people. When Vanja heard this, she said, Daddy, you're forty-five years old. You're a writer. Please, don't do it! It's so embarrassing. She is right, but still it is going to be so much fun. For us, I mean, not the audience! I told no one at the table in Poland about this because after these names had come up the conversation turned to Polish music, how it had been during communism when Western forms of music had to be redefined, given new names and performed with different lyrics so that it wouldn't offend the authorities or be too Western and decadent. I asked Marcin earlier in the day if he remembered anything from those days, and he did, he was eight years old when the Iron Curtain came down. What did he remember? Primarily, the queues, what it was like standing in line for hundreds of metres for basic everyday commodities, one at a time. There were hardly any shops. And there was no life.

Switzerland scored in the last minute, after lots of chances for Ecuador went begging. And my name was shouted over the airport tannoy system – as always, time goes faster when I write, suddenly half an hour has passed without my noticing. Now I am sitting on the plane, high above Poland. It is a spellbinding country, which like so much else I have never really been interested in, never really taken the time to get to know, always thinking it is a little rough, a little poor, a little lacking in taste. It was only when I read Milosz's memoirs, entitled *My Europe*, that my eyes were opened. It does what good books can do, shifts the perspective, makes you see the world from a completely new angle, where everything appears different. Milosz came from Polish-speaking Lithuania, his experience was of a border country where very distinct languages and cultures intermingle, in this case, Polish, German, Russian, Lithuanian and Jewish, through two world wars and a cold war. That is how bloody the previous century in Poland was. When we took the taxi to the restaurant yesterday Marcin told us about the Warsaw Uprising in 1944, when the inhabitants stood up to the German occupiers and were massacred, around two hundred thousand of them. The town was razed to the ground. Not a house was left standing in this ancient European city of over a million inhabitants. While all this was going on the Red Army was not far away, but they didn't lift a finger, they let it happen. And then they invaded Poland. In the building where I was interviewed in front of an audience yesterday, part of the facade had been preserved as a ruin, with bullet holes in the walls, and I saw other walls like this too, otherwise everything was rebuilt in the post-war period. It was strange to walk in the Old Town because it too had been rebuilt exactly as it had been before the war, so all the medieval houses, streets and marketplaces were copies, they just looked old – the Palace residence, or whatever the official name is now, an attractive late-Renaissance building, was finished in the 1980s. It wasn't obvious to the eye, it felt like walking through any ancient quarter of a European city, but it was noticeable, the atmosphere was different. Incidentally, from there you could see the new football stadium that was built for the European Championship in 2012, it looked like an enormous red bucket with spikes on or an upside-down circus tent, impossible to dislike in a town where the predominant colour is grey. I enquired about the Jewish ghetto, nearly all of the Jews who were incinerated in Treblinka came from here. Trainload after trainload left for the village where every single passenger was gassed to death. This happened seventy years ago, in other words, yesterday. My interpreter indicated the area, saying it had been enormous. She also told me the town where she had grown up during the communist period was disappearing, blocks were being demolished and skyscrapers or malls were being built. She said Warsaw might not be pretty, but she loved it and I should come back and ask for an extra day so that she could show me her town. You have been an interpreter yourself, Fredrik, so perhaps you know this experience, the way the interpreter and the interpreted invariably become closer to each other in a strange but agreeable way? For two whole days she was in my language and my thoughts, translated them, and in the breaks we carried on taking about this and that, by the end of the day it was as if we had known each other for years. Sharing a language can be intimate – you notice when you have been abroad for a long time and return home – I notice every time I go to Norway, familiarity increases, you can make jokes again, do the chit-chat, be close to strangers; it isn't intimacy exactly, that isn't the right word, but . . . a familiarity. Even though I have lived in Sweden for years, there is still a distance in me, and that is language-related. I am never quite sure how what I say is perceived, and nor am I sure how what is said to me is meant. All the codes that are embedded in language – for example, those concerning social background, geographical background, culture and class, all these strata of information that exist in spoken language, are nearly impossible for me to catch, so with strangers I am much more of a tabula rasa than a Swede would be. In Norway it is not like that, there I know where I am at once. I was talking about this once with a Swedish woman, she said that was good because what I was talking about was prejudice! So the knowledge you have about people's backgrounds was prejudice because what is primarily important is the individual.

Oh, Sweden, Sweden, what a shit country you come from, Fredrik!

No, no, just joking. The woman I just mentioned was cultural middle class, which is what I am too, and it is this group and its dominance in Swedish society that I always get so heated about. Our neighbours down here, the parents of children at the school, none of them expresses such attitudes or opinions. On the contrary, those who don't ignore them, dislike them. I never talk about such matters, I am not completely out of my mind.

We are flying over Österlen now. It is unbelievably green and fertile. I couldn't find my bearings fast enough, saw Ystad too late, didn't see our house, we must have just flown over it. Now we are landing, so I will have to switch off. But I'll try and catch the Argentina v. Bosnia game tonight, Fredrik, and I'll look for you in the stadium!

All the best,
Karl Ove

Glemmingebro, 16 June

Dear Fredrik,

It is Monday morning, the sun is shining, the children are nagging us to go to the beach. They are on holiday, after all. I say no, I have to work. By work I mean write, and what I tell the children is not strictly speaking honest because writing has never been work for me, it isn't an obligation which, sadly, I have to prioritise over beach life and holiday fun, it is the opposite, writing is my holiday, my beach life. But I told them we can go at three, in another one and a half hours. So I can probably see Germany v. Portugal, another exciting clash to look forward to. This is maybe one of the best phases of the competition, when all the teams perform for the first time. Yesterday it was Argentina's turn. I have seen many of the players, but not the national side since the previous World Cup, and when I sat down on the sofa at midnight yesterday I was really excited. They weren't impressive, like many other teams – Costa Rica, Holland, Mexico, Croatia – nor did they seem very solid or in control like Brazil, whose potential no one doubts – no, damn it, they didn't seem to be the finished article at all. I was in Barcelona this spring, where I met an Argentinian photographer, and while he was taking photos we talked about his team. He said they had tremendous individuals, but it wasn't a team, and they were sure to do badly in the World Cup. I don't believe that, but I understood what he meant after they had played a quarter of an hour. However, getting a lucky goal after two minutes must have had an impact on the game, it was won almost before they were out of the blocks. I don't know, there is a lot of psychology in all this – you mentioned it with reference to the Spain–Holland game, Spain had been the dominant team at first, then went one down just before the break, and when Holland got another, suddenly they were in total disarray. Argentina played OK yesterday, they appear to have a good goalie, the defence worked well, but the midfield seemed to be too quick off the mark – towards the end of the game Bosnia counter-attacked and only Mascherano tracked back, all the others strolled around or jogged slowly as if what was going on in front of their goal had nothing to do with them. Up front there were lots of misplaced passes, I had my eye on Di María, he is a personal favourite of mine, and almost half of his passes must have been off target. Messi? He set off on four dribbling runs, which all failed and were stopped, a couple of them in places that gave the opponents the chance of a counter-attack. Of course he has been injured, out for a long time, and I thought that the worst that could happen was that he would stop trying because even though he is a good passer of the ball – he didn't grow up in Barcelona for nothing – that is not what makes him unique. Fortunately, he kept going, and then it was 2–0. I read the match report on the *Guardian* website after the game, and they said the sight of Messi driving the ball forward in full flight was one of the most beautiful sights in the sporting world. I have never seen him like that, I have never enjoyed the sight of Messi, however supernaturally talented he is, there is nothing in his style that appeals to me. It is strange. What is this about? You touched on it when you talked about Robben, who is also brilliant but hard to like. Take a player like Pirlo though. (Ignore his Italian background for a moment.) When he plays he attracts not only the ball but also admiring gazes. I love everything he does with the ball. The way he traps the ball, his turns and then, my

God, the passes that split open defences. What do I like about him? I like the type, his charisma, it is perhaps a hangover from my childhood, he is cool and he is unorthodox, not like the many magnificent, machine-like specimens there are in football now, all these six-packs and biceps – which Messi certainly isn't either – and I like what Pirlo represents or what he gives football: guile. I admire guile. Ronaldo, he hasn't got guile. Messi hasn't. Nor Neymar. But Pirlo has. And Maradona. However, Maradona was beyond everything mortal. Regardless of whether one likes Messi or not, regardless of whether his driving runs send shivers down one's spine or not, he scored, it was 2–0, Argentina were, like Brazil, on their way. Brazil were undoubtedly better, but something tells me that Argentina have a lot more to come. After all, Higuaín missed seventy-five per cent of the passes he received when he came on, Agüero failed at nearly everything, but suddenly he was there, he whipped the ball back to Messi as he steamed up, then Messi strayed left, causing two Bosnian players to fall over each other, and fired the ball against the left post, it ricocheted off to the right and went in. And there were some other good one-twos, and then you saw what they were capable of. Di María, why do I like him so much? One, he is the spitting image of Franz Kafka; two, his body, long and thin and boyish, is so untypical of a fast dribbler, which he is – and, as we have seen this year, he has quite a range of skills on the pitch. He plays for Real Madrid, as you know, and was used wide until they bought Bale. At first he ended up on the bench, then in midfield, behind Benzema, where he suddenly became a different type of player or showed another dimension of his play, including the raking pass. I wrote a little article about him for a magazine before the World Cup, and for that I watched quite a few YouTube clips of him. Now all players look good on YouTube, of course, most exhibit a couple of good feints over the course of a season, which lacking the context, without the hundreds of unsuccessful minutes around them, look impressive. Nonetheless, I saw Di María lose three defenders without touching the ball, he just ran after it, dummied, and one after the other they dropped off. I saw him place one pass that rendered the whole defence helpless and sent Ronaldo off on a one-to-one with the keeper, and I saw Di María run straight at the keeper, who made himself big and strong and narrowed the angle, and Di María humiliated him with a tiny toe-punt that a child could have executed, holding back long enough for the keeper not to have a chance. It looked a little like what Maradona did to Shilton after the famous dribbling run when he didn't even feint, it was a non-feint, by which I mean a feint was expected but it didn't come, he just swept past. That is guile too. Intuition, improvisation, it hasn't been rehearsed, it hasn't existed before, but it is there because he has read the opponent's mind, and so he does the opposite, or something quite different. And you know all about this, Fredrik. I have played against you, and this is exactly what you do. You have guile. When there is an opening you shoot, cool and calm, and it is a goal. If you have someone tagging you, you outwait them, until your shot can't be stopped. It is hard to understand how you as the possessor of such coolness and footballing intelligence cannot bear Italy, in fact you almost hate them. I suppose that must mean there are other reasons – political (You mention Mussolini, don't you? At any rate, Berlusconi), social (the Mafia), aesthetic (snobs) – but somewhere in your heart of hearts you must admire their football or at least have a sense of it? Football is about winning, not losing beautifully. And Italy win. So coolly, so urbanely and so cynically that it is beautiful or at least worthy of admiration, isn't it? Pirlo, surely you can't dislike him? In my eyes he is the greatest player since Zidane. What he has is the reason I watch football.

No, I know this isn't about football but attitudes and ideals, and it is about childhood. Football is one of the few things children and adults can share and be on an equal footing. So when I look for an explanation as to why I like Italy that is where I have to go. This will be a bit embarrassing, but so be it. When I was growing up I read piles of music magazines, Norwegian and English. A surprising amount of what was written about English bands – we are now in the mid-80s – was about looking good. Ian McCulloch from Echo and the Bunnymen looked good, while his arch-enemy in U2, Bono, didn't. Bono was all about honesty, sincerity, lack of pretence, passion – not completely dissimilar from the perception I had of the Poles this weekend – and that absolutely disqualified him, he wasn't cool, he didn't have whatever it is, hard to put your finger on. It wasn't the clothes because Ian McCulloch looked good in anything, nor was it to do with physical beauty, it was actually about attitude. Arrogance, confidence, big red lips. Paul Weller in The Jam and Style Council looked good, and Noel Gallagher in the later shit band Oasis looked good. I wanted to look good. But as long as looking good had nothing to do with appearance, nor with clothes, I didn't have a chance. I could go to England and kit myself out in whatever bands wore, I still didn't look good. Once I saw a young man on the street in Kristiansand, he looked absolutely fantastic, and I followed him for several blocks, trying to work out what it was. He was wearing normal shorts and a normal shirt, yet he still looked amazing. To my consternation, I discovered that he was Alex James, the bass player in Blur! That confirmed my worst suspicions, he dressed like a Kristiansander, he could have been one of my friends, but there was something about him that didn't belong here, which was bigger, and it was visible even without band associations or attributes. I knew I could never have that. I lived in Bergen, where a boy from Arendal coined the dismissive expression 'the H&M rockers' to describe my brother and me. That was what we were. And so to Italy. For at the same time, the end of the 80s, I was in Florence for the first time, I hitched down from Roskilde with a pal, and there I discovered that everyone looked good. Everyone had it. Here we have the antithesis of Poland and Norway, but also, if I have understood correctly, of Brazil too? Oh, we are talking about stereotypes, but it is not going to be printed in *Dagens Nyheter*, so we can let it stand. Everyone looked good in Florence. The ugly and the beautiful, the young and the old, men and women. Everyone looked good. But also the contexts they were in, the old streets, the new cafés, everything had an aura, character and was beautiful. It was shocking, what was going on here? Why was everything beautiful here and not at home? In Norway nature was beautiful and, without any doubt, an astonishing number of girls, but not in this way, where even the ugly ones looked good. The same applies to football, the players, who look better than the players in other countries (with the obvious exception of Socrates, the king of look-good footballers), but also everything that surrounds football. Italy represents all I want to be (or wanted to be in my childhood and youth, because I gave up a long time ago) but am not and never will be. As regards football, the famous cynicism, calculation and cunning that characterise all Italian teams and trump all notions of honesty, blood and sweat (English) but also honour (they have been known to cheat to win), they are also as far from me as it is possible to be, yet I would like to possess these qualities. I am incapable of lying because I am so bound to the person I lie to, so concerned not to disappoint them, I am always honest, I have a one-to-one relationship with the truth, in other words, I can't play-act. I can't pretend. I am doomed to follow my emotions, even when I know they are leading me directly towards a precipice. I can't plan, I can't calculate, I can't do one thing to achieve another. I can't go for the surface, the outside, I can only go for the inside and the truth. I am an ethicist, and if you are that you also have to be an anti-aesthete. But I don't want to be that, I want to be free, and the only free person is the one who play-acts, who doesn't make a commitment, who goes their own way. They win. Italy as a football nation, their football culture, is like that. It represents everything I don't have but would like to have. They look good and they play a game. I don't look good and am governed by emotions. Obviously I love Italy.

And my books are published by a Berlusconi-owned company there . . .

Now the time for our beach trip is approaching. Four children and a dog get into the car. What a mess. I think Argentina and Brazil will meet in the final. Let's keep in touch about this and more. Enjoy yourself in the promised land, Fredrik – and I'll organise the children and animals as well as I can in your home country and try to talk nicely about it from now on.

All the best,
Karl Ove

Botafogo, 17 June

Dear Karl Ove,

Thank you for the letters. I received two simultaneously, one from Warsaw and one from Österlen.

'It took place seventy years ago, in other words, yesterday.'

Golden words, Karl Ove. And for me, over the years, writing has, to a greater and greater extent, developed into a method of getting to that point, of reaching down through the present to bring this yesterday to life, to make it a now, to feel close to Diderot as he rows his monumental work, the *Encyclopédie*, into port, to reach so far that I can stand alongside Hegel, be a small boy at the edge of the picture who sees Hegel observing Napoleon on horseback, and I appreciate that this scene also concerns us. That same year Napoleon rides to invade the Iberian peninsula, where the first guerrilla war saw the light of day, and thereafter to Portugal; the royal court in Lisbon flees, 15,000 people with John VI at the front, in fifty caravels, the ruling class abandons the common people and suddenly Rio de Janeiro, where I am now, becomes the de facto capital of Portugal. Really. Thus Napoleon is thwarted and – picture it, 15,000 well-powdered ladies of the court and jesters coming ashore at what was then a hole in the ground – Rio becomes a modern city with sewerage systems, libraries, modern avenues, customs and practices.

It only just happened, two hundred and eight years ago.

Messi? I think what you write may have something to do with the fact that he is in part a tender young chicken, taken at an early age from the training ground in Argentina and brought over the Atlantic to the hothouse at La Masia – this may have smoothed away some of his edges, some of what makes him Argentinian, for example, esa locura, this craziness players like Maradona and Tévez have, and that's why he's not so popular in Argentina. Many people there don't regard him as hundred-per-cent Argentinian.

I like your taking me to task over Pirlo and I'm scarlet with embarrassment as I write. I think you may be right, he is one of the greatest players in recent years, but given he's Italian (reread that sentence, Karl Ove, it's insane), I don't like him. And it's not about cultural identity but a footballing culture (Herrera and his catenaccio) in which defence is fundamental. When England go up 1–0 they want 2–0. When Germany make it 1–0 they want 3–0. When Brazil make it 1–0 they want 4–0. When Holland make it 1–0 they want 5–0. When you're playing with your mates and make it 1–0 you want 6–0. When Italy make it 1–0 they want . . .

I think that must be it, I've simply overlooked him because I close my eyes whenever Italy are on the agenda (few things make me as happy during a World Cup as when Italy go out). I've made a conscious choice to turn my back on him, repressed him because he plays in a team with a football philosophy in complete opposition to everything I hold dear. Would you consider this an acceptable response? Mind you, that said, I do recall the semi-final of the 2006 World Cup, Italy v. Germany, and of becoming acutely aware of my hostility towards Italy evaporating as I watched Alessandro Del Piero (now he was my type of player) flying into the opposition half, I could hardly believe my eyes, and was left thinking, why don't you always play this way, caro amico? And because of him the Italian door was open for a little while. It's since been slammed shut again. Speaking of Del Piero and Juventus, in winter 2002 I was travelling, first to Chile, then on to Brazil, and my son William, who was eight years old at the time, was with me.

We'd stayed at the home of my hermano in Santiago, Jorge Calvo, and were on our way to the airport early in the morning on the day of our departure. It was 3.30 a.m., I was ready to pass out from exhaustion, Jorge was in the front passenger seat, and his stepson Fernando was driving. William was wide awake, looking out of the window and he says, Dad, I'd no idea that Trezeguet was part Argentinian! We'd never spoken about Trezeguet, not at home nor on the trip, and I wasn't aware Trezeguet was half-Argentinian either, it was one of the oddest sentences I've ever heard and served to highlight the strong bond Wille and I forged through football at the time, a dream for any father with an interest in the game. I was recently divorced and had the children in my small two-room apartment every other week, El Clásico on the TV and the two of us, sitting close together on a red sofa watching Ronaldinho's fantastic face, all that love, artistry, his flip-flaps, free kicks and then, a few years later, comes the rebellion: Ronaldinho sucks, Dad! Big time! All of us have to become people in our own right, throw off the yoke of our parents, I couldn't believe my ears, nor the grin on his face as he sat at the kitchen table and said it, the defiance in his voice: he sucks, Dad, you gotta see that!

Took it easy yesterday. Bought food in the grocery shop. Ate breakfast in Afonso's kitchen, where I'm feeling more and more at home. Worked in the morning. Sent you a letter and then hopped into the car with Afonso to drive to Polytheama, Chico Buarque's own private little arena. On the way we picked up the musician and poet Paolo César Feital, a big, friendly, garrulous guy, and he squeezed into the back seat before we hit the monstrosity that is this city's traffic. Endless tailbacks. Streets previously unknown to me. The incessant roar and then the landscape suddenly opened up: the Sugarloaf, the Atlantic and Corcovado, with the statue of Christ. Backdrops of immense beauty popped up in all their iconographic beauty among the urban chaos: Jesus with his arms outstretched between two plane trees, and a red traffic light surrounded by hundreds of cars.

The actual pitch wasn't as impressive as I'd imagined, on top of which Chico Buarque has decided to escape the World Cup circus and gone off to Paris to finish his latest book. We play six-a-side in the suffocating heat. As we're about to kick off, I realise the Germany–Portugal game is being played at the same time. A blunder on my part. I wound up on 'Chico's' team (even though he wasn't here), and we played in his home strip. It was now seven-a-side, and myself and composer Ruy Faria, a seventy-seven-year-old who's undergone total hip replacement surgery, form our attack. It would probably be more appropriate to say that I walk forward while he stands in the opposition half. Every time I pass the ball it rolls past him as he needs it played right to his feet. I hear someone shout that Alemanha have taken the lead from a penalty.

As you can probably gather, this is far removed from 'the war' in Duque de Caxias. These are composers and eminent guitarists with long delicate fingers that they're terrified of injuring. Free kicks are awarded for the slightest contact. This is bossa nova football and a slightly relaxed version at that, and, come to think of it, I'm probably more of a samba type, the big beat that makes you want to swing your entire body, the Dionysian as opposed to the gentle sway of the bossa nova. We, the team Afonso and I are on, lose 10–6, the heat is killing me and the fact I score three screamers and that they shout Ibra each time doesn't make me as happy as it did in Caxias, since we're simply not competing at the same level. In Caxias you were given no room, opposition players were on you like wild chimpanzees as if a World Cup was at stake. It wasn't like that here. Paolo is a delight to watch. Big and heavyset, but technically wonderful. He's also had both hips replaced, suffers from terrible psoriasis and has both knees heavily bandaged.

Yet he still managed to score four goals, like Romário or Gerd Müller he seems to draw the ball to himself inside the penalty area and dispatches it just as it ought to be. Impressive. Afonso, my host, is a team player with a simple, direct style. He crosses the ball all the time and never tries anything fancy.

And now I hear that Germany have made it 3–0 and I'm very surprised. I thought a draw was on the cards and had no faith in Germany this year. By the time our game is over and we've found a small bar to watch the rest of the match, it's 4–0 and on a flickering TV screen I see Cristiano Ronaldo's resigned expression and think, you beat us at the Friends Arena in the play-offs and are now being outplayed while we – WE! – fought back from 0–4 down to 4–4 in Berlin against this same German team and we don't even get to join the party . . . a view everyone seems to share, as talk of our own seven-a-side match is overshadowed by the game on the screen. Everyone thinks it's absurd that teams like Poland and Sweden aren't involved, while teams like Iran, Australia and Nigeria are, they all think it's a shame that Zlatan Ibrahimovic isn't at the party. Cold comfort. On the drive home Paolo launches into a potted history of Brazil.

'No matter who you pick, no matter who you choose to analyse, you'll find a little of everything. Of that you can be sure. My grandfather was an Indian, my grandmother was from Portugal. That's the way it is for everyone. In your country, in Sweden, there's a different biotope, so there's a dominant strain, or race, and you're tall, or most people are, and have blue eyes. Here you find everything, small Indians, Asians, light-skinned blacks, very dark-skinned blacks, cafuzos, caboclos, mamelucos. Everything, all kinds. No one is pure here.'

'Was it down to the openness of the Portuguese? The fact they slept with everyone?'

'Exactly. Colonialism here was quite distinct from the Spanish

American experience. That involved Indians being wiped out. Here they mixed with the Portuguese. The Portuguese were softer, more sensitive.' This is grist to the mill for me: the difference between things Portuguese and Spanish. The Castilian mindset is so much stricter, the Portuguese infinitely softer, more melancholic, and that brings us back to Zweig, since in his opinion it was from the Portuguese gene that a new 'race' was born: the Brazilian. Pessoa–Cervantes, Portugal–Spain. Two different temperaments. Two different peoples who changed the world in their own ways.

We drop off Paolo in Lagoa. It's impossible not to warm to him, a person with so much charm and humour. Fica com Deus, he says, hugging me before we part. Stay with God, Be with God. And come Thursday we'll play again.

Germany, Karl Ove, a wonderful team? For me, as a Swede, they've always been like an older brother on the pitch, near-impossible to beat, with such power and energy that they almost always tear us to pieces. I never celebrate when they score or win, but I have immense admiration for them as a team, an intellectually based and slightly resigned admiration. They never touch me in a heartfelt way. A little bit like my admiration for Italo Calvino, Borges, Flaubert or Cortázar. Fantastic constructors, but they never stir me deep down. Not in the way Proust, Thomas Mann, Balzac, Bolaño, Simenon or Ivar Lo can do. The Germans don't have that magic hold over me.

Watched a rerun of Germany–Portugal last night: a magnificent performance, a demonstration of the perfect balance between collective strength, discipline, thoroughness and imagination. They say all the effort put in with German immigrant youth has paved the way for this team, a project aimed at integration that started well over a decade ago with an eye to, among other things, the World Cup in Brazil. We've been witness to it for a few years and in my view it's perhaps one of the best things to have happened to European football, after tiki-taka, and maybe you can look on this German team as a dialectic response to tiki-taka. In any case, it was a pleasure to watch Portugal laid bare in that way, Nani's fruitless dribbles, Ronaldo's sulky expression and his silly stepovers, Coentrão's lonely, bullish runs, and as for Pepe? What a moronic brute. But their play typified what happens when there's not a team, just a group of individuals gathered around a leader who is not only out of touch with them but with himself, and that only serves to make the opposite logical, and thus Mr Ordinary, Thomas Müller, a spectacularly unremarkable player in my view, becomes the man of the match since he's the one German always in the right place when the ball comes in, on hand to make it 3–0 and then 4–0.

I'll conclude my letter here in the Rio night by letting you know you can be eternally grateful you don't have to listen to the Brazilian commentators, a bunch of loud-mouthed imbeciles who scream like lunatics every time someone scores. As Müller, practically on the ground, toes in a ball that the keeper spills, which my eighty-three-year-old mother would have put away, the idiot on Globo screams,

Gooooooooooooooooooooooooooooooooooooooooooooooooooooo
ooooooooooooooooool!

Qué beleeeeeeeeeeeeeeeeeeeeeeeeeeeeeza! Qué alegriiiiiiiiiiiiiiii iiiiiiiiiiiiiiiiiiiiia!

There's stupidity to be found in this country too, Karl Ove, as in all countries, and the way I see it, Brazilian football commentators belong in Dante's seventh circle of hell.

Goodnight. Or good morning. Or whatever it is there now.

Best Wishes,
Fredrik

Glemmingebro, 17 June

Dear Fredrik,

Thanks for your letter.

We are probably two of the most reluctant reporters in this whole World Cup – the pleasure-seeker who plays football and drinks instead of watching games and the Protestant who consistently sleeps through all the matches – and both have great difficulty analysing (reading, understanding) the little football they still manage to see.

We have moved away from the idea that geography and mentality, geography and national character are connected in all areas except in football. There we wallow in such stereotypes – Brazil, playful and beautiful, slow and then explosive. Italy, cynical and efficient. England, heart on their sleeves. Sweden, tactically perfect to compensate for technical flaws: always the collective before the individual. Germany, like a machine. Portugal, moody, inefficient. And then we identify with some of them and continue with a lifelong fascination. The match between Germany and Portugal was an example. I watched it but without much enjoyment, Germany bore me, until they meet resistance I desperately support (always in vain) the opposition. Why? The Germans are a well-balanced side, unbelievably solid in defence, they vary their attacking game and create chances, and they have good finishers who invariably score. This year's crop, the team facing Portugal, is probably the best I have seen so far in the competition. But that is precisely the problem: we don't watch football to see perfection, balance, variation and clever positioning. We want to see frailty being overcome, we want to have a surprise factor, something impossible to predict, we want improvisation, stages, risk. In brief, we want to have life, unpredictability. Or even briefer, we want to have humanity. Not that Germany is inhuman, it would be stupid to say that, nor that they are like a machine, but, well, yes, what they are is successful. Their style is successful. Now I am going against everything I have written before, that the main aim is to win, whatever that means. Germany win, and I don't like them. I don't have anything against them either, but they don't do anything for me. They are bland, in a way. Who could feel any passion for Thomas Müller? Toni Kroos? Bastian Schweinsteiger? Italy aren't bland, they are bad people, they do bad things but they do them beautifully, it is either spectacular or ugly, never bland. Somewhere in this is my explanation for why so few people outside Germany support Germany – I know none (although even this is a qualified truth – I have just heard that someone has seen kids wearing Germany shirts in Oslo, which reinforces the feeling I have that we are living in the Last Days . . .).

In Germany, of course, it is different. I was there after the European Championships six years ago. That was probably when this generation broke through? Anyway, perhaps the most important thing about the championship was that it was permitted for Germans to be patriotic again, to cheer their team on without any sense of shame. I spoke to my German translator, and his eyes went moist when he told me about his son and his friends, how they weren't frightened to wave the German flag, they did it quite naturally like the supporters of any other country. It took three generations for this to be possible. We also talked about the silence there had been in Germany through all the years since the war, how little of what had happened then was spoken about – not in broad outline, not in educational institutions – but between close relations, parents, uncles, aunts, grandparents – no one spoke, no one said anything. And as we know what kind of war this was, and what these people must have seen, done and lost, it is clear the silence must have marked German society in fundamental ways. So the moist eyes were not because of the flag and nationalism, but because those who are young now are the first generation to have escaped the grip the war has had on people and the weight it has been. When you are weighed down with the past, there is little future, attention isn't focused on that. I don't know if you have been to Germany in recent years? I have travelled around quite a bit, in the big cities, Berlin, Munich, Hamburg, but also smaller places in the middle of nowhere, and in university towns. It is such a good country, I think, although I am at a loss as to how to explain in what way. To me it seems open, that is probably the most important point, and then, in some strange way, caring. Without the harshness there is in the US, for example, and all the elements of harsh modernity that exist there – German infrastructure is light and green, American strenuous and exhaust-grey – and also without the extreme class segregation you see in England. Now this is superficial, I have never lived in England, the USA or Germany, but countries exude feelings, you sense a kind of predominant atmosphere, and for me Germany's is openness and caution.

But watching the Germany–Portugal game I was unaware of all this. I can't stand Ronaldo (another feeling I share with almost everyone), and Nani is, if possible, even more unlovable, yet this was the team I was behind. And the sending-off of Pepe? I don't get upset when this sort of thing happens, nor do I think he is brutal and stupid and terrible, on the contrary, I am angry at all the moralistic comments that are made, all the know-all attitudes that follow whenever a player loses his head and is sent off.

For me the situation was clear: Pepe shoved Müller, perhaps it was a free kick, perhaps not, but not remotely a yellow card, and then Müller reacted as if he had been headbutted. Why? He wanted Pepe a) to get a yellow, b) to get a red or c) to lose his head. It was a provocation. And Pepe allowed himself to be provoked. But what did he actually do? He bent down to Müller and shouted. Face to face. But it wasn't a headbutt, it wasn't dangerous, it was over-the-top marking. Fair enough that he got a red. But to call him an idiot and say he ruined the game for the team – well, it is for moments like these we watch football. We want power, aggression, individuality, explosions, unpredictability, and Pepe's reaction expressed all that. Call it the dark arts, the shady side, whatever you like, but it is connected with what we like best. Maradona, the man who had everything, was capable of both: the worst, the dirtiest fouls and the most beautiful and preternaturally clever passes, feints and shots. It is rare for both sides to be in one person, as with him, usually we have brutality (and Pepe is brutal) or elegance (like Neymar – but did you see his elbow in the Croatia game? The way he looked at the opponent before the elbow came. It was dirtier than Pepe's head-touching because it was calculated, Neymar wanted to hurt, Pepe didn't).

Nice to read about your son William – I met him here in the garden, as you know, and he was miles away from the young man who can suddenly talk about Trezeguet's roots; he was a teenager, with the half-gauche, half-sophisticated body language you have then, not quite part of adult company, not quite outside it either, accompanying Dad is still a possibility while you actually consider yourself an adult – I'm not talking about Wille now but adolescence! – you think you know what it is necessary to know. I can still identify with that age, it is as though I will never really become an adult, while it is very different to be in your mid-forties, in the sense that there is more of everything, you have more experience, and the answers to the questions you ask yourself are less sure.

But here, I assume, your experience is probably not so much who was I then and who am I now, but rather my son has grown up to be a man and a person in his own right, no longer dependent on me, perhaps even against me – that is how I interpret what you write about him. Watching football together, which you describe so well, sitting on the sofa next to your son, after your divorce, is no longer what it had been. I am in the midst of this – not watching football together, none of my children is remotely interested, in this respect I have failed miserably as a father – but in the midst of life with children who are dependent on me. I like it, in fact I love it, I think I can say, it really gives me so much; at the same time however everything is ready for them to pack their suitcases one day, get on the bus and go off to start their own lives, leaving us behind perhaps as people who only hindered them from developing? Who never saw them? Whom they have been longing to get away from? If that doesn't happen we really have failed. The greatest danger of all, in my experience, is parents who tie their children too closely to them. There is a strange border there, a border of love: too much love is life-destroying. A danger to life.

I am keen to know what you think about yesterday's game, Fredrik, between Mexico and Brazil. I thought it was terrific, I sat like a coiled spring for ninety minutes, such was the intensity, especially from Mexico's side, they were on fire, fighting for every ball and full of life, and they had the technical ability, whereas Brazil, by comparison, seemed a little lazy or apathetic. Nevertheless, Brazil were the better team – again, as they were against Croatia. I had the impression the Mexicans were playing out of their skins while Brazil were underperforming, yet on a par in the game – and, as for chances, they went Brazil's way. What I liked, I think, was the dynamics of the match. The fired-up versus the laid-back, the frenzied versus the controlled. Nevertheless, the question is: aren't Brazil too easily pegged back? They lack a top player up front – neither Fred nor Jo was particularly good yesterday – and perhaps also a midfield general, what we used to call a playmaker – that isn't Gustavo's role, Paulinho doesn't play like that either – with them play stops when the flanks are blocked or stifled (as yesterday). This is becoming exciting. Now we have seen all the teams. Belgium v. Algeria? The first half was poor, without any pace or energy, but that might have been nerves because in the second they played wonderful football. I felt sorry for Algeria, they had an impeccable first half, very, very solid defensively, and a few swift counter-attacks, but solid then too, so my qualified guess would be they will have to take points off South Korea and Russia to go further.

But post-first round, now that all the teams have been in action, the most convincing performers are Germany, Holland, Brazil, France, Argentina and maybe Belgium too, followed by Mexico, Croatia, Chile, England (whom I haven't seen either), USA – have you any others on your list?

There is a great deal more I wanted to write, but Linda is in Helsingborg today and tomorrow, and I have to take care of the children – I have a nanny for Anne for these two days as well, I rang last night and arranged it, but there are of course three other children here who need food and drink, TLC and instant refereeing decisions. Yesterday we went into town in the afternoon, Heidi, John and I, and bought a trampoline. I have always been against getting one, primarily for aesthetic reasons but also because of a 70s idea that children shouldn't have everything given to them on a plate, shouldn't have it so easy, they should play with what is around them, have fun with each other, oh, this is idiotic, I hadn't been thinking, it was just in my mind somewhere – anyhow, it is so easy for them to sit in front of the TV or the computer, and we think that anything that can take them outside, anything physical, is good, hence the trip to Ystad. We chose one with a radius of 3 metres 60, it sounded suitable, but after installing it last night – it was still light between the two matches – I realised it was gigantic. It looks like a spaceship has landed in our garden. This morning I put up the safety net, which made it look even bigger and more conspicuous. But they use it, they have been jumping up and down all day, interspersed with a couple of quarrels, that is all. And I am not tired any more, I should add, nearing the end of this letter. Tiredness has sapped my attention during the games (I dropped off during one or two more, which I kept quiet, out of fear I wouldn't seem very committed) and last night I fell asleep on the bed, fully dressed, at half past eight and didn't wake up until half past seven this morning, and I needed the sleep – yesterday I wrote three pages of an essay (about fate, the deadline was 1 June and I have had it hanging over me for ages, without making a start on it), cut the grass (which was over my ankles), bought a trampoline and watched two matches, as well as all the usual shopping, cooking and tidying-up. Today I have spent an hour installing the safety net, written half a page of the essay, plus this letter to you. The nanny will be leaving in six minutes, so I'd better stop. Look forward to hearing from you!

All the best,
Karl Ove

Botafogo, 18 June

Dear Karl Ove,

Yesterday was, to put it mildly, a special day. I'd made up my mind to take it easy, but as is often the case with me my optimism regarding time got the better of me and, consequently, I was late for a meeting with the writer Rubens Figueiredo that I was almost tempted to postpone. I agreed to meet him, even though I really wanted to go home, sleep and give my brain a rest after all the impressions from the first week. It's often that way, politeness and the fear of offending others wins out.

I'm happy about that now. You'll soon understand why.

But first the matches. I'd decided to watch Brazil v. Mexico in Tijuca, a district not far from Maracanã Stadium. I got there early, was about to eat my lunch at a cheap restaurant where Algeria v. Belgium was on the TV when I realised that this game left me somewhat emotionally conflicted. I have, after all, backed Belgium to reach the final against Brazil, besides which I like the 'Red Devils', given that they do their bit to hold an ailing nation together, what with both Walloons and Flemings cheering on the same side. Not unlike the Bosnian national team in that respect. Football as a Band-Aid on ethnic wounds.

In any case, Algeria are leading 1–0 and as I'm about to tuck into my food it hits me that it hasn't entered my mind that my brother-in-law Kamel, an Algerian who works as a machine operator, is probably together with my sister in Vasastan in Stockholm right at this moment biting his nails. The Belgians look ponderous and sluggish. Then two beautiful Belgian goals in a matter of minutes change the game, and I can picture Kamel, his distant olive-black eyes, that Algerian defeatism welling up inside. And then bed. He does have to be up at five in the morning after all, to make it to work in Västberga, to repair mechanical diggers, road scrapers and cranes, the lump in his throat, the remnants of that arduous journey we all put behind us when our team is winning and has led us to dream of victory, only to plunge into the void, the chasm of defeat, an emptiness we carry with us wherever we go.

When I get to Tijuca, the place everyone is going to watch the match, it's jam-packed, with almost everyone in sight dressed in yellow and green, women, children, men and boys. I'm wearing my white Garrincha strip. The atmosphere is pleasant and good-natured. People sing. Horns sound. There's an air of expectation, and as the game gets under way I'm taken aback by how good Mexico are, how easily they neutralise the Brazilian attacks, how readily they're presented with chances to score. I think about how the Brazilians probably have the 2012 Olympic final in London at the back of their minds. The Brazilians show respect for their opponents, and the match is transformed into an even game of chess. Mexico keep their shape, are aggressive and confident on the ball. Brazil never get going, never find their rhythm, and I begin to have a sneaking suspicion: I've misjudged this Brazilian team. Maybe they're not as good as I'd believed – or hoped. Oscar is anonymous, Fred is downright poor, and the midfield of Paulinho, Luis Gustavo and Ramires is lacking in creativity. Only Neymar and the defence, chiefly the fullbacks, give a worthy account of themselves, and as the game draws to a close and I stand in the middle of a sea of yellow tops – we are packed like sardines – I begin to hope for a point for Mexico. A slight change of heart, Karl Ove. This often happens to me. Am I an opportunist? No, it's rooted in a love of fairness (though not when it comes to Italy). I think the Mexicans deserve it, and I like that stern Aztec-like quality in some of their faces, and what I'll remember from this game are Neymar's header (wonderful ability, he just hangs in the air, not nodding the ball, but allowing it to strike his head as he simultaneously turns slightly, a sign of his greatness and that all true football artistry has expediency as its lodestar, he does all this for one purpose, to get the ball on target), the Mexican keeper's three fantastic saves (from Neymar's header, Neymar's close-range shot and from Thaigo Silva's header, a real Gordon Banks save that one) and Thiago Silva's chesting of the ball: football as art. And 0–0.

But I'm worried. Something's missing, and as I leave the sea of people and walk towards the metro I search for the words which best describe the mood of the crowd, and just as I make my way down onto the platform it comes to me: cheerful frustration. Not dejection nor anger, but precisely this seeming contradiction.

I'm tired when I make it home to Afonso's house. Just travelling between different parts of this city wears me out, as though this enormous metropolis has placed small weights on my shoulders, and as I power up my laptop I'm inwardly hoping that Rubens has cancelled our meeting. Nope. And so we meet at Starbucks in Copacabana at 8 p.m. He's friendly and open and we're soon chatting away. No beating around the bush. Before long he launches into a tirade on 'Brazilian Society' as if in some strange way he already knew my opinions on the subject.

'The biggest problem is inequality, class difference. The intelligentsia never say this. They only talk about corruption. And they go on about the shortcomings of the public health service and the state of the schools. Not about how too little tax is paid, how we need to increase the taxation of the rich and introduce a luxury tax. As it stands, a lot of the people up here . . .'

He illustrates what he's saying the entire time with the aid of a pyramid he marks out on the table with his thin fingers.

'. . . are paying three per cent on their consumption. Three per cent! And the media is controlled by a small group of actors. And the people won't organise . . .'

All this politics is making for a bit of a stuffy atmosphere and I suggest we take a stroll. We go out onto Avenida Atlântica.

There are football fans everywhere. A lot of Chileans. They're playing Spain today at the Maracanã. As I'm in the process of trying to explain the Swedish system of arts subsidies to Rubens, we see five Chileans with guitars leaning against the open boot of a car. There's a small man next to them wearing an Argentinian top with the number ten on the back. We come to a halt, Rubens and I. There's something familiar about him. He makes his way to an SUV parked a little back from the Chileans' car. I don't know why I follow him, or rather I'm in absolutely no doubt as to why I do. Can it really be . . . Here? Just like that? Everything around him seems so normal and quiet in the dusk. Two men sit in the front seats as though waiting for him. A heavyset guy dressed all in black opens the rear door. He has the look of a bodyguard. I approach him and ask, 'Is that . . . Is that really . . . Him? Es El?'

We see now that the car has Argentinian plates.

'Sí. Es El.'

I'm speechless. This is the man I was obsessed with at one stage in my life and whose career I've always followed, it's the man I've seen do the most amazing things I've ever witnessed on a football pitch.

Es El.

And I stretch my hand into the darkness of the back seat, he sees me, he looks a little older, his complexion a little coarser, his hair still black though flecked with grey, and then I see it, the

Che Guevara tattoo on his right arm, and then he puts out his hand, gives me a warm, firm handshake and says nothing. I can't get a word out. The next moment the heavy door shuts and the car pulls off and disappears down Avenida Atlântica.

We look at one another, Rubens and I, shaking our heads and laughing. Incrível, he says. Incredible. Exactly, Karl Ove. Sometimes it feels as though chance seeks you out. As though he was standing waiting for me. And as we continue our walk along the beach, it's as if our conversation no longer has any weight, as if our words were just soap bubbles because we're both so moved by the incident. It holds us within its grasp and before we part we manage to look at one another, laugh and say incrível, unbelievable, a few more times.

I shook the hand of Diego Armando Maradona yesterday, Karl Ove. Shall we just stop here? Can there be any more to say?

Best wishes,
Fredrik

Glemmingebro, 18 June

Dear Fredrik,

What a fantastic letter! What an experience. Again I have the feeling that I am in a novel, but this isn't a novel, it is something that happened to you yesterday, and instead of thinking nothing can top this and we may as well give up, I prefer to think the opposite, maybe this is the beginning of something new! Something has opened up. From now on anything can happen.

Spain are losing 2–0 to Chile as I write this. There is nothing to say about the score, the Chileans are supremely fast and accurate, technical and aggressive, but if this score line stays it means Spain are out, and that is sad, so sad it almost hurts. I am not sorry for them, this team has won one World Cup and two European Championships, but there is something about their demise it is hard not to feel. Almost all narratives and almost all plays deal with some kind of fall. Spain is the narrative about the team which always had the potential but could never deliver, which never won for so long it seemed they would never be able to win, until their luck turned, and finally they, with all the goodwill and underdog sympathy in existence, became European champions and then world champions. They were the kings, and the story about their path to power has now turned and become one of downfall. When I was young and read about the French and the Russian Revolutions, it was always the king and nobility or the tsar and nobility I sympathised with. Don't ask me why, it may be tied up with a desire to obey authority or a reluctance to accept change. So it is sad they are losing, and the way they are losing, with no drive, no desire, powerless as it were – four years ago they were the ones with the pace, and in every single situation the player with the ball had several options, he had teammates all around him, and the second they lost the ball they were onto the opponent, pressing him to make a mistake while they eliminated his alternatives. You remember Spain v. Germany, don't you? When Germany barely crossed the midfield? And we're talking about Germany here. Now the odd player breaks into a run, but the unit, the astonishingly efficient team pressure when they weren't in possession, and all the possibilities they had when they were, is nowhere in evidence. They are playing as individuals. Chile, on the other hand! They are playing with an inhuman intensity. If they win here, and they probably will, but lose to Holland, it will be Chile v. Brazil in the next round. That could be more exciting than you appreciate, Fredrik, because this Chile can't be a team Brazil want to meet, it must be the worst option for them. Holland, however, Brazil can beat, I think. We will see.

I read your letter on my Mac in the garden, from where everything you write about takes on a dream-like quality because nothing of what you describe exists or could happen in the reality I inhabit. The road outside, always close to deserted, the few houses where mostly pensioners live, and on the other side an enormous farm building with red tiles, all very calm and quiet. Around 700 people live in the village, most on the far side of a little copse of trees a few hundred metres below us, where there is a large housing estate. The garden is full of shadows, dense growth, established and lovely; it is one of the reasons we bought this house years ago. When I read about your meeting with Maradona in Rio I was sitting in the garden with the children, Anne too, who was in her car seat, growling (she has just started doing this), while the others laughed at her. It sounds idyllic, and it is too, but the day has been long and the arguments have been many – my fault really because it is their summer holiday and there are no children nearby, so they are bored, and when they are bored they get irritable, and when they are irritable they argue – then your best bet is to pile them in the car and go to the pool or the beach, and they are as happy as larks for the rest of the day or ring some friends and invite them over, but I have to work during the day, I have a long list of jobs, so I can't do anything with them until after four. Today there was no swim, instead we went to Ystad with Heidi, John and Anne to buy a badminton net, and on the way we got hamburgers from McDonald's, which we ate in the garden with the afternoon wind blowing in from the sea and bending the trees above us to and fro, and the leaves rustling. I intended to answer your letter immediately, but that was impossible with Anne awake, so instead I heated some milk, took her into the living room, cradled her in my arms and gave her some milk while watching the first half of Australia v. Holland. The children were jumping up and down on the trampoline. Australia were the better team, and Cahill scored a stupendous goal, you must have seen it by now, there was a forty-metre pass and he hit it on the volley, it crashed against the bar and bounced down into the goal. Anne had fallen asleep on my stomach, and in the break I put her to bed, set the baby intercom, checked John, who was outside jumping up and down on his own, then sat down to watch the second half, in which Holland woke up and again reminded me of the team that crushed Spain. Towards the end of the game my mother rang, I haven't spoken to her for a long time, she had just been to the doctor, she had cancer not so long ago and is still concerned that it might return, but everything was fine. For some reason or other she mentioned the Swedish kulturmann debate, I don't know if you have come across it, I hadn't, but she said she had read an article by Ebba Witt-Brattstrøm, and she wondered whether *Dagens Nyheter* had printed it to ridicule her. I said no, they didn't print it to ridicule anyone. But it is misandry, pure and simple! my mother said. It is so full of hatred and so stupid! Everyone can see that! No, I said, not in Sweden, everyone here thinks like this. Well, it's unacceptable, she said. After she had rung off, and Holland had beaten Australia 3–2, I went onto the net and read the article. It wasn't hostile to men, it was hostile to humanity, because she writes about people in roles without understanding that these are people whose eyes you can look into, who have their faults and shortcomings but also their own particular good qualities – warmth, ingenuity, devotion, to take just the first three qualities that occur to me. Those who think of humans as systems are totalitarian, and there is no more to say about it. EWB mentions me too, as an example of a kulturmann who has his own spokesman and flag-bearer, you know, the man who walks before the king shouting 'The king is great' – and in my case the flag-bearer is Geir! The man who never allows interviews, who is never in the newspaper, on TV or on the radio, and who rarely meets another living person, but sits up in his office reading and writing, day in, day out. He doesn't have a good word to say about me either, from where he is sitting. What she is alluding to must be the words I put into Geir's mouth in *Min Kamp* about my writing. But that is in a novel, and surely the kulturmann debate is not about that, but about how kulturmenn exploit women, and especially young women around them? In other words, sleep with them. We-ell, Fredrik, what should we say to that? It has ever been thus, a trade-off, ugly old men barter their power for young women's beauty. But it isn't just take, if so it would never have lasted, it is also give. Give and take. Now we are touching on puritanism again, the new morality that is ravaging this country. I am a puritan, as you know, not a bon viveur but a life-denier, but this particular puritanism is too much, even for me. It has such double standards and is so hypocritical because it doesn't take account of what everyone knows: that a man's first thought when he looks at a woman is always what it would be like to sleep with her. How women look at men, I don't know, but it wouldn't surprise me if it was the same. This urge, which is about living life to the full, is ignored. Instead, a satanic, evil male figure is created who damages all the women around him. When I was nineteen I met a girl who had once danced with Georg Johannessen – he was the great Norwegian poet in the 50s and 60s, the learned, socially critical essayist in the 80s, the university lecturer with disciples in the 90s. He, the person with the most integrity in Scandinavia while he was alive, said to her, who was around twenty, twenty-five at the time, while they were dancing, that he would like to take her to a desert island or some such cliché! I was so disappointed when I heard that! How could Georg Johannessen say anything so stupid! Now I think it is fine. Several years after she told me this I met Georg Johannessen, and met his gaze, then his eyes, they were so sensitive that it struck me that everything he has surrounded himself with, writings, thoughts, poems and essays, have been a way of protecting himself, a rampart, because he was so close to the world it was dangerous. Now I know how this will sound – romantic, the male genius blah blah blah – and I am so sick of this, not being able to say even quite self-evident, generally obvious things in Sweden without being subjected to suspicion.

Of course he would have taken her to a desert island if he could.

When I started writing this letter, to respond to your improbable meeting with Maradona, this was on my mind, then the chance event with Johannessen's gaze: I wonder how Ebba Witt-Brattstrøm feels about Maradona? About the hero worship adult men indulge in. Well, it is not so hard to imagine. But it is worth reflecting on. What is it about Maradona? Why does he merit our admiration? After all, he was only a footballer. Perhaps you have to grow up with football to understand, go through all the stages, perhaps it is not possible to understand how liberating it can be, how impossible something is if you yourself don't physically know the ground rules, the framework and its limits? It is a little like writing. Only the person who has written a lot, really tried to form words and sentences for many years, with total dedication, can actually understand and admire the opening of Virginia Woolf's *Mrs Dalloway*, which I have chosen as an example because of the theme, because only someone who has tried themselves will be able to appreciate how extremely difficult it is to breathe life into a character as Woolf does, not only that, into a whole era, milieu and culture, and render it in such fresh, vigorous, indeed such uniquely precise terms. If you have run around the midfield for many years and hit passes to teammates, simple, unspectacular passes, if you have chested balls, laid on crosses and shot at goal, you know in yourself how magical and impossible, original and amazingly unexpected Maradona's play was. I can't think of anyone who has even been close.

But why admire that?

It is only football after all.

It won't lead anywhere, change anything or create anything either, for the moment something is done it has also disappeared. Nothing lasts in football.

The counter-question is why not?

It is a game. It is anti-seriousness. Anti-meaning. Anti-intellectual. It is the kitten chasing after the ball of wool, it is the horse running alongside the fence snorting, it is the falcon gliding on the wind, it is the otter sliding down the snow-covered mountain on its back, it is that which has no meaning, it is only fun. It is a sparkle.

And no one had more of that sparkle than Maradona.

All the best,
Karl Ove

Botafogo, 19 June

Oh dear, Karl Ove!

Oh dear, oh dear. First thing yesterday morning I received an email from Rubens Figueiredo, the writer I'd met the day before. He'd told his wife about the Maradona episode when he got home, whereupon she immediately burst into laughter and told him that there was a Maradona lookalike in Rio and it must have been him we saw.

Honestly, I don't quite know what to believe. The tattoo? The Argentinian number plates? The look in his eyes? Today's paper has a picture of Maradona and a report on his complaints about the poor treatment he received at the Maracanã. So he is here and bears an incredible resemblance to the person I saw the other day.

Ah, well.

Other images from yesterday: the vacant expression on the face of a solitary Spaniard on the metro returning from the Maracanã. He is standing completely alone in the middle of the carriage, wearing an all-too-tight-fitting Spanish shirt with a gold number 9 on the back, Chileans dancing in Lapa, the cocky gait of two young Mexicans at a restaurant in Copacabana yesterday – Somos Mexicanos and we're not afraid of anyone! – a street-corner TV with a poor-quality picture luring the gaze of every passer-by, a lone Australian at one of the bar shacks in Ipanema by the beach, and how he shrieks with joy when the Socceroos go in front against Holland, a drunken Brazilian at a bar ranting and raving about Fred and Scolari. Following up with an attempted impression of Neymar's dribbling, intending to poke fun and almost falling over.

All that is of more interest to me.

What a fantastic World Cup we're witnessing, Karl Ove! Without doubt the best since Spain in 1982. Offhand the only downright poor display I can think of was Australia's first-half performance against Chile, and for that reason it was wonderful to see them redeem themselves by (almost) bringing Holland to their knees. You ask which team has impressed me. There are so many good teams, but so far the ones that have made an impression on me are Germany, Holland and Chile. And of course I should write something along the lines of 'Spain were hugely disappointing.' But no. They were brilliant in the first half against Holland, and yesterday's 2–0 defeat at the hands of Chile was bound to happen at some stage. All empires must eventually fall. Spain has completed its historic mission. Sooner or later every little Napoleon must dismount from his horse. All hegemonies dissolve in the end. That goes for both history and football. Tiki-taka was something new and took the world by storm – gold in two European Championships and one World Cup – and the time has come to abdicate. The world has learned to read Xavi and Iniesta. The question now is what will replace tiki-taka on the throne, the European combination of power and technique (Germany, Holland, Belgium) or a Latin American variant, the Brazilian, I'm still not quite sure what to call it, 'samba football' perhaps, well, yes and no), the 'crazy' Chilean Indian style, supposedly 'invented' by Argentine Marco Bielsa (known as el loco), he was the one who introduced this idea of pressure and pace, which requires an enormous physical effort from the players (Chile continue to play along these lines under the leadership of

Bielsa's compatriot Jorge Sampaoli), and I thought it might have brought them success in South Africa, but perhaps this is their tournament. I could see Alexis Sánchez and his pals getting at least a bronze medal.

I don't believe Argentina will do well this year (Messi looked way too lethargic and laid-back against Bosnia, and the team didn't look like a unit), I think we can discount Uruguay already and neither Costa Rica nor Ecuador will stand a chance when things start to get serious. And Mexico? I liked what I saw against Brazil but think they'll be packing their maletas (bags) after the quarter-finals, which they should reach. As you know, I'm going for Ghana as possible semi-finalists, and nothing would please me more than them going all the way, but there's a curse hanging over African football and it's doubtful it will be lifted here, in the 'Africa' of Latin America. It would be fantastic but is unlikely.

We would appear to be in complete agreement when it comes to the German national team, although I'm probably slightly more positively disposed than you are. You should know that there's truth to the cliché about the German 'machine' – just as all clichés and caricatures contain a kernel of truth – and Klinsmann once claimed it was the most fitting word for German football when it's at its best.

You capture William nicely, at that age when they're almost ready to fly the coop, and you're right about 'love's limitations', and I'm aware of all you said on an intellectual level. He works at the Alfa Laval factory at the moment, making good money, but still lives with us, and I know it's wrong but I still feel panic of sorts: don't want him to leave home. Not yet. Probably because I'm still living in the illusion of a time that's long gone.

The Croatia v. Cameroon game is showing on the TV here in

the room where I write this, what a farce, what a disgrace to African football – 'lions', mice more like. The Croats are leading 4–0 at the moment and two Cameroonians are beginning to fight with one another.

And now the first real cloudburst since I arrived in Rio. And I'd been planning to go out in Lapa tonight to celebrate with my hermanos from Chile.

Watched Spain v. Chile at a bar in Praça Mauá, down by the harbour, and Spain were dethroned by a Chilean side who put in a spectacular performance, but, Bielsas' ideas about an extreme pressing game aside, I think it was mainly down to a difference in attitude. Energy, quite simply. Chile aren't 'better' than Spain. But Chile are on the way up, want to break onto the world stage, have the hunger to achieve something big and want everyone to know. The Spaniards have three heavy gold medals hanging around their necks, and what do you want to win when you've already won everything?

In addition, Chile have the player who could be the sensation of the tournament, Alexis Sánchez, who looks like he's in the form of his life: pace, technique, the ability to read the game and an incredible shot. He has pretty much everything. The way he twisted his body as he struck the free kick that led to the second goal, superb.

You mentioned something in a previous letter that got me thinking about what to me is maybe the most important issue in our time. How the world is changing. I read an article which talked about how the 'economic upturn in the southern hemisphere is historically unprecedented in speed and scale. Never before have living standards and future prospects changed so quickly and so dramatically for such a large number of people.' What the writer of the article is referring to is the French Revolution of our age, a change incomprehensible in magnitude. Hundreds of millions in China alone, millions more in India, as here in Brazil, where somewhere between forty and fifty million people have emerged from poverty to a decent life. One sign of the change that's taken place here is the absence of street children. In the course of this week I haven't seen a single one. Just a few years ago they were everywhere. No matter where you went you saw them. If you were sitting at an outdoor restaurant, sooner or later they'd show up. (They call them crocodilos here because many of them are so small you can only see their eyes sticking up above the edge of the table. Marianne and I were here a couple of years back, I was thrilled to have her with me so I could show her 'my' Rio, and the first night we went to a wonderful seafood place in Copacabana. We were just about to order when I looked at her face and saw how sad she was, for God's sake, Marianne, we're in Rio, why aren't you happy? Finally she told me how that morning she'd looked down onto Rua Sá Ferreira from our little hotel balcony to see five little boys sleeping on flattened cardboard boxes under a tree, and had thought of her son, Arvid, lying down there and had been upset.) People's circumstances have improved in the favelas (many of which are peaceful now, the drug gangs have been thrown out and there are regular police patrols, while the inhabitants have access to health services and schools) and in Duque de Caxias, and Brazil's economy is growing so fast it's creaking. But so are the economies of Ghana and Angola, for example, and that begs the question: in a world where Angola is providing economic aid to Portugal, can we continue to talk of a Third World? Can we use this phrase that Mao gave us? In a world where Brazilian and Chinese capital is extending into Africa, can we really still talk about the Third World?

It doesn't make sense any more. Mao's concept has had its day. And this new French Revolution is happening quietly – in the ports of Brazil, the factories of China and India, deep in Nigeria, in the rice fields of Bangladesh – all very silently, because it's economic, without banners, without barricades, without bloodletting, without guillotines, because it's taking place in people's daily lives.

Hundreds of millions of people across the world, who in the space of a few years have taken the step from having nothing to having something and who can now live their lives the way we, you and I, live ours. It's the biggest change in human history. And it's happening now. Right now, and in addition to the economic change, there's also the fact that violence between people is diminishing. Seen in a historical light, fewer wars take place between states all the time (when I was young, Karl Ove, all of South East Asia and large parts of Africa were in flames), there are fewer and fewer dictatorships (when I was young, Portugal, Spain, Brazil, Uruguay, Argentina, Paraguay and Chile were right-wing military dictatorships, in addition to all the communist regimes behind the Iron Curtain), and democracy is on the advance. Much of this isn't noticeable to us in Malmö and Glemmingebro, but here in Rio you can practically touch and feel the economic and political change, and that's why I sometimes feel that we should raise our gaze a little more often: wake up! The world is becoming a better place! Things aren't as gloomy, from a global perspective, as they are in Europe. The world goes ever onward. Hegel was right. The world spirit grinds on quietly – exemplified by the BRIC countries – and maybe all those European prophets of doom, whether on the right or the left, would do well to take a trip down here or to India, Ghana or China. But what do we do in Europe to meet this challenge? Steam ahead towards a United States of Europe, try to cling on to the status quo or else sink back down into the ancient morass of our own extremism and nationalism.

I don't know, Karl Ove. All I can say is that I'm happy and

grateful to be living in such exciting times. And that it's stopped raining. Onward, to Lapa!

Best wishes,
Fredrik

PS I have an image etched in my mind from an episode you described in one of your first letters, where you and Heidi were stuck in the car, blocked by another vehicle, and of how you had to get out and go over and knock on a stranger's door. It's an unnerving image. I know how the darkness in Österlen can be, like a closed room. It's the perfect opening for a crime novel, but there's something else too: what you write about the man, who he is and what he represents to you. I'd like to delve deeper into this. I'd like to take a closer look at this man, at his house. The man behind the door could of course be anyone, a weary farm worker who doesn't want to speak, a grumpy old fogey with absolutely no interest in politics, but he could also be the prototype of the contemporary European xenophobe, one of those – not infrequently from the working class – now being sucked down into the maelstrom of right-wing extremism. I know several of that sort from my time working at the port in the 70s. At that time they supported communist or social democratic parties. Now they vote SD, Swedish Democrats, and speak warmly about Vladimir Putin and Marine Le Pen. Only their hatred of the USA remains intact. From time to time these old dockworkers have get-togethers, lively, enjoyable affairs, which I attend and where stories from the port, as opposed to any political discussions, usually dominate. Nevertheless, and I've no problem admitting it, now and then I feel the need to slam the door shut and scream: enough! What do you think, Karl Ove, where should you draw the line for socialising with others whose political beliefs are anathema to you?

Botafogo, 19 June

My dear friend,

'Kulturmann'? No, I've no idea what that is or what it's about, but I promise to look it up and get back to you. When I read what you wrote an unpleasant old feeling arose within me, a feeling I experience quite often at home, and which to a large extent has to do with the fear of being singled out as evil. As wrong.

It's been such an intense joy to be here, writing about Rio, Brazilians and the World Cup, and it wasn't until tonight – symbolically enough the rain has been lashing down for hours and I have been sitting alone in the house – that another feeling crept up on me, a niggling unpleasantness around all the dialogue and debate from home. I've been almost deliriously happy down here, and your letter makes me understand one of the reasons why: freedom from what you're describing. Being spared that intense Protestant Manichaeism: you're evil, I'm good, all of you are evil, all of us are good!

That aside, my day has been spent playing bossa nova football on Chico Buarque's pitch. It was wonderful playing in the rain. Felt at home. It's strange how easy it is when you acquire proficiency in something and – the opposite – how bloody awful it is when you're bad at something and overlooked because of it. At the time of my divorce, fourteen years ago, my daughter Amanda was nine years old and had no interest in football. To her a beautiful goal meant the goalposts were adorned with flowers. The day after I moved out of the family home she wanted to join the

Malmö FF girls' team. I didn't understand it at all, she had never played football, had never shown any interest in it, but she was so insistent we went ahead and put her name down. Much later I realised that it was a desperate effort on her part to hang on to me, to hold on to my love, all totally consistent with the logic of a child of divorced parents. It was torture, Karl Ove, Amanda was simply awful, and standing on the sideline at training was agony for us, the determination to appreciate her good intentions and assign talent where it simply was not present, the embarrassment we felt in front of the other parents, the ones who had daughters with ability who could do something with a ball, and then, worst of all, discovering your daughter is nothing in the eyes of the other girls, a zero in a Malmö FF shirt, the colours of Daddy's beloved team. When her mother and I tried to persuade her to quit, she refused, and in the evenings she went down to the school yard with a ball, either on her own or with Wille, hour after hour, day in, day out, and before long she was up to two hundred keepie-uppies, could control a ball played to her, hit a pass, roll the ball with the sole of her foot, shoot – and score. She then ascended in the hierarchy and ended up playing in the final of the Gothia Cup, which they won. An inconceivable progression for us who never thought she had it – what Wille had had right from the start – in her. An unbelievable mental journey that I admire her for, and in the autumn we were eating dinner with all five children and the talk around the table turned to the drift, or not, towards fascism following in the wake of the Swedish Democrats' political gains, I went up to my home office and took out a copy of Primo Levi's *If This Is a Man* and read aloud the paragraph about the look in the eyes of chemical engineer and SS man Pannwits, and about Levi meeting his gaze, and how that look of Pannwits told him he wasn't human, merely a thing, and I went on to talk about the hierarchy among the prisoners in the camp. Amanda said, That's just what it was like on the girls' team at Malmö FF, just like that, Dad, I have to read that book.

But, getting back to the here and now, I certainly feel like a somebody, I'm O Freddy again, or Ibra, and everything is so easy, everyone is so friendly, eager to talk, and after knocking in six goals today I know that I've risen in the pecking order for next Thursday's game.

Watched England v. Uruguay here in my room, and I don't know what it is about England, or how, with their fantastic football culture, they never manage to make a go of it. Why it nearly always ends this way for them. Despite Gerrard, despite having speed merchants like Sturridge and Sterling on the team, not to mention the wonderful Rooney. It's probably down to their predictability, their lack of creativity and pace in midfield. Gerrard is too easy to read with those sweeping long passes of his, and he slows down the ball, allowing the opposition time to dig in before the shot or pass arrives. Uruguay were frighteningly efficient, a completely different team with Suárez than with Forlán, who, in fairness, is past his prime. With two players like Cavani and Suárez up top they can make do without any real stars in the other positions. What we saw today was the Uruguay everyone was talking about beforehand: compact, hard to break down and deadly on the counter-attack. Both of Suárez's goals were superb, the header in particular, given that he was fighting gravity.

So there we have it, Suárez v. England, 2–1, and in all likelihood the Three Lions are out of the World Cup, and I'm sure there were many like me, around the globe, who wondered how it felt for Gerrard and Suárez when they embraced after the match. Gerrard's handsome, sombre, boyish face, his eyes downcast, and Suárez, who must have felt for his friend and captain at that moment. Football, Karl Ove, Jesus, it can really mess up your emotions.

Outside, the rain continues to bucket down. I don't miss home, not yet, but I can feel everything you write about Glemmingebro and Skåne stirring my love for that part of the country and for the landscape there, a panorama that allows you to unwind. Here there's hardly any rest to be had, and tomorrow my trip takes me to Salvador in Bahia, to the black heart of Brazil.

I don't expect to get much rest there either.

Best wishes,
Fredrik

Glemmingebro, 19 June

Dear Fredrik,

Forty minutes to go to the England v. Uruguay game. Linda is back home and sat watching the pre-match build-up on TV with Anne in her lap, and she asked what it is with England, why is it always extra-significant when they are playing?

From a long way off, say two months before the World Cup, when the first magazines containing all the teams and data began to come out I thought how nice it would be if Uruguay did well. I mean, 1950, Montevideo, Suárez, the Forlán family – there is an aura, and even more if you read Borges, because he lightens the sky over Argentina but not the darkness on the other side of the sound, which lies in a kind of literary and cultural shadow – at least for an ignoramus like me. It is exciting. But now, thirty-seven minutes before kick-off, my only thought is England MUSTN'T lose!

Of course this has to do with my upbringing, when English football matches were the only ones shown in their entirety on TV, apart from the two international cup finals in early summer and the Norwegian cup final in the autumn. The rest was Ipswich v. West Bromwich on yellowing pitches, and the heads of my generation are stuffed with names of English footballers from the 70s and 80s. Everyone had their favourite team, and the day Norway beat England at Ullevaal Stadium is still the biggest in Norwegian footballing history, bigger than the Brazil victory in 1998.

I was a Liverpool fan, had a Liverpool bag (but an Everton shirt – just imagine, my mum and dad were in England buying a birthday present and bought an Everton shirt for their son, the devoted Liverpool fan) and was passionate about them until Graeme Souness took over as manager, when I was no longer a fan, only a sympathiser. (By fan I mean it really hurt me when they lost – it doesn't any more, while a mild pleasure can stream through my veins when they win.)

In one of my first letters I wrote that my father took me and my brother to football matches when we were growing up. To check that all the details were correct I sent this letter to my brother too. He answered, don't you remember, Karl Ove? We never watched any matches with him. And then it all flooded back. We went to matches with him but never saw them together because he bought a ticket for himself in the seated area and tickets in the stands for us. Can you imagine, Fredrik? What kind of father does that?

You're right, you have to raise your gaze, look out over our little world. This became especially clear in the letter I sent you before I read yours because it was partly about the Swedish cultural debate and extreme feminism, and it feels so small and narrow and stupid to allow yourself to be affected by that, come on, take a deep breath, it is of no consequence, in fact it is worthless. Having said that though, our everyday is made up of these small matters, this is where our lives are lived, this is what we have to deal with and understand, speculate about and draw our fantasies from. I know I sound like Ekdal in Bergman's *Fanny and Alexander*, when he talks about the little and the big world, but I have been thinking about this a lot over the last, well, perhaps fifteen years, about what is 'local' and why I experience it as so important, and globalisation as a threat, a sort of menace. The reason I give this so much thought is, not least, because the 'local' was so central to the Nazi hierarchy of values. I don't want to go into that now, twenty-two minutes before kick-off, except to say that the Nazis' systematised thinking eradicated the 'local' as an idea, concept, ethical value more than anything else. But in my view there is a lot to this pair of concepts, the local and the global, and there is no doubt that the radical change that has taken place over the last thirty years is a crisis in the sense that we are confronting something completely new, something we haven't seen before. I have my head in the Old World, my body in the New, and am torn between the two. This is what I want to write about, not here, that is, but in the future, start in some way, I mean, write a sentence, let the place where it lands produce another sentence, and so on, until, yes, you know, a novel is the result. That is the best thing about the job we have, or have given ourselves, that it hardly matters what your starting point is, what you actually want to write about, the automatic dynamics of the process are so strong that you still end up in the middle of something different (and much more stupid). Nothing is as great or wonderful as a novel which hasn't been written; nothing is so trivial or stupid as the first pages of the same novel. Oh, I seem to be dreading it already.

Heidi and I in the car that dark autumn evening in Österlen, the anger of the ravaged stranger: that is one of the final scenes I have. Another is an autumn day last year, we were on the beach in Sandskogen, the sky was a brilliant blue, the air still, the sun heavy and yellow, as it can be in autumn. In the distance the boom of artillery – there is a military firing range a few kilometres from here – and if we looked in that direction occasionally we could glimpse smoke. We were three families, many children, they took off their shoes and paddled, ran and played. John walked off on his own, I poured coffee, lit a cigarette, we were sitting in a kind of hollow in the beach, sheltered. Perhaps ten minutes later I remembered John, where he was, I got up quickly, strode in his direction, and I saw him, he was lying on the sand far away. I broke into a run because he was screaming. He lay motionless, screaming, his voice frantic. He was rigid with fear, above him the air was full of wasps. He had stepped on a wasps' nest. Now they were stinging him, and he was so frightened he couldn't move. I ran over to him, picked him up and ran off with him in my arms.

He is still scared of wasps, doesn't dare go out in shorts or a T-shirt, has to wear long trousers and long-sleeved shirts.

It is an opening for something, not so much because of the wasps but of the atmosphere, of a lull, an uneventfulness, time-lessness, and then the booms, and then an unexpected incident.

I am not quite sure why you want to visit the man in the house, what does he represent for you? For me it is simple: he is 'the other'. Or, in Christian terminology, my neighbour. I have written a lot about 'the other' in my novels, meeting his gaze, seeing 'the other'. I have written about Hitler and Anders Behring Breivik and 'the other' not existing for them, they lived in a world consisting of a 'me', a 'we' and a 'they', but not a 'you'. Not a constraining gaze. After knocking on the door in the darkness and being abused by this angry, ravaged man I realised that the universality my books experience is valid only for a certain class, which is more or less similar everywhere in the world. The consequence of this is that 'the other' for me is actually the same. Outside my own class – which is big in Scandinavia, the majority – I very rarely meet anyone who has other values and opinions, I mean, radically different. This man is the real other, who doesn't understand me, who doesn't see the value of what I am doing and whom I cannot understand or identify with. The part of Sweden where I live is the area where the Swedish Democrats have the greatest following, to my knowledge. Let me be prejudiced and assume the man in the house is one of them. Let's say he is a racist. Let's say he is full of hatred. Let's say he is not very intelligent. He doesn't understand that much about other people or the world. In other words, he is a stupid, evil racist. Has this person, who has become hypothetical, from a living being to a character in an analogy, but who still exists – we know that of course, evil exists, stupidity exists, racism exists – is this person worth as much as me? Is he worth just as much as Fredrik Eklund? I see you as a person who wants good, Fredrik, and does good. I would say, instinctively, that you are worth more than him. And I am too. I think the notion that all people are worth the same is superficial, a notion we adorn ourselves with, but actually, deep down, when it comes to the crunch, we do not believe it. There are good people and there are bad people. Isn't that how it is? But it is at exactly that point it becomes critical. It is there Levinas's concept of 'the other' is critical, and it is there Jesus's concept of our neighbour is critical. Not that we should be patronising and say that he is worth as much as us, despite the way he thinks, but that we actually should understand that he is like us, he is like me, he is me. I drive down the road on this dark autumn evening, I find the road blocked and go into my house furious. I open up when the idiot bangs on the door, I shout abuse before I move my car and let him out. I get into bed in the run-down, messy, ugly, abject house, switching off the light and closing my eyes, alone in the world, enveloped by darkness somewhere in Sweden, on this earth floating soundlessly through the universe, surrounded by luminous stars that extend in fields and belts into infinity. What am I thinking? What do I see in front of me? It doesn't matter, for this is my inner reality, they are my thoughts and my images, they come from today, yesterday, tomorrow, from my childhood, adolescence, manhood, and they unfold in the darkness of my brain, hidden from everyone except myself, lying on my back in bed, my eyes closed, my skin wrinkled, my lips thin and my chest slowly rising and falling, I am asleep, it happened quickly, I was tired.

He is probably somewhere far away now, while I am writing this, six minutes before kick-off and would probably think, if he knew what I had just done to him, what I wanted was a smack in the kisser.

I am going to see the match now. Back later to finish the letter.

Now it is my turn to say oh dear! England are out. More importantly, Suárez is absolutely unbelievable. The first goal: Cavani gets the ball, Suárez is miles from the goal, but Cavani holds on to it and then chips it over and behind the defenders, it is a brilliant cross, and Suárez twists to head the ball over the onrushing goalkeeper – this has to be the goal of the tournament so far, doesn't it? And as for the second one, well . . . I haven't seen such desire for a long time. England had their chances, but they performed poorly, without imagination or power, and it is no loss that they are out. It looks like this is going to be a South American World Cup. Brazil, Chile, Mexico, Argentina, Uruguay, Costa Rica and Colombia have all been good. This is normally far from the case! Today a Brazilian newspaper enquired about an interview, and I emailed the journalist saying I hoped for Brazil's sake they meet Holland and not Chile. She answered ha ha ha! We aren't afraid of Chile. But Holland are dangerous. I wrote back my true opinion. If that is the prevailing mentality, that Chile is an easy game, they are in for a shock.

It is half past eleven, pitch black outside, even though the lightest night of the year is only two days away. Tomorrow is Midsummer's Day. This means nothing to me, I would prefer to work, but the children are Swedish, so it will be herring for lunch, a trip to the maypole in Ingelstorp and cake back here in the garden afterwards. Today hasn't been so good, I put Anne to bed so early yesterday that she woke up at five this morning. At half past eight the nanny came, but by then I had been up so long that it was difficult to write – I ought to start the moment I get up, before I have started to take things in. I wrote a page of the fate essay. Then I was too tired, the way I am sometimes, when I find it difficult to do anything at all, barely rise from the chair, barely lift my cup of coffee, barely clean my teeth, and making lunch, as I did, requires a huge effort of will. I went for a lie-down on the first floor and read for an hour – the three oldest children are so big they can take care of themselves and come up if there is a problem, while the youngest one was looked after. I slept for a while or, to be more accurate, dozed, and then I made lunch, wrote a letter to you, saw England lose, deservedly, to Uruguay. Everyone is asleep in the house on the other side of the garden now. A few days ago we were out in the car, and Heidi told me that when she was small – by which she meant five – she thought all the headlamps on cars were eyes, some looked angry, some looked nice and friendly. I asked her what the eyes on our car looked like. She said they looked sad. I laughed but was also a little sorry, I want there to be happiness around us. She laughed too but must have known what I was thinking because when we parked she stared at the lamps and said they looked happy. She added white cars were good, red ones bloody and black ones evil. So it was a whole little universe she had invented while we were driving. Here came an angry, bloody car, here came an angry, good car, here came a happy, evil car, here came a happy, good car. I saw the world the same way I did when I was a child, everything had a face that could be read. I have only fleeting reminiscences now. But I like that world recurring in them, the children living in that reality, which is semi-magical and inaccessible to us. Last year at exactly this time we were going to

Brazil, I had to launch a book there and was taking the whole family with me, the hotel and plane were booked, and then we had to cancel at the last minute, the day before departure. Vanja and John took it well, but Heidi cried, she had been so looking forward to it. Now your letters are the closest I get – and the interview with the Brazilian journalist tomorrow. I am sure she is going to ask who I support. I can't say Argentina, can I. But nor can I lie to please her and say Brazil. And Italy, I have learned, is the worst profanity you can utter there.

More about everything later. Talk soon!

Karl Ove

Galeão, Rio/Salvador, Bahia, 20 June

Dear Karl Ove,

Your England and the football you first fell for was, together with the Brazilian, the football I first fell for as well. I think Linda is on to something with her question. We're all from there in some way or another.

Rooney typifies much of what I think of as English, you can see the defiance in the face of that working-class boy from Liverpool. He's domesticated to a large degree now but in the beginning he was wild and reminded me a little of a former colleague from the docks who had the same truculent features and was always ready to cause trouble, to start a fight, to let chaos loose. This idea of what a man should be that, I imagine, was also to be found in bands like The Clash and the Sex Pistols, with two fingers to the world, as was their wont, and their constant displays of aggression which paved the way for the birth of hooliganism, that English face – the counterpart of quintessential gentleman Gary Lineker's – as I encountered it during the 1990 World Cup in Italy, one of the very few occasions in my adult life that I've been genuinely afraid, after the semi-final between England and Germany. We had checked into a hotel in the centre of Torino, and late at night all hell broke loose, English fans smashing everything to pieces, turning on showers, 'Rule Britannia' resounding in the halls and us not daring to leave our rooms. Englishness for me is also that English violence, the endless confrontations between men from different areas and different cities, this is who we are and we're not like you. In Italy the English supporters never joined the other spectators in the Mexican wave, this to me is also very English, this insistence on masculinity, a malaise that can be traced back to the Empire of course, but also to England's rigid class system. It's a type of masculinity I'm tired of, Karl Ove, which has also to do with the fact that I shun violence like the plague. I used to romanticise a certain kind of violence, not least when it laid claim to being 'revolutionary' – now I abhor even that – and unfortunately this is a side of what is English, a darker side that is perhaps prone to rear its head all too often.

Speaking of gender. Yesterday, after our game at Chico Buarque's place we went to a barbecue at the local bar. There were people from the neighbourhood there. Afonso's musician friends. It was a simple, modest affair, and a small band struck up a samba tune. I watched as a forty-something woman in high heels began to dance with a black man in his seventies – his dancing was supple and rhythmic, his feet and hips moving softly in time. It's easy to become romantic here, but their version of masculinity is different, it's softer and slightly more ironic, not as strict and gnarled as ours – or as in England. I doubt whether Rooney or my old friend from the docks could have danced like that. It's also one of the reasons I enjoy being in Brazil so much. There are other ways of being.

It's the second half of Italy v. Costa Rica now. Costa Rica are holding on to their lead without over-exerting themselves. If either they or Italy win, then England still have a chance. A fantastic free kick by your hero, Pirlo, but the keeper's well placed to save it. The game's heating up now. The action's flowing from one end of the field to the other. Costa Rica are good. They have tremendous energy, like the Chileans. The Italians can't create any opportunities. They, like the other world powers of the game at this tournament, have problems. Costa Rica really deserve to win, they have capable players with good technique but first and foremost they have unbridled willpower. Fantastic to watch. Seven minutes remaining. Italian corner. People gather in groups in front of the TV screens, travellers from all over the world. A collective intake of breath is heard around the departure hall as a Costa Rican attempt goes just over. One minute left. The Costa Ricans are ice cold. Acabou! All over! Applause and cheering all around. I'm obviously not the only one who enjoys Italian defeats.

Happy Midsummer,
Fredrik

Glemmingebro, 21 June

Dear Fredrik,

There was no letter from me yesterday for the first time since the World Cup started. I began the day writing the essay but couldn't manage more than half a page, it is as if the effort it costs me to get into it is too great or, in other words, I am too feeble. This is tied up with concentration, after having been away travelling for three weeks, performing and doing interviews, new people, new towns every single day, I am still restless, out of myself, wanting and not wanting things to happen, and stressed because of all the jobs I have taken on and actually don't have time for, on top of all I have to do at home, not least with the children. That is my explanation, or excuse, for why I am getting nowhere with the essay, which is supposed to be about fate, but which for the moment is about dreams, what dreaming actually is. Afterwards I wrote 150 words about a book I was supposed to recommend for the *Financial Times*, it had to be in English and published this year, so I was forced to take one I hadn't read but seemed interesting by Henry Marsh, who is a brain surgeon and has written a book about his work, brain surgery. I flicked through it, skimmed pages to get a sort of picture and did what was required. Then we went to the Midsummer celebrations in Ingelstorp. This was my thirteenth Midsummer, before that I hardly knew what it was, we don't have anything like it in Norway, as you know. There was a maypole, an ageing band playing Swedish folk songs and locals dressed up dancing around the pole and singing. Most of the faces I recognised, although I hadn't exchanged more than a few words with them, as an immigrant here I am not well integrated. They know who I am – some of them view me with suspicion, some with interest, all without knowing me, such is my situation. I have become a living cartoon character – and if so, not the Phantom, not Popeye, but Gladstone Gander maybe.

When we returned it was Italy v. Costa Rica. This was the first time I had seen Italy and immediately saw how weak they were. Pirlo sent through a couple of defence-splitting passes, otherwise there was nothing but crosses, lounging around in midfield, and the same apathy around him, they couldn't be bothered to run, had no alternatives to offer, played badly, it was poor stuff. In the first half I thought they would win anyway because Costa Rica's back line was well up the field, and Balotelli penetrated it on his own twice, he was the only weapon they had, but it could have been enough, Costa Rica were taking big risks. In the second they fell back and blunted the Italian game, whoever had the ball was surrounded by three men, and without the slightest sniff of a sacrifice Italy didn't have a single chance on goal, apart from Pirlo's free kick. They were apathetic, arrogant and unimaginative. Actually England didn't play any better the day before yesterday, but they had desire, they took risks, but probably lacked, as you wrote in your previous letter, a creative midfielder – that is, someone like Pirlo. England have good wingers, a good striker, and they have Rooney in the hole behind the striker, but no one can set them up, combine with them, open up the defence – they played one on one, and if they beat one opponent, they didn't the next. Same with Italy – Cassano, who came on as the assist provider to hold the ball for Balotelli, failed with almost all his dribbles, he was robbed every time. But the feeling was that Italy really had the ability but not the will, while England had the will, though not the ability. So I think

Italy will go through, they will beat Uruguay in the next group match, that is how they play, Fredrik, they never do more than they have to. Now they have lost, and Costa Rica are through as part of the South American wave we have seen this week. Bolaños was good in the centre – he was the one who played for Start and now plays for FC København, and also the Swedish defensive midfielder Borges (Is that his name? And why don't I remember? The name ought to be unforgettable), he was also good, one of the reasons Pirlo created so little.

What a difference between this game, which was poor, lacking in goals and pace, and the next one, Switzerland v. France! It is strange, but I can't say what made France so fantastically good and Italy so fantastically poor, I mean, with the analytical eye that tells you what France does right and Italy does wrong, I have no idea. With France, everything I saw was elegance, balance and incredible accuracy in their counter-attacks. Their strikers, Giroud and Benzema, were so lively, mobile and dangerous that they were more than a match for Suárez and Cavani. France are definitely the best team I have seen so far in the World Cup, and if the opposition was poor and if Germany were not up to their best because they didn't need to be, France had something Germany don't have, an aura, which counts for nothing when it comes to winning football matches, but I was enamoured. Shame only that Giroud caught the Swiss centre back with a very nasty boot to the face, even though it was unprovoked, it was probably justification enough for a sending-off, and everything that happened, happened in the shadow of that kick.

I apologise for dropping a snake into your paradise by mentioning the Swedish kulturmann debate. On the other hand, this is the biggest issue back home, it is the climate we live in. You don't have to go far from Sweden before it seems weird and actually insane, but if you live in Sweden, it is the reality, it is no good knowing things are not like this anywhere else. It must be two years now since I was compared, in all seriousness, with Anders Behring Breivik in Sweden's biggest newspaper. He murdered seventy-six people, gunned them down, most of them youngsters, all with families, who were utterly devastated. What I did was to write a book about myself. It should not be possible to compare that with the massacre on the island of Utøya. It is grotesque to think like that, even more grotesque to write it. But it is worse that the newspaper actually printed it. That such an act of brutality could be used by a writer in a cultural debate as an argument to support her opinion pours contempt on all those who lost children on Utøya.

This, I hasten to add, is not about being right or wrong. It is about acknowledging that others may have different opinions from you, and that has a value in itself. Anything else is totalitarian. It is striking that in Sweden people think the Swedish debate, Swedish attitudes and ideologies, are universal. According to them, if they don't exist in a culture, if attitudes are different, then this culture is reactionary. The Swedes' view of Denmark is a good example. Or of Norway – there have been, as you know, several articles in Swedish newspapers in which the Fremskritt-sparti, which is now in power in Norway, has been called Nazi or racist, and the Independence Day celebrations on 17 May have even been labelled a manifestation of that. The Fremskrittsparti believes in market liberalism, it was founded to lower taxes and duties and to reduce the power of the state. I don't like them, they represent a lack of culture and a vulgar capitalism that devalues all I consider to be important, but they have nothing to do with Nazism, and what happens when you call a legitimate political party Nazi is that you not only invalidate their opinions but also those of their supporters. They are saying, hey you, you're evil, you're bad, you're stupid, you're wrong. You're uneducated, you're racists, you're Nazis. In Norway, thank God, this rhetoric barely exists. In Sweden it does, and what is happening here? The Swedish Democrats, who do actually have roots in Nazism, have a support of ten per cent and are growing. There is no debate, only irreconcilability and rejection. My standpoint is simple: we obey the law. Is it legal to be against immigration? Yes. It is legitimate. So those who are in favour of immigration should treat those are against with respect. Is it legal to be against equality? Yes. So the same applies. We are living in a democracy, and the party with the greatest support governs. People aren't stupid, people are you and me, that is the most important attitude of all to have, and if a political standpoint sets out to gain support, people have to be won over. If someone says Muslims breed like rabbits and Sweden will soon be a Muslim country, that has to be met with arguments, and whatever allows such attitudes to come into being, namely fear, has to be met with openness and also political action. Why do people fear immigration? Mostly because there are integration problems, not enough is being done in practical terms: how many immigrants live in ghettos outside towns? Linguistically, enough is being done, there everything is morally impeccable, the last remnants of racism have been swept away. Those who live in language, and from it, believe that is where the battle is, but it isn't, it is in real life. Accommodation is substandard, there are job shortages and low incomes, there is debasing work, a lack of power and a lack of a future, gang criminality and a hatred of Swedes. In turn, Swedes are afraid, which manifests itself in hostility towards and a hatred of immigrants. I have friends who have changed their children's school because the one they were in had so many immigrants and all the concomitant issues. These problems are obviously a political question and have to be solved, which they can be, but then people have to come to the table. And that doesn't happen.

Why not? I believe a lot of this is about a perception of propriety. Discussing the issues immigration brings, also discussing the issues of conflicting cultures, opens this Pandora's box of racism, prejudice, fear and hatred that exist in the so-called Swedish soul. The result is that a distance emerges, it grows, soon we have fronts which can no longer be broken down. Distance is dangerous. And it is, at bottom, also elitist and arrogant. Distance says, I am good, I am irreproachable, what I want is the only true, real and morally defensible position.

On a significantly smaller scale I have met this same attitude with my books. I have experienced interviews on stage where everything was focused on what is wrong with them: they, without my being aware of it, I presume, express patriarchal values which are oppressive to women. I remember once having my attention drawn to the fact that only male writers were mentioned in one book (which is wrong, but they are in the majority, that is true), thereafter to a scene about men's and women's relationships with children, where I said something like … as the child has been in the woman's body, and as women feed children with milk from their own bodies, women have a different relationship with children from men. This was also incorrect, I was given to understand, and everything in the questions indicated that the book was a work of misogyny. What I had done, which was to write, was suddenly about what I hadn't written but should have written. So the conversation was no longer about the book but about the values of the woman who had read the book and was now interviewing me. It was implicit in what she said that these values were the correct ones while those of the novel were insane. I had been exposed for what I am. And even more so at a writing academy a year later. I had been invited to a talk, to impart the insights I had gained from writing to young people who were less experienced. But the session concentrated on what was wrong with my books. I fielded question after question about morality, and it was the same angle of attack: the books were oppressive to women and, or as I understood it, evil, or at least informed by evil. It was like being interrogated by a sect. It was frightening because everyone thought the same, there was total unanimity, and for me literature is the opposite, it cultivates differences, ambivalences, uncertainty. These people were certain. And they were so young! They were around twenty years old. The writer who ran the course, a well-known feminist and activist, was also the one who asked the most accusatory questions. So they had invited me to put me on trial and tell me all that was wrong with me and my books. There was no place for doubt in the room. They were right, and they raged at my books with the remorseless fury of the righteous. Now I suffered no injury, and it is not a bad thing to receive criticism, but this wasn't the point, the criticism was so unanimous and these young people were as sure as the young people in the 70s were of their Marxism. I know what this is like, of course, it is good to feel sure, it is good to be swept along in the fight for good. But as I am a writer I know this is death for a writing academy because in literature the good or the right have no place. Haven't they read *Don Quixote*?

When I am interviewed by women in Sweden I am always prepared to be accused of terrible things. When I am interviewed by women in other countries, even by prominent feminists and first-rate writers who write much better books than I do, there are no accusations, there are no attempts to render my books suspect. It is one writer talking to another. Following the Swedish logic, these women are sycophants disloyal to the women's movement or blind. But they aren't, they just have their eyes on something else. Differences, diversity, similarities, dissimilarities; that is what drives literature. A man who looks after children but is bored and would rather write, that is not anti-feminism or Nazism, it is human. I spoke to a woman writer about this, she was thinking of taking a year off to be with her children, she said, but then the thought of standing in the playground day in, day out, in a state of total inactivity and boredom, made her wet herself with fear. Yes, this is a sigh from the heart, Fredrik. I have heard everything, and this resistance from the Swedish Women's Movement is absolutely insignificant, nothing I go around fretting about, but I am writing this anyway because the notion that the Swedish view of humanity and the Swedish ideological standpoint should be universal, that this is the one true path, period, is so utterly and insanely irritating to have to witness. It is totalitarian and deeply misanthropic, while in its own eyes it is open and humanistic.

When I was growing up both my mother and father worked, and my mother was the one with ambitions, who began to study at university in my early years. They shared the housework; at that time and in that part of the world it was not usual to have a father who hoovered and washed and cooked, nor was it particularly usual to have a mother who worked and wanted to have a career. My father was also with us on his own for a year, while she was studying, as she was when he was studying. For me equality between the sexes is blindingly obvious, and I feel stupid writing this, why do I have to write it? It is an insult that anyone might believe otherwise. As regards literature, I like books written by men as much as women – two of the best books we have published at our publishing house, Pelikanen, are written by women, I am thinking of Maria Zennström and Judith Hermann – and for me this is so normal that it shouldn't need emphasising. Another thing, we are both fathers of girls, so it is also odd to be accused of misogyny. For my part, I am absolutely surrounded by girls, we have three daughters, and then there is

Linda, which makes four, in addition both of their grandfathers have died, so there are only women left in that generation, and both grandmothers are often here helping – I live with females aged from five months to seventy years old, as well as John, who is the sole boy. I love my girls so passionately I didn't think it was possible, and I want to do everything for them. However, teenagers often rebel against their parents by acting as or becoming that which their parents like least – if that happens to us my future prospects will be living with three hard-core feminists who despise the patriarch and his blind abuse of power . . . I will survive because I think I have such a close relationship with them that I can look them in the eye, and they and I know what is actually true, what is right, what is important. I have been terribly wrong before, though.

No big matches this evening, but I am still nervous about whether Argentina can sort themselves out. Before that, we are going to a restaurant, the whole gang of us, there has been a lot of sedentary indoor life over the last few days, apart from the regular stints on the trampoline.

All the best,
Karl Ove

Glemmingebro, 21 June

Dear Fredrik,

I am writing this now, straight after Argentina's convincing victory over Iran. No, no. Joke. It was a painful match to watch, not least because I want Argentina, I want their team so much to play fast, intelligent, attractive, spirited football, but they don't, however much I want them to, what can I do, I am sitting on the sofa (and if I had been on the pitch not much would have happened either …). They played just like Italy, stringing lots of passes together in their own half, a slow build-up, every player had three or four touches before the ball was passed, and there was no movement, up the pitch players stood still, and when some impetus did come it was one on one, a dribble, just like Italy. Argentina also played two defensive midfielders, strangely enough, and if they thought they could outplay Iran without making any effort they were completely wrong. Gary Lineker wrote on Twitter that it was hard to judge Argentina until they met a team which wanted to win, and now they are through to the knockout stage they have by far the easiest route to the final – they can't meet France, Brazil or Germany before then – but if they want to advance they will have to play as a unit and not just rely on Messi. Nope, that was bad. I still enjoy watching Di María play, he has so many elegant touches, but otherwise it was simply frustrating. Even though Brazil were poor against Mexico you know they have plenty in reserve. That is not the case with Argentina. Today, by the way, I read Zico's analysis of Brazil in the *Guardian*, he identified a weakness in the centre, with Paulinho, who was totally absent in the first two games, Gustavo was too deep, leaving Neymar all on his own, and the changes forced on them by Hulk's injury meant neither of the flanks worked. He wrote that they could still win, but they would have to do more than just turn up to get the trophy. One thing is good, however, and that is that this World Cup is so volatile it is impossible to predict anything, and some teams play fantastic football. Iran? They played like Norway under Drillo Olsen in the 90s. Hell to meet and boring to watch for everyone except Norwegians. The commentators were wildly excited about Iran, which is underdog fervour, the little hobbit waiting to fell the big dragon, and no wonder, we all lead small lives, which is why we identify with the minnows. I still cheered when Messi scored, and felt bad, a bad person, a white monocultural middle-class man, but then, in the aftermath of the game I remembered that it is Iran which oppresses women, prohibits free expression, hates Jews and builds atomic bombs, while Argentina is, after all, a democracy, and at once I felt a little better.

A dream I have had for more than twenty years, apropos of sitting on the sofa and watching football: I am on the pitch, top-class match, usually for IK Start, but I have also turned out for Real Madrid (don't ask me why), and I play as badly as I do in reality, I know all my limits, I am left standing for pace, nutmegged, and even the simplest passes go astray, I fumble, I am out of breath and the crowd jeers me. It is a terrible dream. It is a scandal I am out there playing. Sometimes the dream starts in the tunnel, and that is the worst bit of all because I know I am not up to it but I still have to carry on. In another similar dream I am standing on the stage in a theatre, it is packed, and I have to sing. But I can't!

What do you think this means?

No, just joking.

Germany v. Ghana starts in nine minutes. Don't know if I can be bothered to watch any more football so soon after the Argentina match. On the other hand, often the champions-to-be drag their feet in the opening rounds. Do enough, scrape through to the big, magical games, where they shine.

Dreams cost nothing.

It is half past eleven now, the game is over, it ended 2–2 and was the tournament's best match so far. I hope Ghana smash Portugal and go through because they were wonderful to watch, and they matched Germany in everything, their defence was so good – what defenders they have! Especially the left back, Asamoah, but they also set up counter-attacks so easily. Did you see the Ghanaian on the left wing who beat two German players and then ran all the way to the goal? If he hadn't shot – what a weak effort – if he had crossed, they would have won. They had such technical ability and they were athletic. What fun it was. A complete contrast to the Argentina match, in the same way that France was to yesterday's Italy match.

Everyone is asleep. I am playing Bon Iver; all the memories from the last time I played it, perhaps two years ago, flood back. Not as images but feelings. Only music can do this, can open the frozen tundra, but it is not only good, it also hurts. So much time passes, so much life is held back.

Are we moving towards Germany v. France in the quarter-final? I haven't checked, but if it happens, it will join a series of classic showdowns because they are on a par now, it seems to me. Tomorrow it is USA v. Portugal and Belgium v. Russia. We'll get in touch again then. You're six hours behind us, so it must be a few minutes after six in the evening where you are. I can see you in a restaurant by the sea, it is dark outside, you have a beer on the table and you are talking to your friend the film-maker, the breakers wash ashore below, and the lamps hanging from a cable above you swing gently to and fro in the wind.

One thing I do know: it doesn't look like that where you are. But for me, until you correct me, it does. As for me, I am sitting in a room that bears a close resemblance to a rubbish tip, the table is covered with cups, many with the festering dregs of coffee in, many full of cigarette ends, a toilet bag on the floor, heaps of journals, a pile of all the books Pelikanen has published – among them yours, easily recognisable by the light green cover – cans of Coke, plastic bottles of Coke, and the floor is strewn with envelopes, newspapers, cigarette packets, more books, several empty plastic Coke bottles, advertising, cardboard boxes, some shoes and shirts. This is the only room I don't tidy up, it gives me a sense of freedom, of escaping my Protestant impulses, I suppose. All the books I bought when I was travelling recently are here – there are perhaps forty of them, mostly ones that came highly recommended – but I don't read them, you know, I only possess them; in total I must have several thousand books I have never read and never will. They are good, interesting, essential, all of them. But there is no time. You wrote in one of your letters that I am well read – I did read a lot until I was thirty, it was about then I stopped, and everything I write now draws on what I read then. What I should do and what I have thought of doing many times is taking a year off and just reading. But I can't, I'm not up to it, it is impossible, I have to work. And for a Protestant reading is a pastime.

It has been a long day, and if not much has happened on the outside, a lot has happened on the inside, I have seen two football matches, one very bad one and one very good one, and I have read a letter from you, and written two myself, in one of which I poured out everything I have against Swedish totalitarian middle-class culture. That did me good. And since it is a letter to you alone, I don't regret a word.

All the best,
Karl Ove

Salvador, Bahia, 21 June

Dear Karl Ove,

I'm sitting in the apartment of Lasse Westman and his Cuban wife Zaylin in a three-storey building down by the beach in the Itapua area of north Salvador, the capital of the state of Bahia (which is about the size of France, it's easy to forget how big this country actually is) in north-east Brazil. Salvador was the original capital of Brazil, and it was through its port that most of the slaves came into the country.

It's wonderful to be here. The air, the wind, the proximity to the ocean, and last night, when Lasse and I went down to the mile-long beach and into the water in complete darkness, with the Southern Cross hanging above me in the firmament, the French goalfest fresh in my mind (I agree with you about the French although I can't say I'm exactly enamoured with them, or the team, but they were so compact, precise and efficient, full of imagination – European football at a high level) coupled with Lasse's warmth, friendliness and sense of humour, I felt pure joy, Karl Ove. Joy and a feeling of privilege at having the opportunity to do what I'm doing, of travelling around like this and, tonight, at being reunited with a person who has taught me so much about the art of creating and of living.

When we were standing in the darkness I told him the story about the cobra and the monkeys on the roof of Afonso's studio. And I asked him how a man would fare in a fight against a primate that size, one about a metre tall. 'You wouldn't have a hope.

147

They'd sink their teeth into you right away, go straight for your throat.' 'So I wouldn't stand a chance?' 'No.' Then he told me he had made a film in the 1960s about Skansen, the open-air museum and zoo in Stockholm, about the apes, and how the zoo-keepers always had to feed them in pairs, one looking into the ape's eyes the whole time while the other dished out the food, and how, among certain ladies in Stockholm that summer, it became trendy to pleasure the apes and themselves at the same time, one hand inside the bars of the cage and the other outside.

'It was the chimpanzees, they were closest.'

'And?'

'Three women ended up dead that summer. Killed by chim-panzees in Skansen.'

I was in the process of pulling on my trousers after our swim and almost fell headlong onto the sand in amazement.

'What? What the hell are you saying?'

'Three women killed. By bites to the throat, like I just described to you.'

'I don't believe you, Lasse, that can't be true. It can't. Tell me it isn't true, por favor.'

'No, really, it is. I made a film about it but it was never screened, the incidents were never made public. They replaced the bars with glass after that.'

We watched Argentina v. Iran at home, and again Argentina were hugely disappointing. They're not a team as far as I can make out, rather a collection of individuals who happen to be wearing the same jerseys, and once more the lazy genius wear-ing number 10 settled the match in his inimitable style during the dying seconds, getting goalside of his man and bending the ball inside the far post, giving the keeper no chance – and from the apartment above, where an ageing Argentinian hippy and his Brazilian wife live, and from which there hadn't been a sound throughout the entire game, a scream rang out over the roof-tops, and, not a word of a lie, Karl Ove, at that exact moment the same neighbours' dog, Bianca, burst into Lasse's living room, tail wagging, with a small Argentinian flag around her neck.

By the way, Lasse told me earlier today that this Argentinian neighbour, whom I've yet to meet, had been subject to racism in his native country, he's evidently not black but moreno, as they say here, and had therefore moved to Bahia, and there we have one of football's emotional paradoxes: the Argentinian hippy on the next floor who hates his country but when it comes to the World Cup screams with joy when his national team scores. And dresses little Bianca up with an Argentinian flag around her neck.

It's quiet and peaceful here now. Lasse and Zaylin are on the sofa watching TV, the day's games and goals are being analysed by Brazilian experts, the sound of the commentators' prolonged, jubilant cries muffled here on the balcony.

Talk to you tomorrow.

Best wishes,
Fredrik

Glemmingebro, 22 June

Dear Fredrik,

Thank you for another wonderful letter. I am still in your Brazil novel, travelling from Rio up to Bahia, where a new character was introduced, Lasse, who also has that magical shimmer around him.

I am sitting in bed and writing. The sun is shining and there is quite a strong wind, as so often in Österlen. Now and then there are booms outside. The wind is a whisper and a rustle in the trees, then it is like a well filling, the sound grows in intensity and changes character, as though the wind is being tightened, it blusters and becomes louder, and then come the booms. When they die down, there is the rustling and whispering again, and I know it has been there the whole time, hidden as it were beneath the other noise. Everything is repeated, the well fills, the wind ratchets up, and then the booms.

I have always had some difficulty with summer days like these, they seem boundless to me, open to eternity and empty. I fear the openness, the boundlessness and the emptiness. I need a framework, routines, limits, rules. I don't know what I am afraid of when I am afraid. Perhaps the meaninglessness, perhaps the chaos that is always close at hand, perhaps the fall from grace.

We have just had lunch, Linda made lasagne. Njal, who is Geir's son and a day younger than Heidi, has been here since yesterday morning. When the children have friends round it is as though they speed up, they run from one activity to another, they are unstoppable, one minute they are naked and squirting each other with water pistols, the next they are dressed and on the road cycling, the next they are playing badminton in the garden, the next they are sitting in the darkened living room watching TV. Actually that is all I want, for them to have a wonderful childhood, and on days like today I know they are doing that.

The story about the women and the chimps in Skansen, what is it about this that has set my mind working? Perhaps just the concentration, in it everything is so close: comedy/tragedy, animal/human, sex/death, truth/lies, reality/fantasy – and their meeting makes it raw and what was unclear earlier clear.

Now the children are screaming and shouting outside. They are shrieks of glee, the difference is immediately obvious; when something happens and the shouts turn to tears or anger it is as though they emerge from the background and suddenly overwhelm everything. Linda is sitting downstairs and talking on the phone. I can't hear what she is saying, only her voice. She watches almost all the matches with me, even if she isn't interested in football, it is more the company and the atmosphere she is after, I think, perhaps her childhood experiences of the World Cup engage here, I don't know. Her father was interested in football, he was the goalkeeper for a local team in Norrland when he was young, probably he sat watching the World Cup on TV during the summers. I met him only three or four times, and we always talked about football. He had no protection against the world, no distance, no irony, and it seemed to me that, for him, everything was equally important and serious. He was a rare human being, not that he did anything rare, more that he had qualities you don't often see. Which made him vulnerable. My father, yes, I know you have read about him, was quite different but ended up in a place not far away, withdrawn from everything, hurt, damaged, isolated and also alcoholic. Linda's father was a good person, that was my impression, my intuition. My father wasn't. He wasn't evil either, but when you were close to him you didn't think of goodness. He died in 1998, at the end of the summer, and it is only now, at this moment, that I realise it was the same summer I have written about in earlier letters to you, when Argentina and England played against each other, and Norway beat Brazil 2–1 in Marseille. These events have been quite separate in my memory. My father's death appeared to take place in a fissure in time, outside everything. But what he did before he died was to drink and watch TV, so he must have sat there watching the same games, alone or with his mother. Perhaps with enough presence of mind to enjoy Rekdal's penalty when Norway beat Brazil? (To what purpose, one might conjecture, when he was dead a month later?) He watched football on TV for as long as I can remember but never played himself (even though he told us he had played for Start). In a diary he wrote a few years before he died, at a rehab centre for alcoholics, he said quite a lot about how lonely he was and that he could always pick out the lonely people in a crowd, they had a certain way of behaving that gave them away. He wrote about how lonely and closed people's lives were in the north, compared with the south of Europe, where the culture is different, warmer, more sociable, more open. He was probably thinking of, and longing for, Spain, but it could just as well have been the Brazil you describe, the happy, outgoing, carefree side of sociability, big families, big circles of acquaintances, dinners out, good food and drink. It was to capture that side he began to drink, of that I am sure – I remember when he got divorced how he suddenly started to invite people home, have dinners, big parties – until all this stopped and he ended up drinking at his mother's, in the house where he grew up, and where he, to wallow in pathos a little more, saw his last football world championship.

The children are asking if we can go to the beach. I have written a page of the fate essay, it stretches to six pages now and is half-finished, and I had thought about doing some office work, paying bills, filling in forms and answering emails, which I have put off for two weeks and can probably put off for a few more hours. So I say yes to the children, we can go to the beach, and I will write more later, this evening after the football.

It is twenty-five minutes past eight in the evening. We went to Nybrostrand, where there are three pools surrounded by lawns, and stayed there for an hour. The blue water against the white side of the pool, the sun's reflections and the hazy whiteness, while the blue is clear and deep, sending an electric charge of . . . well not exactly happiness, but something pleasurable through me. Heidi, Njal and John swam while Linda sat on the grass and fed Anne, and I sat on the bench keeping an eye on the children, or John, who has just learned to swim and still wears arm floats in the deep pool. After a while I changed and dived in, I couldn't resist. Played with them until the sky clouded over and it turned cold, and we drove back home to fetch Vanja and go to the pizzeria on the flat stretch along the road to Löderup and Borrby, where they serve the best pizzas in Sweden, according to people around here. We were there for an hour, went home, and I watched Belgium v. Russia with Linda, the game has just finished, 1–0 to the Belgians after a goal three minutes before full time. All the web pages say it was a boring game, the worst so far, but I didn't think so. Argentina's and Italy's last matches were poor, but I watched this one with interest, perhaps because the teams were so even and they kept trying, especially Russia, they weren't a bad team, they are always good technically and have pace, but this team lacked quality up top, so it seemed, they didn't show much enterprise in front of goal, they could have played for another two hours without scoring. Belgium are very uneven, not in terms of their players, but in their play – last match they suddenly lifted themselves in the second half, this evening they did it in the last ten minutes. What is going on when a team has no ideas and no drive for eighty minutes and then explodes into action, races around and has chance after chance in front of goal? What is missing when they obviously have the ability but can't produce it? With France, Germany and Ghana, who haven't been so dissimilar as teams, well balanced, varied, potent, accurate, the ability is in place from the first moment. There seems to be something wrong with the structure, with the organisation and also with the collective will. Italy and Argentina have completely lacked a pattern of play and a collective will, their performances are poor, as though they have no alternatives, they rely on individuals for ideas, while Belgium have everything but only in brief bursts.

The Algeria v. South Korea game is on, I saw the first ten minutes, Algeria seemed well on top, they are leading 2–0 now, I can see from the Internet. The interesting game will be USA v. Portugal tonight, but I don't think I will make it, it is too late, and tomorrow I have to look after Anne, Linda is going to Malmö for a hair appointment. Then we are into the third round, with two games a day.

One of my favourite Swedish novels is *The Draisine* by Carl Henning Wijkmark. It is about two human-like apes that cross the sea from Africa to South America in a draisine. They pass through St Helena on the way. It is a long time since I read it, and I remember almost nothing of the plot or why I was so absorbed by it, except that the distinction between human and animal, civilisation and nature, was drawn differently, and that the pages about the place where Napoleon was imprisoned, the abandoned nineteenth-century house, were absolutely fantastic. It just struck me now, after your story about the women and the chimpanzees.

Our eldest daughter has just been to see me, she told me about all the latest facts surrounding the *Titanic* she has found on the net. I listened and gave her a tender kiss when she had finished. She has been so engrossed by the tragedy and the film for a couple of weeks now. I tried to remember if I'd had any similar fascinations when I was young. Can't think of any specific ones. Football, that was ongoing, there were no demarcated limits, it was never about one game because as soon as one was over, there was another. But it was possible to take one match at a time, concentrate on only these ninety minutes, chart all the incidents, all the moves, also all the names and not just follow them on the pitch but in life, their stories before the game, parents, grandparents, brothers and sisters, friends, what happened after the game, the following years, the career that finished, life in a satellite town outside some Colombian or Iranian city, for example. The ninety minutes were inexhaustible. You could spend a whole lifetime on them. But that would be against the nature of football, which is that it appears and is concentrated in the here and now, and then it is gone, only to appear somewhere else. Writing about football is actually nonsense. All the pleasure lies in seeing it unfold before our eyes, this minute, happening right now, and it is unpredictable. That is, teams try to make it predictable, but the whole point of the game is to break that. When football is written about it is already over, and when the article is read there is no longer any value in the match; all that exists is the value of the writing. So you are absolutely right in your attitude towards analyses. But it is tempting to do it anyway, it is about understanding what is going on, seeing the underlying patterns, which are why what is happening develops in the way it does. As this is a game it is in fact possible, whereas in life, which I think is the reason for the desire to see structures, it is impossible. I am writing about fate, as I have mentioned several times, and this is connected, there are two parallel realities, one we see and walk around in, the other we don't, but it is still active, it is the beyond, it is heaven, the divine, the Kingdom of God, and in it everything that happens here is already determined. Then there are the passageways between the realities, such as dreams, visions, revelations or, in some religious communities, speaking in tongues. This is a way of organising the world, a way of understanding what is happening to us, making it meaningful. Nowadays that has disappeared, nobody believes in fate or heaven any more, but there are still systems we relate to, which actually are less fantastic than the notion of an invisible reality where everything that happens in the visible reality is predestined, only we don't think of them as such.

I received a phone call from Tore this evening, the guy I will be performing with this autumn. Among other things, we talked about the World Cup. He wanted to talk about Suárez. He said Suárez was at a stage in his life where everything was possible. He is absolutely limitless. He grins on TV, he laughs, he sits in a wheelchair, he scores goals at every available opportunity. Everything is going his way. And he is in contact with all his emotions and reveals them without shame. He is completely free, and if you are free anything is possible.

In other words, this will be Suárez's World Cup.

I think what I wanted to say with reference to the ape books is that the line between humans and animals is so relative, so changeable, and that now it is not only a chasm which you can feel when you look an animal in the eyes, the chasm has gone too, as we no longer live close to animals, they are no longer animals but producers of meat and are out of our sight. There is something there, in the exchange between animals and humans, in all the old adventures and myths, which has stopped, and does something to us, the way we see ourselves in the world and which books like this confront. After all, we are animals. (And now I am not talking about only men.)

Portugal are leading 1–0. It is twenty-five to one. I have to go to bed, I have to make a packed lunch for the girls early tomorrow and drive them to the rehearsal, where they will be all day. Next week they have the premiere of *Hairspray*, the musical. So this is over and out from the Österlen darkness.

All the best,
Karl Ove

Salvador, Bahia. 22 June

Dear Karl Ove,

Strange reading about your dreams. For me dreams are literary modelling clay, something you can knead truth from. Your one about IK Start is very similar to a recurring dream I used to have for what must have been close to two decades. But I only had it about once a year, never more frequently. I would dream I was pulling on a Malmö FF first-team jersey and running out on to the pitch at our stadium. It was often the most vivid, realistic dream of the year. The changing room, the tying of boot laces, the camaraderie with the other players, the noise of the crowd in the background, then the walk down the 'tunnel', which you also describe, through the inside of Malmö Stadium (where I spent so much time as a boy and junior player) and sometimes right out on to the field of play and then, as you wrote, that awful moment in the dream when you realise it is only a dream. The markings on the pitch are wrong and everything has to be done all over again, or I'm wearing my right football boot on my left foot and need to return to the changing room, or the laces on my boots are so long it's not possible to tie them, or, the most Kafkaesque, I get lost in the bowels of the stadium and can't even find my way out onto the pitch.

There is something archaic about both cases, whether IK Start or Malmö, these are dreams about becoming somebody, about affirmation, about being seen. The difference between us, I think, is that I wanted to be a professional footballer and by chance became an author, while you've always wanted to be an author and of course became one, and never really wanted to be a footballer, or am I wrong?

Two thoughts occurred to me yesterday as I lay twisting and turning on the mattress behind the sofa in the living room. The importance of football to my family. The evening before I left we had a going-away dinner and ended up watching a holiday video from our trip to Cunit, just a little down the coast from Barcelona, in 2006. The film included a game of football on the beach between los hermanos menores (Arvid and William) and las chicas (Amanda, Anni and Rita). Referee: me. Cameraman and commentator: Marianne. The match was the final in our family championship (Marianne and I, los padres, went out in the 'semi-final') and is the type of family film we can watch over and over again: me in my ridiculous summer hat, Willie (IF Alianz) and Arvid (IF Alianz) with their combative and competitive streaks, Anni (Malmö FF) with the air of a midfield general, Amanda (Malmö FF) with her winning mentality and deft sole rolls, and finally the temperamental Rita (kickboxing and tennis, never football), fast as a ferret in the sand. You should know, Karl Ove, if you don't already, that the make-up of our family is peculiar, although perhaps typical of our times. There were two families, neighbours, living next door to each other in a small apartment building in the heart of Malmö, when Marianne – the wife of the man next door! – and I fell in love. Something which resulted in the tearing apart of two families, a cleaver through two domestic idylls. The children were shocked when they understood, Amanda laughed hysterically before beginning to cry inconsolably, the children were best friends, Wille and Anna were even in the same class, I felt such agonising guilt for betraying, not only my ex-wife, but Marianne's husband as well, that I suffered from terrible migraines and had to visit the doctor, I thought my head was going to explode and I know, have learned to accept, that I'll bear feelings of guilt for the rest of my life and can only hope that Marianne and I have shown the children enough love, have tried to make their lives as happy as possible, so that one day – and perhaps they already have, it often feels like it – they can forgive us.

Now and again I still wonder if I destroyed their childhoods by falling in love.

Wandered down to the beach on my own. Not a soul around. As I went a little way out in the water, I felt the enormous power of the Atlantic, the pull towards the deep. Moments before, in front of the laptop, I'd had a feeling of omnipotence, of being able to create and recreate the world – and then in the water, that power drawing me out, the opposite feeling to the one writing can give me: of being nothing, merely a body, insignificant, replaceable.

Watched Belgium v. Russia at Lasse's local. A beer and crab meat with rice and cassava flour. The match is boring and the Belgian team, which I had such high hopes for, are disappointing. Most of the clientele in the almost-full restaurant seems to share my opinion. People's interest in the game is minimal. Hazard makes no impact, is man-marked, and the Russians seem like a decent enough side, but as the game wears on I have a sneaking feeling that they lack substance. The Belgians are more complex, not only in their play, but it feels like there's more to them, they have more in reserve, while the Russians seem to be playing to the best of their abilities, a little like you wrote in your analysis of Brazil v. Mexico.

In the second half the massive Brazilian jogo-bonito-loving crowd at the Maracanã begins to chant 'Segunda divisão!' – Second-division football! – and I'm inclined to agree, but I have hope, as well as an inkling of what way it's going to go, and as the match nears the end Belgium wake up, like they did against Algeria, and for a quarter of an hour we're treated to powerful, beautiful 'European' football, less space and more tackling, lightning-fast counter-attacks and Hazard looking more like the star he is, inflicting damage down the Russian right wing, and in the eighty-second minute the inevitable happens, when after some wonderful footwork by Hazard, who takes the ball right to the byline before knocking it back at an angle, bang, 1–0, and Belgium through to the next round.

A fair result as far as I'm concerned, and the big question is how this, at times brilliant, Belgian side will do against teams like Holland, Germany, Argentina or Uruguay. Quite well, I think, and I'm still confident of them making the semi-finals.

Germany v. Ghana yesterday? As you wrote, the best match so far, a duel that had it all, beautiful football, was tough, tactical, had quality goals, and not least real excitement. We watched in a local café and the roof almost came off when Ghana took the lead. As an old woman at the next table with a huge underbite said to us, Temos outras raizes aqui (We have other roots here, with reference to the large black population of Bahia and how sympathy with Ghana goes without saying). I enjoyed the display of German discipline, the equal parts of skill, composure, strength and imagination on show, but also relished the wonderful potency, skill, composure and energy of the Ghanaians, who at times managed to outplay a team which everyone believes will make it to the final with ease. Ghana showed up the Germans' weaknesses, no real leader and a defence which, apart from Lahm, isn't world class, not like the rest of the team, something an ailing Sweden side proved in qualification, with seven goals against them. I think Germany will go out in the quarter-finals.

The most notable moment of the match? Did you see when Philip Lahm broke through five or six minutes from the end, when the score was still 2–2, and was presented with a chance he should have taken? What does Lahm, a German, do instead? He back-heels the ball – like an African or a Brazilian! Absolutely incredible. Fantastic too, as it meant the game ended in a draw and kept Ghana in the World Cup, but not only that, it showed me how global this sport has become. A German player would never have done such a thing in times gone by, choosing beauty and dancing on the edge of the precipice over the safe option.

I blow a big kiss to Lahm from here in Itapua, Karl Ove.

And on the TV in the living room I see that Algeria have just got another goal, to make it 2–0, a beautiful header from a corner against South Korea, and I immediately place a call across the world, to my brother-in-law and sister's small flat in Idunsgata in Vasastan, and my sister takes the phone straight away: 'Thanks! Kamel has already been dancing around ... We have hope, we have hope ...' and I also suddenly hope that this terribly troubled nation can, through victory and progress in the tournament, find justice after the scandal – and now they make it 3–0! – of 1982, when Austria and Germany conspired to play out a 1–1 draw in one of the most infamous games in World Cup history, which resulted in Algeria, who had beaten giants West Germany, going out. I remember watching the game at our summer cottage together with my sister, my brother and some friends, it was Midsummer, holy for us Swedes as you know, and being ashamed on behalf of Austria and Germany, and I also recall the spectators in the stands getting to their feet in protest and waving banknotes, and those bloody players just continuing to knock the ball back and forth while waiting for the referee to blow the final whistle.

And everything just continues, Karl Ove. The world turns, the World Cup rolls on without cease, that's the way it feels.

All the best,
Fredrik

Salvador, Bahia, 23 June

Dear Karl Ove,

Woke up early, it's a quarter to six in Itapua and the world is quiet except for a bird of some kind nearby making a peculiar chirping sound. My head is clear, and I have a strong desire to get some thoughts down on paper, despite a relatively 'hard' session last night with Lasse and the Argentinian who lives above. We went to a newly opened cheap local pub, where by mistake I, believing it was beer – the bottle was identical to the brown bottles that beer is served in here – managed to fill our glasses with cachaça, the Brazilian sugarcane spirit usually reserved as an ingredient in a caipirinha but which can also be taken neat.

So the night wore on, and pretty soon Lasse was as drunk as a fiddler, gesticulating wildly, chatting to one person after the other in the pub, and, without our asking, the waiter was putting fresh rounds of beer in front of us the entire time, USA v. Portugal played on a screen high up on one wall, yet another good match in a succession of dramatic World Cup encounters. Klinsmann's USA impress me, they have a Yankee energy I find appealing, but I'm also impressed by their technical ability and tactics, yet another sign that the global football map needs to be redrawn, and the fact that a player comes from one of football's old powers (England, Spain, Italy or Portugal, for example) means in itself nothing at all. The USA, in common with others like Costa Rica and Chile, to name but a couple, display a splendid lack of respect, and we saw that in the game between the USA and Portugal as well, not least when Nani and Ronaldo executed their comical stepovers. There's so little to be gained from showboating when playing against a well-organised defence. And this is coming from me, Karl Ove, a man of feints and tricks who loves dribbling and dummies more than anything else on the football field. However, in today's game you need to have both a finely honed technique and exceptional speed to get past defenders and then manage to leave them behind you, and the only two players I can think of in this tournament who are capable of that are Eden Hazard and Arjen Robben. 2–2 was a fair result, and I celebrated when Ronaldo's beautiful cross led to Portugal's equaliser because it meant that the door is not quite closed on Ghana going through to the second round.

I want to go back and open another door. I want to return to that slightly unpleasant winter night in Österlen when Heidi was in the car and you went to knock on the door of that house.

Let's say the man who opened the door is also the kind who hates women, and apart from any sympathies he might have with the Swedish Democrats, or loathing he might feel for Jews and Muslims, what I'd really like to know is what is it inside him that makes him hate women in particular. Most Latin American countries have gruesome traditions of violence (although not Costa Rica, oddly enough, who are charming us in this tournament), violence that stretches back to, of course, colonial times and has taken on modern forms, first and foremost political under the many right-wing dictatorships, but also as a part of the Che tradition, the romance of guerrilla warfare, and in the form of the violence of the drug cartels. And that brings us to

Ciudad Juarez, El Paso's counterpart on the other side of the border from the US, and to Roberto Bolaño, one of your, and my, favourite authors.

The first time I heard about the corpses of the dismembered, raped and murdered women who had been found over the years, and are still being found, in the countryside around Ciudad Juarez, I thought it had to do with Los Zetas and the cartels; gradually I understood that this wasn't the case, when I read the fourth, or was it the third, part of Bolaño's *2666*, in which he, with chilling, anatomical precision 'performs a post-mortem' on hundreds of bodies, of mostly poor young Indian women from the south of Mexico. Bolaño found this deeply fascinating and enrolled the help of an investigative journalist to come a step closer to this hell.

And that brings me to the edge of the abyss: the online trolls in Sweden who threaten and play with words on Twitter, Facebook and other sites, who use terms like 'cunt' and 'slut' and issue threats like 'I'm going to slice . . .' All this was reality in Ciudad Juarez, truly the worst place on the planet in terms of violence and hatred against women. In Bolaño's literary universe there's a masterfully depicted serial killer, and theories about murderers and copycats who have specialised in abusing, raping, killing and mutilating young women have long abounded in Mexico to explain this grotesque violence. I view these theories with scepticism and believe in a simpler, sociological explanation that I came across a few years ago: nearly all of the victims are young female Indian factory workers, naïve girls who come from Chiapas and get jobs on production lines, las maquiladoras, in Ciudad Juarez, right beside the US border, and they are good workers who carry out their work dutifully and the 'ordinary' men, the working class if you like, in Ciudad Juarez lose their jobs to these Indian girls from the south.

And consequently lose everything, their livelihood, their dignity. And therefore want revenge.

I don't know, Karl Ove. But this has something in common with what Swedish feminists are being subjected to on the net, something repugnant.

Best wishes,
Fredrik

Glemmingebro, 23 June

Dear Fredrik,

Thanks for your letter, Fredrik. I see where you are going with regard to my long letter about Swedish feminism, for you have gently turned my argument against me and indirectly point out that the people I write about in such hostile terms are human, not stereotypes, with their faults and shortcomings, their warmth and tenderness, fear and happiness, and one must never forget that. To quote one of the consistent images in these letters: it is important to look the other person in the eye. You are right. But this is not about individuals. The people I am writing about are representatives of an ideology who appear to think that statements or opinions that contradict the ideology are dangerous, evil, repressive and actually shouldn't be expressed or uttered. This is what is so awful. The puritanism that insists whatever is immoral should go, the unflinching certainty that in its extreme form is fanatical, this is what I am against. It is the tyranny of the good. In your letter you are turning the whole issue one hundred and eighty degrees when you write about misogyny, primarily Internet misogyny, but also what in South America is manifested in the wholesale murder of young impoverished women, which Bolaño describes in his brilliant contemporary dystopia *2666*. Let's leave that aside for a moment and stay in Sweden with Internet misogyny, which is largely directed against women in the public arena, it is obviously misogynistic and as such deplorable, but it still doesn't prove that there is a general hatred of women in Sweden, in the same way that there is no general violence against women. One slogan which I must have read thousands of times in this country is 'Men's violence against women.' I am a man, I have never been violent to women, I have never struck a woman and I have never raped a woman. Hitting a woman, abusing a woman, physically or psychologically, or raping a woman are for me and everyone I know so dishonourable, so spineless and so degrading, so far from the person I want to be that it could never, under any circumstances, happen, and if it happened in my presence I wouldn't accept it. That is what being a man means to me. Here I belong to white middle-class culture, and it is its values I am describing now. In other words, my own and those of people I have grown up with, studied with and associate with. I know of one man who hit his partner, you know who it is, I don't know him myself, but I heard via a mutual friend what then happened: all his male friends distanced themselves from him, all of them protected her, there were no grey areas, there was no defence, the limit was set: this is something you never do, ever. Yet still we read 'Men's violence against women.' This is fraudulent rhetoric because even those who use it know this is not how it is. We know there are women who are violent to their children, but surely no one would ever dream of coining the slogan 'Women's violence against children.' Violence against women is the exception, not the rule, and it invariably has social causes, so there are other factors than gender which have to be in the equation. The same is true of rape. This is divergent behaviour and few men would accept it, it is perhaps the most degrading thing a man can do. The same is true of Internet misogyny. Like violence against women and rape it is absolutely reprehensible, punishable by law and repugnant.

It isn't 'men' who hate women, there is a group of men, and what they have in common, I would imagine, is that they score low on quite a number of parameters. I am guessing here, but this is not a treatise, it is a letter from one friend to another. They don't have influential positions in society. I think we can take that for granted. The Internet has given them an opportunity to gain some power over those they insult and harass. It is a pseudo-power, built on fear and very seldom acted upon, but it is effective, their words reap a rich response. Why do they hate women? For the same reason they hate immigrants or, two generations ago, hated Jews. It is a social problem, it is also violence against women, and it is rape, and it has to be solved in the same way, through the legal system, the judiciary. But I don't want to be drawn into this, I am not an accessory to the crime because they are men and I am also a man. And this misogyny does not reflect a patriarchy, it reflects the opposite, the sudden powerlessness of the patriarchy. It is pitiful, stupid and terrible, and akin to anti-Semitism and racism in general. And in the same way it is basically a social problem and has to be solved as such, through political means. The slogan 'Men's violence against women' obfuscates this. Men's Internet misogyny as well. But the suggestion that a hatred of women is part of male culture, that is simply not true.

Isn't it a little sad to write so much on the subject? Isn't this supposed to be a book about football, a celebration? Of life that is fun, not life that is serious?

I promise to return in a different mood, a bit like Brazil did yesterday (when they brought on Fernandinho and for the first time in this tournament had a midfield that attacked and defended) or how I hope Italy will come back today, in a match that will be exciting whatever the quality, I can't imagine anything else because now it is make-or-break time, sudden death, and Suárez and Cavani, Pirlo and Balotelli are coming.

Look forward to talking about that and much more!

All the best,
Karl Ove

Salvador, Bahia, 23–24 June

My dear friend,

They're celebrating São João here, our Midsummer, and the bangs and explosions are making the house shake. A little while ago I heard what sounded like an exchange of gunfire between two warring gangs, and the smoke from the fireworks and flares people are lighting in the streets is seeping into the house. The bats on the balcony appear absolutely terrified, or it could be I just don't know enough about bats. Maybe they always fly in such a wild and irrational way.

I took it easy today. Zaylin, Lasse and I went to a restaurant with a view over the beautiful bay of Salvador. We could discern modern high-rises on the skyline between swaying palm trees in the heat haze. Big waves were roaring in from the ocean. We ate moceca for lunch, a fish casserole, a fantastic local speciality, with charr, shrimps, saffron and coriander, yes, I know, you're not a foodie, but I am, and when food is good, like it was today, and I get a whiff of coriander, then nothing else exists for me at that moment.

Watching football with Lasse and Zaylin is like watching football with two children: you have to explain the rules to them the whole time, the groups, the draw, what is meant by the last sixteen. Nevertheless, the enthusiasm and enjoyment they display, their outbursts, laughter and joy, were no less than with those who 'understand'.

Holland v. Chile? A game of chess in which both teams held

back for a long time, feeling each other out, Holland were satisfied with a single point and Chile bided their time, waiting for an opening. No openings, no pawn sacrifices, no risks, resulting in a dull and pretty tough game between two good teams in which Robben – ugh – the disagreeable, gifted Robben, finally prises open the Chilean sardine tin with two beautiful, clinical passes, one leading to an unstoppable header from Fer to make it 1–0, the other Memphis sends into an empty net to make it 2–0. Robben v. Sánchez, 2–0, sending Chile to meet Brazil in the knockout stage, meaning my two favourite teams will face each other and I don't like that. Arvid, my stepson, has some Dutch blood in his veins, and the older he gets the more Dutch his footballing sympathies become. Some time ago we were sitting in the living room watching the Dutch play Sweden off the park, and when after a while he began mocking the Swedish team, I felt real anger begin to bubble up inside, out of nowhere, as though he'd flicked a switch, a nationalist nerve deep inside that must not be provoked, and all of a sudden we were screaming at each other, really bawling, the pair of us, who share a love of Malmö FF and always get on well together, so strange that football can cause these chasms to open up between us, Karl Ove. One of the worst episodes of that kind I've witnessed occurred on one of the pitches at Limhamn last winter during the final game of the year, the day before New Year's Eve, when we'd brought along some glögg and planned to have a glass after training to celebrate the year that had gone and wish each other a happy new year. In the middle of the game a fist fight broke out right in front of my eyes, between Nikolaj, a Russian, seventy-three years of age but still going strong and an extremely tough tackler, a Siberian tiger who always, even in the dead of winter, takes a dip after training, and Sana, an Iraqi who works as a taxi driver in Malmö. One of them went in too hard and in a matter of seconds they were embroiled in a fight, two grown men, with strangle-holds, kicks and biting – biting! – apropos apes, animals and everything else we've discussed in this exchange of letters, I was shocked and it took all our combined strength to pull them apart. As I made my way to the car after our post-match toast with glögg, after we had of course forced them to shake hands, I thought about the Balkans, about how close relationships between people must have been before war broke out, about how unthinkable it must have been for people in Sarajevo, Vukovar or Osijek in the time before the war that in only a few short years they would be prepared to kill their neighbours.

After eating lunch and watching the game, we walked down to the beach. I went for a swim and revelled in being buffeted by the waves. Lasse, camera always at the ready, took photos of everything he came across: fishermen, dozing dogs, down-and-outs, palm trees and the ocean. I lay down on the sand, the others beside me, and Zaylin began talking about Cuba, about how people in the favelas here were better off than those in Cuba, how life there was marked by carencia, a shortage of everything; all the same she said (and I was finding this very interesting, Karl Ove, but the day before had taken its toll and I felt myself dozing off on the sand and heard her words mingle with the roar of the waves), 'There's one important thing I've learned, Federico, when everyone talks about materialism, about possessions and property, I've learned the most important thing, curacão, heart, the fellowship of the heart, remains greater than all else.' That was what I caught before I drifted off, and if there's one thing I'm interested in it's exactly this, and for a number of years I've had a sentence ringing in my ears: 'Are we there yet?' And I want to use it as a starting point for a larger project, an essay perhaps, about modernity, about its effect on countries like Sweden and Norway for example, and if we are there yet, if this is as far as we can come, and if so, shouldn't people be happier, or is that the price for our form of societal progress, this existential emptiness I seem to see pretty much everywhere at home?

This sentence can pop into my head anytime, these words pursue me, sometimes day and night: Are we there yet? But given that I was so drowsy and only wanted to fall asleep on the sand, I didn't get a chance to hear Zaylin's, no doubt interesting, perspective, but allowed slumber to win me over.

We watch Brazil v. Cameroon at the same restaurant where we had eaten a few hours earlier. Cameroon prove tough opposition in the first half and I'm surprised at how well they play, the ease with which they neutralise the Brazilian attack. Apart from Neymar, of course. And I find myself quietly cheering on Cameroon. There's something about the huge yellow mass of supporters, the self-assurance, the arrogant commentators and general expectation of success, an enormous yellow and green wheel everyone presumes will roll the whole way to the final on 13 July, a wheel everyone expects will crush everything in its path, and I suddenly turn my back – me, the Brazil fanatic – and when the Brazilian goals start flying in, I feel nothing and don't do anything, just scribble down a few notes, nothing more, just dry words on a piece of paper: Daní Alves downright poor, David Luiz and Thiago Silva shaky, the midfield completely anonymous, Fred up top completely pointless, Oscar invisible, Neymar – a genius! and I'm not sure what it is I'm looking for, what it'll take to impress me, but then, just before half-time, it happens, an outstanding combination of passes with Neymar playing the principal part and Hulk as the intended finisher, but no goal, that was it, the magical dance that is and always will be Brazilian football, and the whole restaurant gets to its feet, but then Neymar is substituted and, no, I don't know what to make of this Brazilian team and I'm suddenly struck by another thought, an almost sadistic one, that I want Chile to knock them out in the last sixteen, just to be here and document that anticlimax and the upset it would cause throughout this vast country.

And I wonder, as I look at what I've written, if perhaps this 'sadism' has to do with a feeling of them having let me down, of them not having fulfilled their mission here in life: proper jogo bonito.

24 June

Another morning. My last day in Salvador. I'm sitting on the balcony stripped to the waist finishing off this letter to you. I find myself pondering that story about the chimps in Skansen, and apes in general, but also the fight between Nikolaj and Sana on the training pitch, and the animalistic within us all. Now and again, more and more the older I get, I think that this is our great misfortune, being so drilled in the notion that we're human, culture making us forget that we too are animals.

Football appears and disappears, you wrote '. . . the nature of football, which is that it appears and is concentrated in the here and now, and then it finishes, only to appear somewhere else'. That's well put. Appears, disappears and reappears. And right now, I'd imagine, the Australian, Croatian and Cameroonian players are getting out of bed in different places all over this huge country and preparing to pack their bags. It's all over for them. The end of the party. Their dreams shattered.

One more thing from yesterday. When I was lying on the beach with Zaylin and Lasse, I was absentmindedly flicking through *A Tarde*, one of the two local evening papers in Salvador. I turned a page and happened upon a picture of you, with that serious, penetrating gaze of yours. There's no getting away from you, not even here, on a beach in Bahia! It was a lengthy article, well written and favourable, actually I've only just noticed that it's a translation of a piece from the *New York Times International Weekly*, but that's neither here nor there. And it reminded me of the first time we met, it was before the first book in your series had come out, and you were going to play your first game with the rest of the Swedish authors on the Galleri 21 team. You had to bend down to get through the hole in the fence at Malmö sports field. Tall and shy, that was my first impression. Karl Ove? A Norwegian writer apparently, he's trying out for us. Magnus invited him. You were a new player who just turned up in the autumn darkness, and even though I knew you were an author, like me, the only thing I was interested in or curious about there and then was: can he play? (And if I had to describe my impression of you as a player after your first match for us, put in terms of this World Cup and the players in it: no Suárez, no Messi, more a Mertesäcker, good in the air and tough in the tackle.)

I have a question. You're currently writing an essay on fate, if I understood you correctly, and when you were in New York recently there was a queue around the block at one of your book signings. Did you ever, in your wildest dreams, imagine that it could turn out like this, with a Knausgård wave rolling out over the world, and now even over North and South America?

Best wishes,
Fredrik

Glemmingebro, 24 June

Dear Fredrik,

That was a match and a half. I am referring to the Italy v. Uruguay game. It finished an hour ago, but I am still shaken. Not only because Italy are out, after controlling the proceedings for an hour in a match that seen from a distance must have been boring but if you were involved definitely wasn't. These are perhaps the world's two most cynical teams, and the most negative; no one can kill a game like Uruguay and Italy, and neither of them shrinks from 'playing ugly'. Italy only needed a draw, and they continually slowed the pace, whenever they got the ball it either went back or to the side, and they were forever playing for free kicks, throw-ins and interruptions. They disrupted Uruguay's attacking flow, Cavani and Suárez had one chance between them all ninety minutes, which Buffon saved. Uruguay, for their part, nullified Pirlo by sacrificing Cavani, he marked him out of existence for the first hour, with the result that Italy lost their edge and Uruguay their penetration. It was attritional warfare, and it was exciting, especially as Uruguay had something Italy didn't have, a world-class striker, Suárez, whom they were clearly relying on – sooner or later he would get a chance and Uruguay would take the lead. But Italy, with their excellent defence, had Suárez completely closed down. The feeling was that anything could happen, but in fact Italy were in control and the game was where they wanted. Then Marchisio was sent off by an officious referee standing half a metre away from the incident, and I think that is the explanation because stamping on an opponent's calf at the end of a slaloming run was not much worse than what always goes on in tight situations, certainly between these two teams, although usually it happens with the referee at some distance. This time he was close, and as the offence is officially a red card, that is what Marchisio got. But a studs-up challenge at speed, when one player launches himself at another, is dangerous and can break a leg, it is quite different from this, there was no speed, they were almost standing still, and Marchisio actually had the ball under control, so it wasn't particularly dangerous, and even though it was what we used to call a 'late tackle', I have no idea what it is called now, it wasn't brutal and nor was it final, Marchisio was actually already past his opponent and on his way. But all right, red card, Italy down to ten men for the last thirty minutes. I sincerely hoped Italy would still do it because although this team hasn't been great and they were several notches below France, for example, it turned out I was rooting for them, I wanted them to go on in the competition, and there we have abandoned any desire to see good football, the odds of Uruguay delivering were greater, and we were into something else, equally important as far as football goes, namely partiality. I have touched on this before, but the sly, cynical, calculating element is so far from my personality that it holds a deep fascination for me. I know you cannot understand this, I am talking to deaf ears, writing to blind eyes, as it were, nevertheless, it is true: I love Italy.

Uruguay's goal came as no surprise because the balance between the teams, which had till then cancelled each other out, had shifted with the sending-off. Italy fell back deep and defended the scoreline, and when the goal came, they had neither the strength, the creativity nor the goal-scorers, they had blown their chance, they were out. And they had only themselves to blame. Had they raised their game against Costa Rica they would have avoided the knife to the throat this evening.

But that is not why I am shaken. It is because of Suárez. Two days ago, as I said, Tore was talking about him on the phone, he said all channels were open in him, he had unfiltered access to all his skills and emotions. And I agree, there is something limitless about him, as though everything in him is freed up, he goes on the right runs, gets himself in the right positions, shoots and heads right, no thinking, pure intuition, he follows his impulses and wants goals more than anything else. He cried after the England game, but like a child. What happened today, towards the end of the encounter but before Uruguay had scored, was a part of the same limitlessness, he raced towards Chiellini, lowered his head and bit him, threw himself to the ground and rolled around as if it was him who had been hurt. They keep showing the incident on the TV stations now, and then an image of the bite mark on Chiellini's shoulder. They also show two earlier cases of him biting an opponent, one at Ajax and one in Liverpool. The latter in particular, when he bites the Chelsea defender, is scandalous, you see him opening his mouth and sinking his teeth into him, and we haven't, or at least I haven't, seen the like of this before. He really looks like an animal. But it is that very lack of control that makes him such a unique footballer, there are no limits for him, he is in full flow, he is twenty metres from the goal when Cavani gets the ball against England, and there is nothing to indicate that the cross will come, it is much too far forward, but he runs, Cavani holds the ball and chips it, Suárez shifts his weight, twists in mid-air and heads the ball into the corner past the oncoming keeper, without any back-thrust, the ball just seems to hit his head. It is an unbelievable goal. For the next one he sets off on a run so fast he is on the verge of falling, then he lets fly with his boot so hard the goalie has no time to raise his arms, once again a perfectly executed goal. It is not strange he also follows his impulse to bite because that is what he does, he obeys his emotions. What is strange is that it should be a bite. There is something inhuman about it, hence our reactions, it is absolutely unheard of, something animals do, and our children before it has been socialised out of them. An adult man who bites, that is shocking. He has done it three times. The consequences for him were serious the other two times, and he knows that. He also knows there are not only TV cameras all over the pitch, there is also one following him exclusively. So he knows everyone wants to see him do it, and that the consequences will be dire. Nevertheless, he sees Chiellini, the red mist descends, and he bites.

Zinedine Zidane's headbutting of Materazzi, which was also dramatic, was different: it was almost as though he had made up his mind to do it, and then he did it, he was decided and ready to take his punishment. Materazzi had gone too far, said something Zidane could not tolerate, and he nutted him to the ground. The deliberation makes it different, and even the headbutting too, that is how you fight if you have been brought up in slightly tougher surroundings than the Norwegian middle classes. Zidane's behaviour was in a way, within a certain logic regarding honour and retaliation, entirely rational. Suárez, bearing down on Chiellini, opening his mouth and taking a chomp, acts quite irrationally. Actually it is only a minor transgression because it isn't dangerous and can't have hurt that much, but it becomes so much bigger because it breaks all the conventions of how to behave, also in a footballing context, where violence is ever-present, like stamping, holding, shoving, tripping, elbows to the head, feet to the head by Balotelli (he should have been sent off for that). Even in this context biting is unheard of. 'That simply is not done,' as they say here. Both commentators on SVT,

Hamrén and Nannskog, struggled to articulate their feelings after the incident, words such as sick, crazy, perverse and incomprehensible were used, and Hamrén also said Suárez should receive professional treatment. This is entirely understandable, but there is something else about it, something fantastic, we watch football because it is theatre, it is drama, it is different from our lives, and when something unheard of takes place, the intensity and value of what we see is enhanced, sometimes radically. You mentioned Schumacher's charge on Battiston in 1982, and it was upsetting, but it is also one of the few things I remember of 82, and it is part of the game's own aura; everything happened in it, even that. This match won't go down in history, now all we will remember of it is Suárez's bite, however we will remember it all our lives and perhaps also reflect on it. Especially the fact that it is actually such a minor thing, so harmless, innocent almost, while its symbolic value is so great, the brutishness of it so present and so final, it is unendingly fascinating, why did he do it when he had everything to lose? How is it possible to lose control of yourself in that way? What is it about him? Who is he? Immediately afterwards, when Uruguay scored, he cheered like a child, and everything was forgotten. After the match he was interviewed by Uruguayan TV, they didn't ask him about the bite, but he was still clearly subdued, as though something in him knew his race was run, actually his World Cup was over, because of what he had done, which he might not even have remembered clearly.

Everything in him is open, this too.

It says on the net that he could be banned for two years.

It won't happen. But he can forget the World Cup.

I didn't write a letter yesterday, there wasn't enough time; in the morning I had to make packed lunches and drive the girls to the theatre, they have rehearsals from ten to four every day next week, then there is the dress rehearsal and they have twelve performances. It will take all their time, and a little of mine too, because it will mean two hours' driving every day. But I do it gladly; I like driving, I like driving through this area and I like the girls spending their time singing, dancing and acting. When I got home I had to read *Njal's Saga*, I have to write about it in the fate essay, and I don't remember much from it, mostly that it is so bloody long! After an hour I made lunch, then I did various admin jobs, scanned contracts, wrote letters, emails and paid some bills. Afterwards I picked up the girls again and watched the Holland v. Chile game until Linda rang and asked to be collected from Ystad. I put Anne in the car and drove in listening to the football on the way, and once home I found out about the two Dutch goals, feeling no emotional or mental involvement; to have that you have to be able to watch the whole thing, and if you have watched as much as I have over the past few days there has to be something at stake to get involved. The next game, however, was different because Brazil had lifted themselves, suddenly they were playing with tempo and intensity and the players flooded forward. The opposition may not have been the greatest, and perhaps Cameroon made it easier for them by standing as far up the field as they did, but Cameroon provided resistance some way into the first half, they cut through Brazil and had chances and even a goal, but I never thought the result was in any doubt, as a team Brazil danced to a different beat, and when Fernandinho came on in the second half they had something they had missed terribly before, a centre of gravity between Gustavo and Neymar, a ball-winner and a ball-distributor and a marauder. Suddenly they were on a par with Germany and France. And I don't think it is important that they were playing one of the weaker teams; now they have been there, now they have felt they are there, at the level they have to maintain to sweep the board. The future is looking bright for your team, Fredrik, especially little Limahl, his first goal, the simple first-time shot from a cross is what great players do. The second was also delectable, he dummied the keeper on his burst through the defence and the ball was in the net with his next touch, that too apparently effortless, as easy as taking a stride.

I fell asleep on the sofa at some point towards the end of the second half and woke up in front of the TV at half past twelve. Everyone was asleep, and I went in and lay down beside Anne's cot, five hours before she would wake me asking for food. Two hours later Linda left for Limhamn, with Anne, and after driving the girls to the theatre I was back home with John. I wrote a letter to you, and he sat in the living room watching YouTube, films of people playing Minecraft. Watching a film is one thing, playing Minecraft is another, but watching people playing, is there anything more passive or meaningless than that? He, six, going on for seven, finds plenty of meaning in it. I took him out and jumped on the trampoline with him, but after only a few minutes we lost interest, so I skipped the rest of the working day and took him to the pool in Nybrostrand. We swam, then he had a hamburger, followed by an ice cream, and we went back home. On the way he said, is there anything better? A swim, an ice cream and some pop – that's living!

After Italy v. Uruguay there was a little incident here, one of the girls made her sister cry, and she didn't say sorry either, she was cheeky and toughed it out, that is one way of maintaining a distance from what happened, and I was unable to close the gap, but I did see she was sorry, her eyes were sad behind the hard facade, and in the end she came to where I was writing about Suárez and asked if I would read to her. All the others had gone to bed. So we sat down on the sofa, she snuggled up, and I read the book about Silver Lake, you know, Laura Ingalls's series, the most famous story is *The Little House on the Prairie*. She loves the stories, perhaps because nothing happens, it is just long descriptions of nature, of the animals, what they do in the house and outside, what they eat, how they get food, make clothes, everything in very slow detail. Have I mentioned this in one of my earlier letters? At any rate, the opposite of Harry Potter – not a bad word about that series, but the calm you find in Ingalls's books is absent in most children's culture, and it is good to be immersed in it with her.

Argentina and Bolaño will have to wait for another letter, it is getting on for midnight here and I have a sleep deficit, and tomorrow I seriously have to get down to the essay.

All the best,
Karl Ove

Botafogo, 25 June

Dear Karl Ove,

I'm in Rio again. It feels good to be back, and right now I'm enjoying the almost monastic quiet in my room here at Afonso's. I am,
as you've probably gathered, very fond of Lasse, and he's taught
me, and continues to teach me, a great deal: to see details, see the
world, see the people, in other words what pervades his film-
making, nothing is too big, nothing is too small. And he, like
Suárez, is also 'unfiltered', as you put it.

Yesterday was my last day in Salvador, it was beautiful and
sunny and for the first time during my stay we went into the city
centre, Pelourinho, which was once the hub of the Brazilian slave
trade and is still the heart of black Brazil. There is a different,
slightly wilder, simpler beauty about Salvador, the sea and sky
merge the whole way along the horizon when viewed from the
top of Praça do Sé as you stand looking out over the port and city.
As I've said, it was my last day with Lasse, and being together
with him is to spend time with someone who manages to open
up the world the entire time, through his conversations with
others, as well as through documenting it with his little camera.
There was, for example, not a single stray dog in Salvador that
didn't get its photograph taken yesterday.

When we were at Café Gourmet I wanted to confront him, not
about his curiosity but in relation to what has I suppose become
my mantra in the past year, that the world is becoming a better
place the whole time, that right now the future of mankind is

brighter than ever, something I knew from beforehand that we don't agree on.

'Everything is improving, Lasse, I and many, many others share that view, but you don't agree, why not?'

'Because I see that the middle class has more purchasing power, something which does not equate to happiness. And what about everyone else? They get to sit on rickety buses, part of a public transport system which never improves.'

'But Lasse, forty or fifty million Brazilians have been lifted out of poverty in the last few years, is that not progress?'

'And how the hell do they know that? Which bureau of statistics says so? This is the most mendacious country in the world, from the president right down to the slums.'

'Why is it that way?'

'You can blame it on colonialism and neo-colonialism, and that Brazilians are afraid to protest. It wasn't until recently, just prior to the World Cup, that they took to the streets, as well as which they were young middle-class people, not the working class, not at the beginning, who have real cause to demonstrate.'

'But isn't that a good thing?

'Yes, of course it's good. But then the authorities clamp down on demonstrations by sending in the police and military from the favelas that have been "made peaceful".'

'A lot of people would say that this "peace" is welcome, that the criminal gangs have been chased out and the people there now have access to health and schools . . .'

'But what did the criminals do? That's the next question. They went elsewhere, to Salvador, here, for instance'

'So Terceiro Comando gangsters are here now?'

'Yes, we watched pictures live on TV from the Rocinha favela in Rio! You could see them fleeing, the gangsters, over the mountains, exchanging fire, and then they wound up here instead. In

Salvador. It's easy for them to get to, just hop on a plane. It wasn't wrong of them to go into the favelas, but they should have done it long ago.'

'So you think I'm mistaken? I haven't seen a single homeless child on the street in Rio in the entire week I've been here, they used to be everywhere, I've hardly seen any hookers in Copacabana, and even here in Salvador, where everything looked so run-down last time I visited, now the facades are positively gleaming . . .'

'But where did all the street children go? They can't all have become football players! Many of them were merely transported elsewhere, the ones who were around the Maracanã, for example, they tore down their shacks and shelters, put them on trucks and drove them somewhere far off, outside the city, to places where they didn't know a soul!'

'Isn't it possible, Lasse, that those street children are simply better off now?'

'It's possible some of them are, but they were shooting them in Fortaleza prior to the World Cup. It was filmed and everything. There were businessmen in the city centre who . . .'

And so our conversation veers off in other directions. Afterwards we take a stroll though Pelourinho, where tourists are pouring in in droves, mostly Bosnians and Iranians since their teams are to meet at Fonte Nova the following day.

We watch Italy v. Uruguay at Cantina da Lua, a place owned by a guy who was a friend of author Jorge Amado. It was, in my view and contrary to what you think, the most boring match so far. Anti-football from start to finish, one long protest against what I regard as being the very idea of the game: to score goals and do beautiful things with the ball, exhibit control with feet as though they were hands, which is after all, in the light of my previous musings on apes, a simian characteristic. On the second floor of the restaurant my attention is drawn to five young Englishmen sitting next to us, the sad, empty look in their eyes which is the sad, empty look you get when it is all over, and this makes me think of Bradford, Manchester, Leeds and Bournemouth, perhaps they hail from one of these places, have saved up for several years, worked extra hours and taken overtime and dreamed, dreamed, dreamed, Karl Ove, of a great England, an England that could surprise the world, and under the leadership of Rooney and Hodgson go the whole way to the Maracanã. I feel for these young men, who have seen their dreams cruelly shattered, and when my eyes return to the screen I find myself wanting to look away again, as though unable to bear this wretched excuse for a game. Free kick. Play is interrupted. Players protest. The referee reprimands them. They gesticulate. It's like American football: the movement on the field occurring in fits and starts with never any flow. And then we both notice simultaneously, Lasse being the first to comment on it, that Pirlo looks just like you, and that brings us on to something else, then he starts talking about film-making and nothing can reignite our interest in the game. At around the hour mark, Marchisio is – as you wrote – wrongly sent off, and at this point I begin to sympathise with Italy, your Italy, Pirlo's Italy, which suddenly becomes Pasolini's Italy and Cultural Italy AGAINST benighted Uruguay, because I think the Uruguayans are beginning to reveal that Latin American Janus-faced characteristic, that shadowy side of beauty, the darkness, violence and the abyss, and it struck me that I've never liked Uruguay or Uruguayan football, and when IT happens (the Rio newspapers are filled with vampire cartoons today, each one funnier than the one before), it is in my view in line with a deeper logic about predators disguised as footballers.

If FIFA doesn't ban Suárez from playing for the rest of the tournament then that organisation will lose any last shred of dignity it has. Felt sorry for Pirlo, Buffon and, not least, Chiellini as they walked off the pitch, and when they showed a close-up of Suárez I noticed, as you did, that he didn't look happy, there was no Made it to the Last Sixteen! Yippee! in his face, but something else, perhaps an insight into what he sees across the sea of people, two things: I'm not like you, I'm a vampire AND this was my last moment, this was the last time I can bask in the light because if the eyes of the world saw what I did it's over and back home to Transylvania.

I hope that elegant Colombian team dance all over Uruguay when they meet, whether the vampire plays or not.

After the game we caught a taxi to Itapua and took a walk along the beautiful seafront there. The sea shifted from turquoise to blue, the surf rolled white, and on the beach you could see groups of boys playing football. An hour later it was time to say goodbye. Two prolonged hugs, first Lasse, then Zaylin, and the thought crossed my mind: will we meet again? I'm sixty-two, he's seventy-five, both of an age where you can't be sure you'll see each other again when you go your separate ways and say au revoir, auf wiedersehen or vi sees.

I want to return to what you wrote in your last letter about structure and ideology, in relation to some of the feminists we've talked about, and my reasons for skewing the perspective to bring in Bolaño and Ciudad Juarez (Santa Teresa in his novel). There are more issues here to deal with. And with regard to your unwillingness to deal with them – not everything is supposed to be fun!

Thus one more thing, in conclusion, and it concerns what you mentioned in an earlier letter, how you sometimes feel ill at ease when being interviewed by Swedish feminists. There's a profound irony here. In *Min Kamp* you have, among other things, depicted the life of a Scandinavian family with small children, the love between a man and a woman, changing nappies, collecting kids from the kindergarten, preparing baby food and all the things that weren't the remit of men until relatively recently, which, I imagine, the men of my generation, born in the fifties, were the first to start doing. We realised the ideal of equality everyone believed in and fought for in the 70s and you tread in the tracks we made. In other words, in your life you do exactly what all feminists wanted, and want, men to do.

And that's the biting irony in all this, because you don't act like Hemingway or Mailer, you don't boast about erotic conquests, unceremoniously dump one woman after another, you haven't, like Garcia Marquez, lived half your life in the brothels of Barranquilla, in institutionalised misogyny. And yet, all the same.

Who is 'little Limahl'?

Fantastic reading about John and what he came out with on the way home from the beach: 'A swim, an ice cream and some pop – that's living!' There you go, a connoisseur of the art of living in your immediate proximity. I like reading about your children, what you all get up to. It reminds me of when Amanda and William were little and how wonderful it was being around them.

Best wishes,
Fredrik

Glemmingebro, 24 June

Dear Fredrik,

Only a few minutes ago I sent today's letter to you, and then I read what you had sent, thinking I might as well carry on because that is what your letters do, they open something up for me which I want to respond to, though I seldom can. Not themes, I think, not so much anyway, it is more the descriptions of the world you inhabit, and the way your associations work, how you dig up memories from Malmö or Paris, for example, and write about them with the same lively fullness, which seems to prey on me: I have to describe this, the summer in Österlen and what is going on here with the same detail! But then I start to write, lose sight of this, my mind comes up with the odd idea, much more arid than I want, and it is, in my view, because at the moment I am arid inside, I am out of kilter, not in repose, even though the days here are sun-drenched, and the air stands still in the garden, quivering in the heat, and the clouds tower up in the most unlikely of beautiful shapes, white and grey and bluish, with a depth I have seen nowhere else. It is like enormous ships coming in. Or enormous airborne mountain formations. The Andes, the Alps, the Dolomites in white smoke. This time, however, it was what you wrote about animals, footballers on the Limhamn pitch, where I also played when I lived in Malmö, I was there on New Year's Eve and celebrated with aquavit, and I remember Nikolaj well. He and Sana bit each other, you write, and you say we are animals – and then Suárez bites Chiellini. It was in the air, you felt, didn't you? It existed, it was a possibility and then it materialised.

We have both touched on the differences between humans and animals in earlier letters, how much closer we are to them than perhaps we believe. The difference between us and them is the difference between culture and biology of course, and if animals seem further away to us, that is due to changes in culture – we barely see animals any more, their rearing, which used to take place at many farms, happens now at huge, industrial-sized complexes, and the result, what we eat for lunch every day, bloodless pieces of meat in plastic, has nothing to do with living beings. So no life, no death, no blood, no sound, no smell, no taste, no movement – animals have gone from our lives, and then perhaps animalistic behaviour also appears out of the ordinary, something we reject, while it actually expresses the opposite, something deeply human, the human as a biological creature. Suárez may, when it comes down to it, behave in a more human way than you and I, Fredrik.

I supported Cameroon yesterday, naturally enough, but we still must have been watching a different match, for there was a sharpness about Brazil that they haven't had before. I agree that Alves was poor – in all three matches so far the opposition has broken through on his side – and Oscar was invisible for as long as he was on the field, and Fred is no world-class striker, but as a team they were better, and it seemed as if they could burst through Cameroon's defence at will, all they had to do was put their minds to it. Was it just Neymar? Perhaps. They will have a tough time against Chile anyway. It will be a fantastic match. Chile have everything to win, Brazil everything to lose. And I don't think Chile will allow themselves to be outplayed, allow themselves to be opened with slick passing and ball skills; energy and explosive power will be required.

One of the best things about the World Cup is the history behind it. There are classic encounters that go back a hundred years – Brazil v. Uruguay of course in this competition, but also Germany v. France, if they meet. Sincerely hope they do. There are Schumacher and Battiston, Roucheteau and Giresse, Platini and Rumenigge somewhere in the background, extra time and penalty shoot-outs.

The only World Cup I didn't see was, typically, the one where Sweden got into the semi-finals. USA in 1994. I saw the group-stage games, Norway were there – they beat Mexico, drew against Ireland and lost to Italy, and as far as I remember those four were level on four points, and Norway didn't get through. Our friend Drillo was manager then, and he was probably satisfied with the results and thought they would scrape through. They didn't. Four years later they did, but then we met Italy in the next round, and they didn't give the ball to Norway, who were unable at any point in the game to take control, they just defended and counter-attacked, so that was that. But in 94 I was working 'on the slide', as Norwegians said then, concreting using sliding formwork; when they work on oil rigs they need lots of people, and it is a Bergen tradition for students to travel down and get work. At first I got nothing, but I didn't go home, I waited for two days, then they needed more people and had no choice but to take us. On with overalls, a safety helmet and goggles, out with the ferry to the rig, which stood in the middle of the fjord, and up we stared at one of the four legs. It must have been twenty metres above the water. The job was easy: either filling a wheel-barrow with cement and emptying it down a shaft or stirring the wet cement in the shaft with a vibrator. Round and round, twelve-hour shifts, day after day, until the leg was a hundred metres above the sea. It was fantastic working there at night, with all the lights and sounds, surrounded by darkness. The lunch breaks, when we ate ten open sandwiches, at least, while the older workers told us what it had been like in the 70s, when everything was new and safety minimal: people got injured and died. I said nothing to anyone, just listened to what was said. At the weekends buses came and drove us to a disco in the nearest town. A lot of drinking. Living in huts; this experience is probably the furthest from the life I have chosen. Then I got the sack; the closer we got to the top of the rig, the fewer workers they needed, and I was last in, so first out, of course. But when I returned to Bergen I rang another company building a rig in a dry dock – or whatever they are called – I said I was experienced and could start next day. While I was there the World Cup was in America, and so I never saw the golden generation of Swedes, who are still in the public eye – Brolin, Ravelli, Thern and so on. Nor the final – was it Italy v. Brazil? All the other World Cups I have seen, from 1978 onwards.

My father was a pathological liar, he lied about everything, mostly trivialities, which brought him nothing. But if he told us lies and we knew he was lying, we never confronted him, at least I didn't, and I don't think Yngve did either. One of the last times I saw him, perhaps the very last, at any rate it was the year before he died, he said he had cancer, he had been to hospital and they had operated on him, but he couldn't be saved. 'I'm going to die, Karl Ove,' he said. And I knew he was lying! What could I say? I couldn't say he was lying. I couldn't react with horror at the news either. I looked down, said, oh, that's terrible or something. There we sat. When I told my mother, who had been married to him for twenty years, she told me that once, when he was eighteen or nineteen, he had told her he had testicular cancer. So, in a way, the circle was closed. What he said then, by claiming he had testicular cancer, was perhaps no more than that there was something wrong with him, he was sick, at least there was something not right. When he told me he had cancer it was simpler, actually all he was saying was that he was going to die. And he did. Another thing my mother told me was that one of my father's friends had taken her aside and informed her that he, my father, told lies. He was well known for it. I don't know, Fredrik, now I am forty-five and actually I just feel sorry for him. Somehow he had got it into his head that what he had wasn't good enough, he had to lie about himself, and after a while he couldn't distinguish between the truth and the lies. I once had a friend who was like that, he told transparent lies too, and when we didn't say anything, even though we knew, he knew we knew, and the situation was irredeemable and just sad.

Sunday-morning football on the Limhamn pitch, where people just turn up to play and have done ever since the end of the 60s, if I have understood correctly, is one thing I miss. It reminded me a lot of how it was when we were children, the anticipation, who is coming today, how many, will it just be the four of us, as it was sometimes in the winter, or maybe eight, then football is completely satisfying, or, as in the spring, maybe twenty? The attachment you form with everyone there, at once you know who are the football types, what they can do, what you can expect, and the great earnestness, everyone giving it all they have, and strangest of all: nothing has any importance except for what is happening there at that moment. All the men are divested of their private lives, who they are elsewhere counts for nothing, here it is just who they are in the game that matters. I have met several of them in other contexts – the chatty Frenchman, for example, he sold carpets in a shop I went to, and the man with the high forehead and glasses works as a journalist, I discovered when I met him at some library do. I knew none of them, but it is still a community I miss. Now, smoking forty cigarettes a day, not having run a metre for the last five years, it feels like a long,

long way back, so far that I probably won't go back, however much I'd like to. I was down at the pitch here two years ago watching the local team, they play in the sixth division or something like that, I was considering training with them, but they were eighteen, nineteen and ran like crazy men. I just had to give up on the idea.

How funny you reading about me in a Brazilian newspaper; you are so far away that I still can't take it in. But I did an interview with a Brazilian journalist a few days ago, as I think I said, it was the usual questions, the title, what did my family think about it, have I got any friends left, how does it feel knowing so many people know so much about me, but finally we got round to football, and I was able to say we were writing this book, you and I, you were there, in the cauldron, and I was here, as far away as it is possible to be, if not physically, then mentally. She asked me who I supported. I said I couldn't say that to a Brazilian newspaper, it was impossible. Because, as you know, I support Argentina. She laughed and said, so it definitely wasn't Brazil. We talked a bit about the next round. She wanted Chile as their opponents, said they usually beat them. Today I saw that Scolari had been warning Brazilians about Chile as far back as December, he didn't want them, he would rather have a European team. After seeing them, I can understand why.

The swimming pool in Nybostrand. I wrote about it earlier, the hazy white walls in the sun, the deep-blue water, the atmosphere – which reminds me of one of two really wonderful days we had on holiday in Las Palmas many years ago, a restaurant by the sea in disrepair, bricks and tiles, water lapping over it – and the sun shining, the wind blowing, and the sense or insight: the days are so many and this building will only be standing for some of them before it has completely disappeared, while the sea and the sun and the wind carry on. Eternity, in other words. It isn't often you sense it, is it? It has happened to me only a few times. The last time was exactly one year ago. Linda and I were in Sydney, in the evening we ate at a fantastic restaurant, up on a cliff over a beach, it was called Iceberg or something like that, and was built in an Art Nouveau style, beneath it were pools on the edge of the sea, and from the panoramic windows high up we saw the waves crashing in over the white brick pools, wild and ruthless, the darkness was thick, the sky black, and the waves towered upwards and were hurled forward. It was so beautiful it hurt, and I had the same insight, the days are so many.

Well, not much substance this time either, only thoughts – but the World Cup is long, there are still lots of letters to write before it is over and we can meet over a Brazilian cauldron in Limhamn.

All the best,
Karl Ove

Botafogo, 26 June

Karl Ove,

Thank you for yet another amazing letter filled with vivid images and life, one of your best yet, although you don't seem to agree ('Well, not much substance this time either, only thoughts . . .') – 'only thoughts'? Your father's grievous lies, the clouds over Österlen, the depiction of the oil platform and its dizzying height, dinner with Linda at the restaurant in Sydney – and you call me a romantic! (Incidentally, the oil-rig description reminds me of a night in Salvador when Lasse and I tried to explain the beauty of the snowplough to Zaylin, how its monstrous form appears out of nowhere in a cloud of snow, the thrill of seeing sparks fly when the blade scrapes the tarmac, the sheer power, like the locomotives in Turner's paintings, and how frightening it is, how you can't see the driver, and I told them about my ex-wife, who grew up in Norrland, in the north of the country, and her relating to me how afraid she used to be going to school in the snow, terrified it would turn up while she was en route.)

Sometimes I imagine you can open up reality anywhere at all if you're just attentive enough, open it up to 'eternity', or whatever it should be termed, whatever it is that flows through us with indomitable power and which we so often keep the door closed on and protect ourselves against. To take that thought further, have you noticed that the teams and the matches in this tournament have been akin to a big Advent calendar, you open a door to a country and the associations spill out and we stand in the cascade interpreting and putting together our sporting and ethnological jigsaw puzzles? I also think that these doors, or flaps, are part of the mystery of writing, and that if you dare to open them – the societal as well as the personal – they lead all the time to new doors, and it's language and writing that help us gain entry. To open the Alexis Sánchez flap and wind up with Bolaño in Ciudad Juarez, with Walter White in Albuquerque or with Jorge Calvo in a flat by Möllevångstorget in Malmö, perhaps it is precisely this that gives the greatest pleasure in writing, lies at the very heart of what we call creativity, simply watching as the flaps are opened.

It was quiet last night. As I walked down the dark path from Afonso's house onto Rua Assunção, I heard sounds and discerned movement in the darkness above me: nine monkeys swinging cheerfully on the telephone line leading to the street. Their faces looked small from down below and they hurried off as though they'd been up to no good. I went to Cobão, a market here in Botafogo with a lot of outdoor bars. There I watched France–Ecuador with Pascal, one of my old friends from Rio, a Frenchman who's worked as a translator and interpreter here for over twenty years. He was with a French friend, Stephane, who's also a translator. It was Pascal who helped cure me of my fear of violence here in Rio on my first visit in August 1997. I'd been invited by the Biblioteca Nacional to give a lecture on the reception of Brazilian literature in Scandinavia, which for a long time I intended to deliver in Portuguese – in spite of the fact I couldn't speak the language at the time!

What is it, Karl Ove, that makes us want to approach the edge of that stomach-tingling precipice where absurdity displays itself in all its glory? Could it be what you write about your father, the desire to lie to make yourself bigger than you are? Could it be that simple? You feel small and want to be bigger? Sometimes I have to shake my head in disbelief at the things I've done, or in this case planned to do. It ended with a thundering headache and me doing it in Spanish, which went well and was appreciated. This took place at the Méridien, a luxury hotel in Copacabana, which I hardly dared leave. I was scared of Rio and was convinced the streets weren't safe to walk. Then Pascal came over, thanked me for the talk and suggested eating lunch at a place a few blocks away.

That was how we became friends. It was he who opened up Rio for me, who stripped the city of the horrors I'd adorned it with. He seemed so young, boyish and bashful back then, and I looked at him tonight as we sat in front of the TV, and it was the same face as seventeen years ago, the same soft boyishness, but now, I saw, his hair was flecked with grey and the bags under his eyes were a little bigger. I asked him how old he was, and when he answered fifty, I nearly fell off the chair. That set me off thinking about time again. I've been to Rio fifteen or sixteen times, and we always meet when I'm here, once or twice at least, and the strange thing is I consider him a close friend, one I have complete trust in, but I don't really know him. I don't know a great deal about his life. Only that I like him, his smile, the way he speaks Portuguese, and tonight it felt like I had once again dropped into his life simply to ascertain that he has now become a man, and then my thoughts took off in other directions, like how most of the Europeans I know here are together with black Brazilian girls, or at least mixed-race, and it hit me how that's also true of several of the Brazilian men I know at home, only the other way round. Pascal's partner is called Sheila and is a real stunner, a mulatta who seems hewn from the very ideal of beauty that prevails here, where mulatta women rank at the very top.

I think there might be more to this, that countries like Brazil are God's gift to those of an austere disposition, the simple sensuality that exists helps smooth the sharp edges we puritans have. It would seem Brazil has been good for Pascal, in the same way as France and Brazil – countries where I've discovered other parts of myself – have been good for me, made me bigger, more whole, and I write this without lapsing into any kind of cultural self-loathing. I love Sweden, its language and its culture just as intensely now as I suspect you love Norway and its language and culture. There is in my view no contradiction in loving your own country, where you come from, and the countries you travel to and make you feel more complete as a person.

Brazil has, in other words, been good for the former young communist from Nîmes, self-described as strait-laced back when he was active in the youth wing of the French Communist Party. He has now built himself a life here, and I've been able to follow his progress. To begin with he hardly had any translation jobs, now he's used by large French companies, the French embassy, the Canadian embassy, and his job requires him to fly all around the world. And every time I meet him, I think of that first walk we took, from the Méridien hotel down Avenida Princesa Isabel to Copacabana with the sea on our left, and of my peculiar lecture on a subject which, when all was said and done, I didn't know that much about, and of how I stuttered my way through it in Spanish, and of how enthusiastic people were at hearing reactions to their literature on the other side of the globe, and then the two hundred metres to the restaurant where we had lunch and that feeling of freedom it entailed. You can actually walk the streets of Rio without being shot! But I ponder also that we can sit quietly together, the conversation not flowing endlessly (the Lasse syndrome). And there is nothing wrong with that. The silence is not uncomfortable, and if anything should happen to me here in Rio – should I get winged by a stray bullet, run over by a taxi – I know he, Pascal, would be the first and most frequent visitor to my hospital bed. Strange, seeing as I can in no way say we really know one another.

The game wasn't good. France seemed to treat it as a practice match, and I thought about what you wrote, about your admiration for this team and that you were 'enamoured' with them. All I saw was eleven footballers going about their work, determined not to pick up an injury, half an eye on the match in a couple of days, against Nigeria in the last sixteen. Ecuador were weak, and on a TV in the other open-air bar beside us I saw Switzerland book their place in the last sixteen with a convincing win against Honduras, and the only thing I noticed about that team, Honduras I mean, is that they have a black player called Jerry Bengtsson. So the football yesterday was a bit of an anticlimax, and the day's reward for me was listening to Pascal and Stephane have an intense discussion about President Dilma Rousseff, the former president Lula da Silva and the demonstrations last year. Pascal was direct and firm in his opinion, sounding, I can imagine, much like he did as a young communist leader in Nîmes in the early 1980s.

'What started out as something legitimate, a popular demand for free public transport, Pase Livre, and sprang from ordinary people's anger at the atrocious transport system on offer, was hijacked by the middle class to attack Dilma. People on the right took over the whole thing and tried to steer public discontent against the Partido dos Trabalhadores, the Labour Party, Lula and Dilma. That's also why there was such support for the anti-World Cup demonstrations, because it was Dilma and PT who'd brought it here. And that in turn was why the foreign media wrote so much about how nothing was going to work in this country during the World Cup, they bought into the false picture of the situation peddled by the national press, who are also very much to the right. But everything is working perfectly. The stadiums. The airports. Everything.'

And I agree with him completely. The World Cup is proving a success in every way, it's been one big party up to now and I cannot see any reason for that not to continue. I consider it a privilege to be here, but I can't help but think forward to 2018 and the World Cup in Russia, to that thug in the Kremlin, how he'll be sitting at the opening ceremony with that steely gaze of his, and I wish we could somehow renege on awarding them the tournament in protest at their annexation of Crimea. And subsequently 2022 in Qatar, the emir there and . . . well, maybe this is the last tournament I'll have the opportunity to experience in a respectable footballing country.

Impressions from last night: the statue of Christ, as so often before, made an impact on me, standing there, illuminated, seven hundred metres up on the peak behind us. My eyes were drawn more often to that than to Ecuador's desperate attempts to get the ball in the net. Another image sticks in my mind. As we left we found ourselves in a street from where we could see the Dona Marta favela (where the Michael Jackson video for 'They don't care about us' was filmed) protruding like a constellation in the night sky. This is also part of Rio's beauty: when darkness falls and the lights come on in the favelas, the lights of the thousands of houses encircling this vast city.

All the best,
Fredrik

Glemmingebro, 25 June

Dear Fredrik,

It is now ten past eight in the evening, it has been a hot day with sun and a blue sky, Anne is asleep, Vanja and Heidi are watching the Pajama Club on the computer, both wearing pyjamas, as is only fit and proper, John is watching children's TV, Linda is in Helsingborg overnight, she went early this morning, comes back tomorrow afternoon, and I have just seen Argentina beat Nigeria 3–2. At long last they played to the level they can, at long last we get to see some lightning-quick one-twos between Di María, Messi, Higuaín, Agüero and eventually Agüero's substitute, Lavezzi, who really set out his stall, at long last a varied attack with some long crosses over the defence by Mascherano, with some slow back and forth in the midfield, moving forward metre by metre, until they suddenly upped the tempo and broke through the middle. Long shots, crosses from the flanks. It was so simple, Nigeria attacked, wanted to be forward and unlike in the Bosnia and Iran games there was room for the Argentinians. I like this team, Fredrik, I already liked it when they were playing badly, and now I am excited and happy, even if they stopped playing football after an hour. I think there is more to come and we have some really big games ahead.

The free-kick variant between Di María and Lavezzi, where Lavezzi passed to Di María, who dinked a cross over the defence to Lavezzi, who ran through and hit the ball on the volley, was clever and beautiful. They can do things like that, it is hard to resist, they do it for us. I switched over to Danish TV a couple of times, which is always amusing because the picture might be the same on both channels but the commentators are always very different in tone and what they talk about and fixate on, and the Danes just said Argentina were world champions in attack, but not in defence. They let in two goals, and Nigeria came close a few times, while I think the back line was good – I am thinking of individuals in one on ones – especially the right back, Zabaleta (he put in a perfect tackle when Musa was through, it was quite brilliant) and the central defender Garay, whereas the left back was more tentative, a little like the Brazilian backs, good in attack but too easy to get past. Mascherano was terrific throughout. In principle, Argentina were through to the next round the moment Messi scored his first (after Di María had done the legwork), and I think the areas that opened in the defence were because of that. The defence as a whole will look different in the upcoming matches.

It is also true that, as a TV viewer, it takes time to get to know the teams and players, and familiarity increases the value of what you see – if you follow the English Premier League, for example, after a while you know the players at Chelsea, Manchester City, Liverpool, Arsenal, etc. and then you read the game better – that was how it was for me with Brazil during the first game, in fact they have almost the same team as last summer, during the Confederations Cup, while with Argentina I know only the front line, plus Mascherano. (For Nigeria I knew only Mikel from Chelsea and Odemwingie from Stoke.) In the final, which we hope and pray will be between Brazil and Argentina, it will be like neighbours and familiar faces on the pitch.

I reckon the quarter-finals will be: France v. Germany, Brazil v. Colombia, Argentina v. Belgium, Mexico v. Greece (possibly Chile instead of Brazil), and then the semis: Germany v. Brazil and

Argentina v. Mexico, and the final: Brazil v. Argentina. But I hope France will beat Germany. That would be wonderful and fitting revenge for the 1982 semi-final. If Chile beat Brazil, I think Germany will be in the final. So either Germany v. Argentina or Brazil v. Argentina in the final.

What do you reckon?

Today was almost a replica of yesterday. I got up with Anne at half past six and fed her, slept through till eight while Linda had her, took over again, made lunch for the girls, the nanny came, and I drove the girls to the stage, which is in a barn between Skillinge and Brantevik. The way there is an adventure in the summer, especially on mornings like this one, when the sky is a perfect azure, the air is still and the low sun in the east a burning yellow. First, there are the cornfields – they are still green with a hint of yellow, and they ripple in the light breeze, like a sea. And once you have seen the greenish-yellow, dense, rippling corn as a sea, the isolated houses, all under immense trees, become islands. There are no forests here, just plains and islands of trees and houses. A glimpse of white walls, timber frames, barns of brick or wood beneath the thick, luxuriant foliage. Some of the trees – which is all you see if the distance is far enough, for everything here is flat and you can see for kilometres in all directions – are huge, and if you imagine that they are creatures, that they are living and have stood there for maybe many hundreds of years, it is difficult to keep the car on the road – this morning I had to swerve back three times because I was heading for the ditch as I stared. Second, there is the sky – the clouds far away on the horizon, which hang there every day, towering up, are hypnotic, like something from a different world. Third, there is the sea, which isn't my sea, I will never write an ode to the Baltic, its waters aren't even salty, it is a semi-enclosed sea, but seen from the road, from the depth of meadows and farms, the dark blue rim, which no islands punctuate, is what defines the beauty of the country-side, the background it contrasts with, for if everything I see and drive through every day had been deep, deep into the country, like in Russia, say, it would have been unbearable and not beautiful in the same way, but here it ends, here it comes to a stop, here it is framed by something else.

No ode to the Baltic, but perhaps the best collection of Swedish poetry I have read is precisely that, I am thinking of *Baltics* by Thomas Tranströmer. By best I don't mean objectively the most successful and impressive, but something very personal; it was the first collection of poetry I read that actually spoke to me, which I could take in and relive. The description of the sounds of the sea passing through the trees, which I seem to remember is at the beginning, reminded me of what it was like to walk through the woods on the island of Tromøya, out by Spornes, when I was a child, it opened up that space in me, and afterwards nothing was alien, in that oblique way that poetry collections can be alien, though nor was it familiar. There is such an appeal in those poems, and so much space, and so much time.

On Tromøya, where I grew up, there is a church on a low hill above the sea, visible from afar and for many hundreds of years it was a landmark. It was there long before I read Tranströmer, but it was this poem which either gave it meaning, the feeling of time that has passed in this one place, that it is unchanging while the days race through it, and people rush into it, or which confirmed a feeling I already had, though tentative and unformulated and unseen. That is how the best literature works, isn't it? You see something you haven't seen before or which you have seen but you haven't realised, and the world opens up for you anew. This feeling of time and place, bound to Tromøya through Tranströmer's poem about the Baltic landscape, lies at the base of everything I have written.

Tranströmer is perhaps first and foremost a solemn poet, he is almost sacred, but in a sober way, if such can be imagined – the sacred element comes from the movement, I believe, what I would call 'rhythm' if the word were not so hackneyed and reminiscent of writing school, but this is what it is about. Not rhythm as in a drummer's rhythm, the marking of the beat, but in the way the spaces give way to each other and the phrasing of the voice. The poems are Protestant, this isn't Rabelais, this isn't the rabble and laughter, bums and farts, rubbish and exaggerations, this is one person in the world, or the world in the person, monotheistic poetry. Stern, beautiful, serious, monotheistic poetry. It is what is associated with Scandinavia, and rightly so, but it didn't need to be like this. Today I have read *Njal's Saga* and secondary literature about the sagas, about Norse culture and religion, because I am writing about fate, of course – and what characterised Norse society before Christianity arrived was first of all that the concept of an independent individual did not exist, you were primarily a representative of the family, and that is why being outlawed was the worst punishment there was, without the others you were no one – and there are references to this in *Njal's Saga*, it is about the whole society, in which everyone can make themselves heard and has a voice, high and low, slave and chief, man and woman – in the epilogue it says that 140 characters speak – at the same time we don't find out about anyone's inner life, everything is about interpersonal relations, it is these infinitely complex relations which drive the plot, not the individual's will or psyche. In Dostoevsky's novels, which were the starting point for Bakhtin's theory about the dialogic novel, I have read there are around forty characters with a speaking role. So the Icelandic saga is a kind of collective novel, written in the thirteenth century, at a time when nothing of its kind existed. Another interesting point is that there is no expression of personal guilt, or of guilt at all, no one has a bad conscience about what they have done; they can feel shame, for this is a question of honour, and that is what governs this life: if you have killed someone, you don't feel guilt because this is an internal, personal matter, no, you bear guilt, it is objective and can be redeemed: you pay so much for a murder and then the balance is restored. Even more interesting is that *Njal's Saga* also talks about the Christianisation of Iceland. In the course of a couple of pages they changed the system of faith, although this affects neither patterns of acting nor thinking, but that followed later, it is what has left its mark on us, or at least me. Enclosed in myself, filled with feelings of guilt and shame, which are actually irredeemable, even though they do fade with time. I presume that is why I am so fascinated by other eras' fundamentally different ways of understanding themselves and the world because it means belief is relative and consequently random.

This began with the Baltic, continued with Tranströmer, who I think became so important for me because the time of a place, the inconceivable chasm that separates us from those who were in the same place in the twelfth century, is about roots, about belonging, which I have always lacked or thought I have lacked. You touched on this in an earlier letter. It is a timeless longing for belonging, roots, because now identity is a construct, you can be whoever you like, wherever you like, and everything that happens to us happens because we are the way we are, because we have certain qualities and a certain psychology, life meets us and we react to the encounter according to who we are – and so on, almost into determinism, but not quite. Character is fate, they said in ancient Greece, and I think it is true. That is my fate belief.

It is Thursday, 26 June, a few minutes after half past six. On TV the match between Portugal and Ghana ebbs and flows. Portugal have just scored and are leading 1–0. Yesterday I sat down to see France v. Ecuador but fell asleep at some point in the second half and went to bed before the match was over. Woken at half past six by Anne making disgruntled noises. I fed her, put her on the changing table and placed a mountain of clean clothes in the cupboards, emptied and filled the washing machine, changed the bedding and tidied the rooms to make the job easier for the cleaner, who comes every Thursday, then I made lunch for the girls – fried fillet of chicken, pepper and a wok sauce with noodles, and then fruit, slices of bread, water, pear juice, yoghurt and pancakes – at half past eight the nanny arrived, and at half past nine I drove the girls to the theatre, through the sun-filled, luxuriant and sated countryside, stopped at the local shop and bought our lunch, then sat and worked on the essay for two hours, one page. Spoke to Geir on the phone for an hour. Fetched the girls, who were happy, it is still five days to the premiere so they haven't started to get nervous yet, did some shopping, drank coffee with Mia, who is the mother of Heidi's friend Megan, and Linda, before starting on this letter.

Such is life here. Nothing spectacular, nothing memorable, with someone I pay to clean the house, someone I pay to look after the children while I am working, a life filled with children, cooking, driving, football on TV and sleepy evenings, all set in countryside full to bursting with gentle beauty.

'Little Limahl' is a joke – Espen texted me and said that Neymar looked a lot like Limahl, the 80s pop star, English, if you can remember him. (In the same way that Suárez looks like Freddy Mercury.)

All the best,
Karl Ove

Glemmingebro, 26 June

Dear Fredrik,

I agree with your verdict on the France match yesterday and admit that the word 'enamoured' was hasty – but whose amour isn't hasty? That is the whole point of it! And there was no reason for them to exhaust their repertoire and sap their strength; they have, if they beat Germany against all the odds, four matches left in this World Cup. Before the last group game, which starts in ninety minutes, there are seven teams from South America, six from Europe, one from Africa and then the USA – fingers crossed for Algeria this evening of course.

I believe in your 'door/flap' theory because I experience it every day, the way one thing – it can be anything, a smell, a landscape, a football match, a face, a sound, a snowplough racing at full speed through the night somewhere in Scandinavia, whirling up snow – contains the second, which contains the third, and so on ad infinitum. This is about personal memories, but also about the collective, the stream of images from the world that passes through us from when we start to find our bearings, from when the world is lit in us, to the day we die and it is extinguished. But also the physical, material world opens up for us, if we want – usually we don't, we have to keep it at a distance so that we can live our lives more or less purposefully. In the garden outside, for example, there are enough phenomena to keep a mind busy for a whole lifetime. Not so long ago I began to wonder what the situation was with material, such as a door handle, tabletop, brick wall, windowpane – what was it actually? I read about atoms, and about atomic physics, about radioactivity and the quantum leap. I understood nothing, but I persisted because even the time when they made these great discoveries in the world's smallest constituents is fascinating, in my opinion; in the 20s, for some frenetic years, they made one discovery after the other, in a whole variety of fields and countries, it was like a fever, until the area lay fallow and certain knowledge was established. Some of them were obviously brilliant scientists, but not all, many were average, but they were still part of this wave, and their names are still remembered. They were also young, many of them. I still can't connect the world I can see with the subatomic reality they describe, the leap is too great. But what the alchemists tried to do, change one material to another, they did the same. We are no longer surprised by this, no one shows any reverence, it has become an accepted part of reality. Paracelsus belongs here, he was an alchemist, and he had the pre-Enlightenment urgency to understand and change the world – this is actually a Faustian story – and Pascal belongs here, the man who wrote about internal eternity and external eternity, and was frightened not only by the emptiness this revealed but also our desire to chart it. You see: this was the door to the garden. Then we have the door to the brain, where all memories and all knowledge, everything we know, want and believe in, are to be found. Recently I read a book by Henry Marsh, a neurosurgeon who operates on brains and has written about his work. It is endlessly fascinating for many reasons, I am stuck to my chair as I read, I really ought to take a day off to finish it. They clamp the head in position when they operate, then they saw through the skull or bore with a drill, and when the brain is open they go in with their instruments. They see everything through large microscopes, and from his description it is as though he is wandering through an enormous landscape, and the beauty of what he sees, which he is open to, is reminiscent of the beauty of the galaxies in space, perhaps because the names are so exotic, cold and attractive. It is like a landscape, with long valleys and mountain ranges, rivers and plains, which he cuts through, millimetre by millimetre, to locate and suck out or cut away the tumour. There is the constant risk of a blood vessel opening, then there will be chaos, you can see nothing, everything is red and you have to act blindfold. I imagine myself driving, clouds descend, the windscreen is suddenly all white and you are driving fast. You can brake, signal right, stop and wait until it is over, but he has to do the opposite, he has to act fast, blindly, and quite often, it transpires, it is in vain and the patient dies or is left disabled. During the operation he sometimes tries to understand what he is seeing, that what he is cutting his way past is thoughts, feelings, memories, knowledge, this person's whole world, but the notion is impossible to grasp, for the grey jelly-like matter shows nothing of this – in a way the feelings don't belong to it, but only to that something which is in it. And what might that be?

There is a lot more to this book than that, and from here, in the nerve centre of the body, the doors open to everything that exists and has ever existed. I will let them stay closed and return to your Rio de Janeiro, the river of January, which you have not only opened through your letters but also kept open during these World Cup days, in the same way that a novel does. The novel is the only medium I know that shows that things are not as we believe. Nothing is as we believe. Even our own world, which we know inside out, is not as we believe. What we believe protects us against the world. And that protection is necessary – I must have said that before – one of Borges's fantastic short stories is about someone who doesn't have that protection, someone who remembers everything he has ever heard and seen, and he is numb, paralysed, incapacitated – but the protection has the effect of making the world freeze, and die, and then we live like the living dead, safe but frozen. I am talking about myself. My way into living, my way of opening the channels to the world, is through writing. What I want though, really, is to open myself, and not what I write, to living. At least that was what I wanted when I was twenty. It didn't turn out that way, it became something else, and here I am. Children, they cut channels in the ice and give everything warmth and life and meaning. They must never find out, I think now, that I need them.

Two of the children have a sleepover with friends, the youngest is asleep and the eldest enjoys being alone. She was just here, sitting on the sofa on the other side of the table, and asked what I was working on. I told her about this book. Told her you were in Brazil and I was here and we were writing about the football World Cup. Who's interested in that? she said. I replied that lots of people were interested in football. But you aren't at the World Cup, she said. So what can you say? I answered that I was watching it on the TV. She smacked her forehead. Who's going to read it?! she said. Is he in the stadium watching while you watch TV here? Yes, I said. But I write about other things too. Like what? she said. Whatever's on my mind, I answered. Don't write what you're thinking about, Dad! she shouted. That's what I do, I said. Today, for example, I've written about the drive to the theatre. How nice it was. Oh no! she said.

She was here because she wanted the computer. I promised her I would download several days of Minecraft for them, and now I will keep my promise, so this will have to be my lot for now. Looking forward to the next round. Hope you get a ticket for some of the coming games. She was right, you know, my daughter. It is not a bad idea to attend the World Cup if you are writing a book about it!

All the best,
Karl Ove

Dear Karl Ove,

Two powerful, overwhelming letters from you today. I sat in a street café near the metro station in Botafogo reading them, and suddenly the World Cup, the reason I'm here after all, seemed very far away, and you, and the world you wrote about, seemed much more important and immediate. Tranströmer, for instance, your first encounter with his poetry which you describe so vividly, how he opened up that space inside you connected with a place on Tromøya, the island of your childhood, and how the spaces gave way to more. How his metaphors opened the world for you and made it more visible. I find this particularly interesting to read as he had a similar significance for me, albeit not in such tangible detail. Other collections of his, *17 Poems* and *The Half-Finished Heaven*, meant more to me.

My life had taken a new departure, I had finished military service and moved into my first flat, Spångatan 30, eighteen square metres, toilet outside on the stairs, ninety-eight kroner a month in rent, working at the port, and some mornings I got up very early, at 5.30, to read Tranströmer before cycling down to report for work, the mornings electric in their beauty, Malmö dark and quiet, the smells, and Tranströmer's poems carrying me on my bicycle all the way to the harbour, where they evaporated in the often raw reality.

It was a time in my life when I didn't consider being an author a realistic option. My interest in football had waned and I was gravitating strongly towards politics and Maoism. But Tranströmer and Vilhelm Ekelund made it possible to create a parallel world that Maoist dogma couldn't touch. Odd, really, but since my whole life has been characterised by uncertainty and division I see the logic in it now. I didn't at the time, however, and both these founts, poetry and politics, helped make the world decipherable and bearable at a time when I didn't know quite where I was heading.

Your two letters today were so thought-provoking that I'm not quite sure what tack to take. Perhaps it doesn't matter, somehow or other it feels like paths lead us where we want to go anyway. So I'll continue with Afonso, my placid host, he picked me up at a quarter to twelve and we drove out to Recreio, the part of town where Chico Buarque's football pitch is located. It's nearly an hour's drive, and we were the only ones in the car today. Wonderful silence, a few short exchanges, no lengthy discussions, leaving lots of time to gaze out over the city and the ocean, and as you exit the tunnel that connects old Rio with nouveau riche Barra, and turn your head to the right, you see possibly the largest favela in Latin America, Rocinha, situated right next to Rio's best golf course and the affluent area of São Conrado, a sight both strange and potent that gives you the key to understanding what makes Rio unique, because the rich and poor live side by side here, not what you usually see, with the poor on the outskirts of town, but literally right next door, and ironically it's not uncommon for the poor to have the best views. If I were to transpose this to, say, Stockholm, you would need to picture a one-hundred-and-fifty-metre-high hill covering the entire park area of Karlaplan with small breeze-block houses on the slopes and at the top, where jungle-like growth dominates the terrain, sit a horde of gang members, armed to the teeth, controlling people's lives – ordinary workers, domestic helps, cooks, nannies, doormen – with what's known as the lei da bala, the law of the bullet, which means that if you or your wife inform on them, they'll shoot you, her or one of your children the same night and leave the body out on Karlavägen, at the entrance to Fältöversten Mall, to strike fear into others as well as to make it clear you don't mess with them, but many of the ordinary people on this hill work in São Conrado, or on the other side, in Gávea, so it only takes them a few minutes to get to work in Narvavägen or Tysta Gatan and it's this cheek-by-jowl existence that characterises Rio, which feeds the middle class and elite's perpetual fear of the people in the favelas – the same people who run their kitchens and look after their children – but which also, inevitably, leads to unexpected encounters and love across class divides.

When we got to the pitch I met a journalist from O Dia, one of Rio's biggest dailies, I had an interview scheduled with him to talk about samba football, this book and about the film Lasse and I made about Garrincha's son. I talked and talked and suddenly felt completely empty, as though words had lost their meaning, and I just stood there, a babbling head in football gear, a sixty-year-old Swede explaining the history of Brazilian football to him, a thirty-year-old journalist from Rio, and then our match kicks off and the photographer he had with him, a woman about the same age, takes up a position behind the goal where those who call me Ibra expect me to dispatch a few scorchers, but there are four or five others on my side who have never seen me before and view me as just an anonymous gringo, and one of them consistently refuses to cross the ball to me, in addition to calling me Dutchie, and I'm aware of an unpleasant feeling welling up inside, a feeling I recognise from long ago – the team regarded you as crap and never passed to you – in addition to which, I fail to control the first two balls played to me and receive only abuse from these new 'teammates', carhalo (what the hell), puta que te parriu (whore that bore you), and am told to pass the bloody ball and they make resigned gestures, and the *O Dia* photographer is kneeling behind the goal and suddenly the joy football always gives me is gone. Bastards! Who do they think they are with their bossa nova football, and when, finally, after half an hour, things improve and I make sweet contact with a volley, making the net bulge, the guy who was giving me the most grief comes over, genuflects as if worshipping a god – opportunist prick – and then ten minutes later, the episode takes place that is my real reason for writing about the Chico Buarque gang again today, our nine- or ten-year-old left-winger – this same boy who has dazzled with scissors moves, crosses and even scored a goal – fails to trap a pass, whereupon the guy who was on my case and fell to his knees afterwards gives the kid such a telling-off that I can hardly believe my ears, in terms so terrible and words so vulgar that I can't commit them to print, and the little boy breaks down in front of my eyes and plunges deep into a child's bottomless despair, he cries, takes his top off and flings it on the ground, goes and sits on the sideline, screaming that he is never, never going to play football again and begins yelling insults back at Grandad, who turns white with rage, and this mutual bawling and bellowing continues, rendering me speechless. I can't believe a grown man could treat a child that way, but after a chaotic five minutes or so (with someone in the background screaming é brincadeira, é brincadeira! It's only a game, we're playing for fun!) we get on with the match, the inconsolable boy is replaced by someone else and then we attack, Grandad sets up a goal and everyone celebrates, except for me and him, and I catch sight of his face, he's devastated, reality has caught up with him, he understands what he's done and says as much out loud, me desanimei (you could translate it as I've lost the desire, but with the double meaning of animo, desire/soul, it's also possible to think as I did, I've lost my soul, because that's what I think happened when he treated the boy so brutally), and his expression is blank, as though he too is going to burst into tears, and that puts me in mind of my last letter and what I wrote about Rooney and masculinity, how there is a softer masculinity here, which makes crying like that possible, because, generally speaking, men here are more in touch with their emotions than we are, where you are.

Can you imagine a first-team footballer at Glemmingebro IF berating a youth player to such an extent that the boy breaks down and walks off, and then when the game resumes, the player stops in the middle of the pitch with a vacant gaze and tears in his eyes, and says, my soul has left me?

I can't.

Morning. Peaceful. Children babbling away in the distance, and a machine of some sort which, now and then, sounds like the Brazilian commentators when they shout gooooooooooooool! Suárez? I've read, or heard, that he suffers from tacomania, a pathological compulsion to bite, which is apparently related to schizophrenia, and as I watched him yesterday on Brazilian TV receiving word of his ban on a mobile phone, breaking down and being enveloped in a hug by someone in the Uruguayan management team – I thought of that boy from yesterday, at Chico Buarque's place, and then I felt sorry for Suárez, my heart went out to him. That's how much of a softy I am.

It was hard to concentrate on all the football being shown yesterday, and it made me think of Lasse Westman again. He told me he'd been in Paris in 1980 when Sartre, who as you're no doubt aware was extremely wall-eyed, passed away, and the following day there were posters of Sartre's face plastered all over Paris, which left Lasse wondering which direction to look in: on every street corner this impossible gaze going in all directions at once! That's what it was like for me yesterday with South Korea v. Belgium, Algeria v. Russia, USA v. Germany, and Ghana v. Portugal all showing on different screens.

I had to zap back and forth on the TV while checking the laptop at the same time, and, to take South Korea v. Belgium first, it feels as though South Korea and Japan have everything except good finishers, and what's more they look physically inferior from the start. Too slight for corners, spot kicks and tackles, which means that well-organised and physical European teams, like Belgium, eventually grind them down. Belgium are, in my view, precisely how you described Brazil after the first match, it feels as if they have more to give; they've won all three games in their group, but it doesn't seem as though they're firing on all cylinders yet. I still think they'll make it to the semi-finals though.

Algeria v. Russia, from what I saw, wasn't much of a game, but it had a wonderful, almost religious intensity, and during it I was, as you'll understand, back in Idungatan, Vasastan, Stockholm, and the Algerians' joy when they made footballing history by going further tops all the scenes so far in this World Cup, and when I pictured Kamel, at that moment lying on his back under diggers and crane trucks on Västberga industrial estate, I could almost see the inner energy filling him, and him – should he hit on the crazy idea – walking from Västberga to Idungatan with a digger on his back (because that's the power of football when everything goes our way), and should the impossible come to pass in the last sixteen – inshallah! – and Algeria meet Germany and are afforded the opportunity to redress the disappointment and scandal of 1982 then my cup runneth over.

Ghana v. Portugal? I feel for the Ghanaians of course, but you have to be blunt and say African football still has too many moral and political problems for them to have any real chance of success on the field. Nevertheless, we will see an African team win the World Cup one day. It'll take time, however, all the crap surrounding football in that part of the world needs to be sorted out first (player revolts, suitcases with three million in cash in the dressing room, Boko Haram bombs exploding and killing twenty people right before they board the airplane). Africa is at an impasse but will one day take its rightful place in football's Valhalla. Portugal? Catholic icon and diva football. Did you see Ronaldo after he made it 2–1? There were still ten minutes left and if Germany had scored one more goal in their game and Portugal had managed two, then Portugal would have gone through, but not so much as a smile from 'the world's best player', only a sulky pout from the boy from Madeira, and none of his teammates went over to hug him. Not a single one! Had it been a usual day at the office, he could easily have scored at least four goals, such were the chances that came his way, and that brings us to yesterday's undoubted highlight, USA v. Germany, yet another World Cup clash that had pretty much everything: a no-holds-barred contest within the laws of the game, tempo, rhythm, spectacular shots, dribbling, beautiful play that ebbed and flowed the length of the pitch and an ice-cold finish from Müller to win the game. He fascinates me more and more. In my eyes a very ordinary footballer who also seems to be devoid of charisma as an individual – and yet a world-class player who does almost everything correctly and is always in the right place when the ball arrives.

Germany were of course impressive, but so were the USA, and while watching it occurred to me that both teams play Protestant football, which is the antithesis of the Catholic diva football Ronaldo represents. There were two telling moments, one during the game and one after the final whistle: 1) After Müller coolly dispatches the ball into the net, a goal bearing the hallmark of a simply executed masterpiece, he's engulfed by joyful teammates, true joy, and none more so than Klose, who in all likelihood in the course of the next game or two will be crowned as the player with the most World Cup goals ever, not a hint of 'It should have been ME that scored,' and that kind of collective spirit can take them all the way, but they have, as I've mentioned, an Achilles heel, their defence and the lack of a natural leader should they face real adversity. 2) The faces of the Americans after the game. Whereas I'd expected to see delight, their expressions spoke of disappointment. They were through to the last sixteen but instead of being thrilled they were furious at having lost – against Germany! That, Karl Ove, is a testament to their self-confidence and morale. The footballing map has been redrawn, and the USA, under Klinsmann, are one of the teams holding the pen and ruler.

'What do you reckon?' was the question you put regarding the last eight and the semi-finals. This is what I think.

Quarter-finals: Brazil v. Colombia, France v. Germany, Mexico v. Costa Rica and Belgium v. Argentina

Semi-finals: Brazil v. France and Belgium v. Mexico

Final: Brazil v. Belgium (3–1)

There you have it.

The other day you wrote that 'Men's violence against women' should be rewritten as 'Some men's violence against women' and of course I agree with you on that, and I think that type of campaign, where a whole group, in this case men, are assigned blame works in the same way political correctness can, creating fear within, making you afraid to write and say obvious truths, just as here, we're only talking about some men. Not all French people hate Jews, but some do and that's a problem. But I wanted to flesh it out and go further, that's why I brought up Bolaño and Ciudad Juarez, and even though we probably agree that there are sociological explanations (unemployment, new ideals of the man's role, economic problems, culture clash), I believe there's more there, something I can't quite put my finger on. That was my reason for wanting to go further, to go deeper into Bolaño's dark heart.

I don't know what this something is but believe it exists, and I want to know more.

With regard to the man you mentioned, as you are also aware of, we were quick to protect his wife, as you wrote, but we did so in solidarity with him, so that he would seek treatment, get help for his behaviour. It ended with my losing a good friend, and the following year he went to prison after having beaten her up again, and when I see him in town now I feel afraid, Karl Ove, he's bigger and stronger than me, and when we meet on the football field, it happens, I feel fear and a profound sense of unease. The fear is palpable, but I'm also afraid that I have a 'Suárez' within, that to protect myself I'll injure him before he injures me. That can also be seen as one of the consequences when 'normal' men, who don't beat women and are in the overwhelming majority, stand up for what's self-evident: that violence and the threat of violence continue on, towards 'us'.

I found what you wrote about *Njal's Saga*, about guilt, honour and shame, interesting. After all, there are now many people coming to our home countries for whom these concepts still have the greatest resonance. For us, who now trust in the state (whether it be Norwegian or Swedish), relatives and family hardly mean anything, but they mean everything to people arriving from countries where the state is seen as an enemy and a malevolent power. For us the health services are 'family', social security is a caring grandmother.

Best wishes,
Fredrik

Glemmingebro, 27 June

Dear Fredrik,

It is close to midnight on this, the first football-free day in two weeks, and I have been tired all day, writing emails and talking on the phone for most of it. I'll have to pass. I can't answer your very full letter now; I'll do it tomorrow.

All the best,
Karl Ove

Glemmingebro, 28 June

Dear Fredrik,

It is Saturday morning, I have driven the eldest two girls to the theatre, no sunshine today, an almost white sky and a chill in the air, and Linda has gone to Ystad with John and Anne, so I am sitting in my study with the dog by my feet, listening to Harry Nilsson, an American artist from the 70s, after having read yesterday's letter one more time. I am struck by how much it contains and how seamlessly it moves back and forth between Rio de Janeiro and Malmö, the present and the past, theory and practice. In this letter you move from Rio to Stockholm. What happens then? We suddenly see Rio clearly, and we suddenly see Stockholm clearly. The image made an impression on me, for now I saw how foreign and inconceivable that world is here. And how fantastic it is. All cheek by jowl, all side by side, all overflowing – violence, love, wealth, sounds, tastes, smells. Now we can, and perhaps also we want to, romanticise everything, apart from poverty and deprivation. I learned something from the Swedish author Kjerstin Ekman – she is clever, wise, whenever I hear her say something on the radio or read something she has written, I pause and listen – she spoke once about the past, the old days, which I often yearn for, the manual world without cars, tractors, planes, trains, mass production, commercialism, and said we don't want to go back there, we mustn't romanticise it, poverty, material and spiritual, is terrible. She didn't use those words, but that was what I heard. Romanticism is also dangerous because it soon becomes theoretical, dealing with an idea rather than the reality. Having said that, we have lost something, something has been lost or perhaps it has never been here, but it is the abundance, the squanderable superabundance, not of money, not of things but of life – you wrote about a man shouting at a boy who becomes distraught and leaves the pitch in tears, then suddenly the man sees what he has done and is sorry, now that it is too late, and says he has lost his soul. What is that about? A man completely dominated by his emotions – at first he is furious, incapable of reining himself in, showers the boy with abuse, then he is endlessly sad and he cries. We are in the land of myths and stereotypes, that is how I have always imagined Brazil, and actually almost all Catholic countries, there is a much greater degree of acting-out emotion, a much greater degree of community, more of everything, a surplus of everything – happiness, sorrow, pain, pleasure. This is a stereotype, like the measured, controlled Scandinavian is a stereotype, but there is something in it, we cannot get past that. Brazil is an opera; Norway and Sweden are a string quartet.

Tell me, though, Fredrik, when you describe your work in the port as a young man, you say about Tranströmer that his poems 'helped make the world decipherable and bearable'. I am curious: in what way was the world bearable for you then? It must have been that which led you into writing, at any rate I don't know of any other reasons for writing other than it heals, is healing. There is a lot of happiness in the description of the port, but what was the pain? You don't need to answer if the question is too personal – I was only curious.

If I went to Brazil and experienced the partly foreign and partly familiar elements I would accept them at once, everything would be natural, the monkeys in the trees, the green mountainsides, the extensive shanty towns and shopping areas, but I would do that only because the criteria for my judgements have also changed. And your image breaks the familiarity: if there are enormous mountains in the middle of Stockholm covered in favelas, the foreign stands out as foreign and is in fact inconceivable.

And that brings us to the high point of the last round: Russia v. Algeria. I agree that the quality of the football was perhaps not the best, but I think you hit the nail on the head with your comment that Algeria had 'a wonderful, almost religious intensity' – I have enjoyed the USSR's and later Russia's expansive, flowing football over the years, but this team had no colour, too much Capello, too little Russia – after all this is a nation with passion and heart, but in the face of tragedy, not comedy, if we stick with the reality of stereotypes – while Algeria played with a contagious wholehearted commitment, I wanted them to win. They have many players of the type that France produces; hardly surprising, many were born and grew up there, to my knowledge. But did you see the interviews after the game? I saw one with the team captain. He thanked God for their victory, and then he dedicated it to the Arab world. It was fantastic, especially the sudden presence of God, which was quite different from Maradona's Hand of God, here we saw gratitude, elation and pride, here much more was at stake than football. The fact that they would be meeting Germany in the next round didn't dampen their enthusiasm. Ghana holding the Germans to a draw and at times running them ragged – that is, running through a defence that was suddenly wide open – may give Algeria hope, but they haven't got an earthly.

Your faith in Belgium is fascinating. I can see Eden Hazard twinkling and glittering like a diamond, with his blistering runs and masterful ball control, he is one of the best wingers in the competition, and to some extent I can see Dries Martens, who has had a big impact when he comes on the field, but I can't see many others. Defensively, the side is solid, well, they do have Vincent Kompany, but they are also a little unimaginative in attack – so I assume it is their potential you can see, and it is one of the strangest phenomena in the World Cup you are hoping for, a team slowly improving over the tournament until it is bursting with confidence, playing above itself when it counts most – that is, in the semi-final, because the finals are always poorer performances, at least from a spectator's point of view, than the semi-finals.

Belgium in the final is noted.

I didn't see the TV shots of Suárez when he was given his punishment, but I saw pictures on the net of him, apparently inconsolable, being hugged, and photos of him arriving home in Uruguay and unloading bags from the car in the evening or night, and the clip of him standing with his children, one on his arm, smiling. I felt sorry for him, he was on the way to being one of the big stars of the World Cup, and then he ruins it for himself. It is like a Greek tragedy: what makes him exceptionally talented is also the cause of his downfall.

But we wouldn't have been without it, would we?

The World Cup is a theatre, it is the arena of great feelings, the anguish of being knocked out, the euphoria of winning, and every other feeling in between. The genius of it is that feelings are not binding emotions, it is not like in a war, with the sorrow of a child or a sweetheart or a friend dying or dead enemies as the price for the joy of winning – no, there is no price except for possible self-denial on the part of these eleven players and, in rare cases like Suárez's, total humiliation before the whole world.

If Norway had qualified I would have been thinking about their games all the time the World Cup lasted, and would have been disappointed and sad for perhaps three or four days after they were knocked out (anything else is unimaginable) – but then that would have been that.

Dostoevsky, how often did you think about him when you watched Russia play? Jane Austen when you watched England? I have a notion inside me about what characterises these countries when I watch them play, but it is as though their literature doesn't belong here, perhaps because it is created despite its country of origin. This ambivalence makes it impossible to take a writer as representative of a country, as you do with a football team, there is no ambivalence there, and that is good, we need that. But I am interested in the ambivalence, the idea of belonging in a language but not in the country of the language, because, as I have mentioned before, I would like so much to belong somewhere, to have a home, to say 'this is home', and everyone who lives here belongs, there is a 'we', and this 'we' has certain ways of doing things, that which is called culture and is unlike all other cultures. This longing has nothing to do with exclusion (even if it could be the consequence), nor with conservatism, the way I understand it; is not reactionary. What I want in literature is differences. All the nuances in style, voice, tone, line of argument, creation of associations. And what I want in reality is differences. Not the same everywhere, not similarity, not mass thinking, mass production, mass culture. Not the global mass commercialism. Nor nationalism, which is of course also only an ideology, a superstructure, a theory which blinds you to a view of real life, reality as it is, or changes real life into something else. Nevertheless I am drawn by the depth of myth, the power of it – which, for example, was activated in the Balkans in the 90s, and which is obviously destructive or a counter-productive force in all societies, something attractive but also dangerous. Myth doesn't exist, I mean in reality, it is just something which colours reality in our perceptions.

I want to go home, but I don't know where it is.

Yes, of course I do, the house here, it is the first house I have lived in where I have felt at home, which I have felt at one with. And the family, that is where I belong. It is home in the most fundamental sense. But at a higher level, the one connected with culture, that in us which says 'we', there I have no home. And to some extent because of that, I think, I wrote what I did about the Icelandic saga, in which belonging is so self-evident that we are nothing without it. You mentioned the clan society, the archaic but still current way of organising societies, which contrasts with our state, and it is right, old Norse society was like that, and it was extremely violent, but what I was searching for was the non-individual, the collective, a natural belonging. To which one might object: if you are against mass culture, which naturally enough is characterised by a non-individual belonging, how can you want the collective? Isn't that an unresolvable contradiction? Yes, it is. As it was with the big political youth movement in the 70s, which was also about a collectivisation. And it is not the self-sacrificing collective I mean; I would never have survived that. Perhaps it is simple. Belonging is an abstraction, a notion, an idea which actually has no correlation in reality: family belonging, come on, what is that, are we going to sit having a cosy chat with our uncles and aunts, with whom we have nothing in common? And are we going to tie our children to us so that they don't get the freedom we longed for when we were young?

The divide is between reason and emotion. Feelings are so much stronger. I wrote in one of the first letters about the roar you can hear from a full stadium as you pass, a chill always runs down my spine when I hear it, it is so alien and so compelling – but if you hear it, then you aren't in the stadium, you are outside. The power of emotion, it was particularly manifest in Norway after the tragedy on Utøya, the collective grief, the intensity of it. It set in motion so much in me. But the feelings football arouses are an imitation, that is, the feelings are genuine enough, but they are not binding, they are not tied to any reality but one which is artificially constructed for us, twice forty-five minutes: Imitation of life, as REM sing.

Today the knockout rounds start. The football-free day was enough for me to renew my keen anticipation. Chile v. Brazil, that will be exciting. I am going for Chile but have feelings for Brazil and the Brazilians, it won't be the same World Cup without them, and I would like to have Brazil v. Argentina in the final, which would be the ultimate. But where your real sympathies lie is revealed the minute the game begins, then there is no doubt.

I am also looking forward to seeing Colombia, it is the only team I haven't seen, except in passing, and everyone seems to think they are the best team so far. I want Uruguay out as soon as possible. I don't suppose I am alone in that?

All the best,
Karl Ove

Botafogo, 28 June

Dear Karl Ove,

All I want to put down on paper today are two texts that captivated me, both in different ways, as I sat on a deckchair on the beach at Ipanema yesterday:

From the Rio newspaper *O Dia*, 27 June 2014:

Outrage in Costa Barros. Yet another innocent child. Funeral wake for three-year-old boy turns into public protest. 'He was sleeping like a little angel. Why did this happen?' The harrowing words of Jurema Rangel Bento yesterday at the funeral of her three-year-old son, Luis Felipe Rangel Bento, at Irajá Cemetery. The little boy, whom relatives described as a happy lad who loved football, died on Wednesday from a gunshot wound to the head, received as he slept in his mother's bed, in the Costa Barros favela of Quitanda. The incident occurred during a police operation carried out by the 41st BPM brigade in Irajá during an operation to recover a stolen car.

Below the text there's a photograph of a little girl of about eight, crying as though the pain of every child in the world is concentrated in her face. She's wearing a T-shirt with a picture of the little boy on it, while somebody, a big sister perhaps, is standing behind attempting to console her. An ordinary newspaper photo that opens the door to the pain we can all feel when someone we love disappears.

And the following is an excerpt from the crime novel *Berenice Procura* about a female taxi driver in Rio. Berenice, who is the main character in a series of crime novels by Luiz Alfredo Garcia-Roza, undertakes her own investigations into various cases. A street boy, Russo ('the Russian', fair-haired people are often given this nickname in Brazil), who may have been present on a beach when a murder was committed, attracts her interest:

On the beach, everyone is all but naked, but the difference between the rich and poor was still striking, or rather the difference between those who live in the area and those who have come, packed on buses, from the suburbs. The first thing the latter did when they got to the beach was to jump into the waves and then roll around in the sand. Looking for all the world like human fish fingers. At night, activity shifted from the beach itself to the esplanade along Avenida Atlântica. During the day a drowning might occur; at night or in the early hours, a stabbing. The visitors in the daytime were different from those at night. They belonged to different universes. At night the bars were filled with tourists, tat vendors, prostitutes, transvestites, pimps, people from northern Rio and the suburbs. The Russian did not belong to any of these categories of beach 'outsiders': He was born there, in Copacabana, and he identified completely with the area. And all he owned was what he had in his pocket.

He could not remember living anywhere else than on the street and in different children's homes. He did not know who his parents were, and had not so much as a distant memory, no matter how vague, that could serve as a reference of any kind. In his life the only thing that could come close to something resembling a mother were some transvestites on the street who had acted in a maternal way towards him when he was small. The little he did know about his real parents, which he was not sure was true, was something he had heard years ago: a story about a fair-haired foreigner having a relationship with a woman who lived on the street. Maybe it was accurate. It would in any case explain why he was blond and had freckles. Hence the nickname, the Russian. Towards the end of childhood and beginning of adolescence, he also earned the sobriquet Rat, because he was so adept at stealing from tourists and then quickly disappearing down into the neighbourhood's subterranean tunnels and sewers. He had not changed much since then. Merely honed and improved his survival skills, and as regards his foreign appearance, it had become more prominent as the years passed.

Brazil v. Chile in just under three hours. I don't like it. I feel mild trepidation at the thought of the two of them meeting. I want both teams to remain at the party.

Best wishes,
Fredrik

Glemmingebro, 29 June

Dear Fredrik,

We don't lack for levels of reality. You write about children killed
in their beds by random bullets in Rio de Janeiro, I write about
privileged children rehearsing for a musical in Österlen, and
between them we have yesterday's matches, the first at the
knockout stage, Brazil v. Chile and Uruguay v. Colombia, seen,
respectively, on the big screen with a massive crowd in Rio and
on the TV in the living room here with my family in Glemmingebro. One is life and death, the other entertainment, but not
without overtones from the former, setting the stage, as it were.

When the whistle blew for the start yesterday I supported Brazil. This had nothing to do with the football they play, but my
sensitivity to other people's disappointment; I couldn't bear the
thought of all Brazil, all 200 million inhabitants, being out of
the competition while Chile was there against the odds, and it
would be easier for Chile to cope with being knocked out. This
isn't something I am proud of, supporting the superior force
because for them failure is greater; however, I have to confess
this is how I felt.

Brazil didn't play well, didn't play like champions, and if you
home in on the individual players' performances, many of them
were poor. Both flanks were weak, Hulk and Oscar – although
Hulk was better than in a long time, he broke through the
defence in his brutal, muscular way several times, had a dangerous shot and a goal disallowed for hands – and the midfield too,

with Gustavo and Fernandinho, was overrun for periods. Fred and Jo were shadows, and innocuous. Jo, who is a giant compared with the Chilean defenders, barely won a header. But the reason was Chile, their incredible stamina and aggression, there was always a swarm of Chileans around the man on the ball, the pressure was uncomfortably intense, physical contact constant, and for large sections of the game Brazil were held. Not all of it though; they had several chances, and even if Neymar was less visible than he has been before, he showed a couple of fantastic touches, such as his take in the penalty box, there was a cross from around forty metres, he chested it down and left the defender for dead, it was stunning, quite simply stunning, suddenly he had the ball and was on his own, but of course two Chile defenders were not far away and he didn't get past them. What Brazil lacks is a creative midfielder, someone who can lower the tempo, raise it, distribute the ball, marshal the game, in other words, a Xavi or a Pirlo. You say Germany doesn't have a leader – isn't that also true for Brazil? They have Neymar, but he is no more a leader than Messi is. Brilliant, the best in the world, but individuals.

What a game it was. Poor play, lots of free kicks, but the intensity, the desire, the energy was red-hot. Medel for Chile was particularly impressive. I followed his season in the Premier League as he played for the team Solskjær managed, Cardiff City, but there he was a defensive midfielder for a team which was strung out, nervous, the very opposite of this Chile, who have been so compact and so confident in everything they have done that they could easily, with a bit of luck, have reached the final. Even their attack was good, I mean Sánchez, his goal: a tiny mistake by Hulk and bang, straight into the box, and Sánchez, one touch, bang, past the keeper.

Brazil had the first half, Chile the second, while extra time belonged to Brazil, and that was where Chile made a mistake in my view, they were playing for the penalty shoot-out, fell deep, went defensive – then the penalties were an aim in themselves, so getting there was an achievement, and perhaps, the way I see it now, they were much more tired than Brazil when the shoot-out started. I don't know. Penalties are just psychology. In training the players score in nine out of ten cases, all of them. Now Chile have missed three out of five, Brazil two. And it was a feat by Brazil to have scraped through, we are talking pressure of incomparable proportions, Brazil have everything to lose, and because they survived, in spite of this, I think they deserved to win. The match against Colombia will be different, they are going to win by a comfortable margin; the game yesterday was the hurdle.

Linda watched it with me, she can't bear penalty shoot-outs, they are inhuman, she says. Those who miss are scarred for the rest of their lives if they lose. Cruel, she says. And it is. But that is what we want! The tension when the whole game depends on one kick of the ball. The calamity is immense, but the reward for success even more so. All or nothing, heaven and hell – and afterwards everyone is in tears, the Chileans and the Brazilians.

Uruguay v. Colombia, that was quite different. Without Suárez Uruguay had no attack, and even if their defence is brilliant they couldn't keep out the two goals by James Rodríguez. The first was sublime, he chested the ball down with his back to the goal, turned and whacked the ball before it hit the ground, but with such power and accuracy that the keeper didn't have a hope in hell. The second was even more delectable because it came from open play and because the cross from the flank wasn't headed towards goal but played back to Rodríguez, who hit it straight into the net.

As I write this, evening has fallen. John is at a friend's with his gun, Heidi has a friend here, they are playing, Vanja is sitting with a game in front of her, Linda is on the sofa beside me feeding Anne, and the Mexico–Holland game has just begun: Robben is on the screen. Mexico are wary, so it seems, few players going forward when they win the ball. A one-two between van Persie and Robben already. They can unpick any defence, so Mexico will have to score more goals if they are going to get through. The feeling now, after three minutes, is that Holland will win. Isn't it the same with football matches as with books, you can judge them after the first few lines?

I will send this off now and concentrate on the game, knowing you are sitting there and watching the same images. Talk soon!

All the best,
Karl Ove

Botafogo, 29 June

Dear Karl Ove,

Yesterday was, as I'm sure you understand, agonising, and I still feel hot and woozy as I write this, as though I've been through an emotional spin dry.

The bar on Rua Assunção was full, about one hundred people inside and out, most of them wearing yellow jerseys. A group of drunken Englishmen were sitting at a table towards the back, with lots of caipirinha, beer and meat lined up in front of them. I sat squeezed behind two guys nervously drinking the whole time. I thought Brazil seemed uncertain at the start and was impressed early on with the Chileans' composure, tempo and how they played themselves out of every situation. Sánchez was good from the start, while many of the Brazilians were clumsy and awkward on the ball. Alves in particular, but also the midfield, comprised of anonymous donkeys like Luis Gustavo and Fernandinho, likewise the enigma that is Oscar, who I don't see doing anything (he is probably closing down space or something, but in my world he does nothing). Add to this, the mystery of Fred up top, all at sea, whereas Hulk appears to have woken up and suddenly gets right to the byline and finally manages to hit a cross in. The people around me become frustrated. They see what I see. This is not a pushover Chile (like in France in 1998 or in South Africa in 2010), this is a great Chile, this is Alexis' Chile, but then Brazil are fortunate and make it 1–0, and I start thinking it might be over all the same, the Chileans won't be able to pull level. But they continue playing as they have, with lightning counter-attacks, tons of aggression in the midfield, neutralising Neymar, who doesn't once shake his markers loose, and then, all of a sudden, he's there, Sánchez, inside the penalty box and makes it 1–1. Ice-cold. Clinical. And it's at that moment, but only then, as everything around me goes quiet, as the colour fades from those lively, happy faces from moments ago and they each assume a more neutral expression, that what I've been saying all this time, this Chile is a great Chile, becomes a reality.

It is true, I realise. And then, Senhor Knausgård, the fear creeps in that the improbable may come to pass: Brazil knocked out. It is really happening, and when Sánchez opens up the entire Brazilian defence at one point with a beautiful lob from standing, the feeling is even stronger. The match moves in waves, but what's striking in the second half – and only serves to further increase my unease – is that it is Chile controlling the game, as they say. Sánchez toys with the Brazilian midfield! I can't believe my eyes, and all around me frustration has given way to simmering anger, and every unsuccessful Brazilian attack is accompanied by loud swearing and abuse directed at the referee:

'Careca!' (Baldy!)

'Puta que te parriu!' (Whore that bore you!)

'Filho de puta!' (Son of a whore!)

And last, but certainly not least, since it's what you hear most of the time, 'Porra!' (A strange expletive, equivalent to something like Fuck! but which actually means cum.)

The drinkers in the street knock back beer after beer. The unease is palpable. The English guys mockingly – true to form, their arrogance almost tangible – chant, 'Shakespeare, Shakespeare, Shakespeare!' (?) and as the ninety minutes draw to a close, the verdict of the people is clear. Not even Neymar appears to escape it, porra from start to finish, as is the team and Felipe

Scolari, who looks quite pale and isn't waving his arms or jumping around as usual.

Jogo bonito? A joke. Not one move, not one feint or dummy, hardly a single incident that could fall under that definition. It's a team with quality in defence (Thiago Silva, David Luiz, Dani Alves, Marcelo as well as Gustavo and Paulinho), some players with special skills (Hulk's shot, Oscar's technical ability) and one genius, Neymar. Fred is a joke. Yet despite their skills, the sum of the parts don't add up. And there's no one on the bench who can improve things. Brazil have no playing style of their own and are all too reliant on Neymar in the same way as Argentina are dependent on Messi.

Extra time serves to confirm their shortcomings and the porraistas around me only get drunker and grow paler, outside a cloud envelops the Sugarloaf Mountain in white mist. Hardly any cars on the streets. And so we come to the penalties, and as I watch Neymar, Thiago Silva and Felipe Scolari make their impassioned speeches and pleas in the team huddle, I think: they'll win. They have such strong morale. They do have leaders after all, and then I imagine how David Luiz feels walking to the spot – I've done the same a few times, once in a match to decide the Malmö Championship against Valby, on the pitch at Vintrie in front of about five or six spectators, but my knees still shook as I made my way from the centre circle to the penalty spot, and I barely made contact with the ball – with the entire world watching and over one hundred million Brazilians demanding a goal. As Luiz puts it away I jump up from my chair and shout and dance around. My eyes well up, I'm close to tears, then Chile misses, César's save, Willian's miss, this torturous roller-coaster ride, and then the final penalty for Chile, it hits the post behind César, and back out onto the pitch. Is this for real?

Yes, it is. And the song Chile adeus, adeus! resounds and the people around me, fainting, halfway to a heart attack, order more beer, more cachaça, and as for Shakespeare, I think, looking over at the English guys. *Hamlet* and *King Lear* versus this? Sorry. Nothing can move people like this kind of game. And as I was on my way 'home' to write this, I thought about all the Chileans in the world, about my Chilean friends, Jorge from Santiago in Fuerte Valdivia, his sisters and children, he had been right in what he wrote to me on Facebook yesterday, this is a new Chile team, a great Chile team. It was, and I hope Pinilla's shot against the crossbar leads them to create beautiful subjunctive worlds about what might have been – but was not to be.

Uruguay v. Colombia? A deserved victory to Colombia even though Uruguay lifted themselves towards the end, but prior to any analysis of that I need to take a detour, or a short cut, to Simon Kuper, with whom I was in Copacabana the day before yesterday. We met at Posto 6 before making our way to a small street café on Rua Gonçalves.

Kuper has travelled all over Brazil in the last fortnight and already submitted ten articles to the *Financial Times*, for whom he's written for many years. We were both lavish in our praise of the tournament so far. He believes 1982 is the only one comparable. I'm leaning more and more towards the opinion that the current one is the best ever, better than 1982, better than 1970.

'But what's going on? How has it happened, such amazing matches, so many goals?'

'Attacking football has been winning everything over the last few years, the quick passing game, movement up the pitch, the ball on the deck. No team set up defensively has won anything lately . . .'

'Chelsea?'

'The exception that proves the rule. And there's no contradiction between tiki-taka and German football, between Barça and

Bayern Munich, it's the same football applied in different ways. Guardiola, who learned from Cruyff, is the link. Granted, Bayern's play is that bit faster, but this is the style that's winning now: Chile, Colombia, Germany – Klinsmann's football – Ghana, USA – also Klinsmann's football, Holland, although the Dutch variant is based more on counter-attack. This is the style I'm talking about, and its origins go back to Cruyff's time at Barça. It was he who laid the foundations for it. Play the ball fast and star players don't matter, the specialists, the ones who are good at one thing, are on the way out. The footballers of today can both attack and defend. That's why Argentina and Brazil are having problems, they're each dependent on their respective wizards, Messi and Neymar. As well as the fact that their midfield is too slow.'

And that, I think, is it. Teams like Italy and Uruguay, whose fundamental philosophy is one of defence, are having problems dealing with this 'new' football. The way I saw it, Uruguay didn't stand a chance against Colombia, who, let's not forget, have given us what appears to be a new superstar in James Rodríguez, whom the Brazilian newspapers are already comparing to Messi and Maradona.

After a while we go our separate ways, Simon Kuper heads back to his hotel room and laptop, and onward the following day to new stadia, I on my way to other meetings. We part with a firm handshake and an expressed hope to meet again before the World Cup is over.

Tranströmer and 'what was the pain?'

My experience of Tranströmer was not the same as yours, I didn't encounter a clear, distinct metaphor that opened a world I subsequently felt I could write about, for me his poetry was more a source of solace. I found in his work an ordered world, meaning if you like, and I think now that you press me, he may have acted as a substitute for religion, he made the world whole. Pain? I was twelve when 'God' – read: security/order/meaning – vanished somewhere along ski tracks as I poled my way along behind my mother, and a hole suddenly opened up in my existence. A void. That hole reappeared, regularly, throughout my childhood and younger adulthood (beginning when I was twelve, and again when I was sixteen, nineteen, twenty-one, twenty-three and twenty-seven, at which time it went on for, at its worst, six months. Towards the end of that period I thought for a while that suicide was the only way out, but, it's important to point out, I never stood with a rope in my hand, a box of pills by the quayside, was never on my way to the railway track) in the form of a series of psychotic breaks which we, my family and I, tried to defuse with the phrase 'terrible thoughts'. Freddie is having terrible thoughts, was the dictum when I thought I was going to succumb to angst, a condition where I was non-communicative and sometimes just screamed and screamed and screamed. What prompted these episodes was not fear of death. I was not 'afraid' of death and still am not – even though I suspect that such a fear may lurk when things are at their worst. Nothing seemed to help, not medication, nor conversations with a psychiatrist, nothing, and since my uncle, one of the people who meant most to me in life, was lobotomised to cure his anxieties, the curse of insanity hung over me, a dread of having what he had. Over the course of a six-month period in 1981 I made an interesting discovery, which was that literature didn't help, offered no consolation, couldn't lead me out of it, and that while certain pieces of music provided temporary relief, the only thing that really helped was time. Time and work. I began studying French in Lund, and the concentration required for that, plus my feelings for the woman in front of me at the lectern, changed my life, led me out of the darkness and back to humankind.

That was 'the pain' I was referring to. As regards Tranströmer and Vilhelm Ekelund existing in a parallel world to the political, I found small bridges between these worlds – Maoism and true art – which paradoxically fortified my political beliefs, Tranströmer had poems that I read from a political perspective, and when I learned that Vilhelm Ekelund's *The Ancient Ideal* had inspired the Swedish trade union movement in its infancy, I fancied I was on the right track, a feeling only strengthened when I discovered that Mao Tse-tung was also a poet.

Your musings on nationalism and a yearning for a home trigger many thoughts, but I don't have the space for them in this letter.

Best wishes,
Fredrik

PS Lapa was buzzing last night. Never seen anything like it. Packed with happy, smiling Colombians singing, drinking and dancing in the streets, and the scene put me in mind of Rabelais again, and how the Latin Quarter in the early sixteenth century might have looked, back when as a young medical student he trod its cobblestone alleys with Notre-Dame immense in the background.

Glemmingebro, 30 June

Dear Fredrik,

My head is beginning to spin now, so many matches, so many letters from you that are so rich in content, so much driving to the theatre and back with the girls, so much writing, and in recent days it has occurred to me that autumn is approaching – all publishing houses know this, they have everything ready for the autumn before the summer, but, as you have probably noticed, we are no normal publishing house, so on Saturday I had to get to grips with this, I read a manuscript, then it was Brazil v. Chile, I rang the author and talked for an hour on the phone, just in time for Colombia v. Uruguay. The following day, which started with Anne at six and continued with a drive north with the girls, then a letter to you, ended with first Mexico v. Holland, then Greece v. Costa Rica, which went to extra time and penalties and didn't finish until close on half past twelve. By that time I was on my knees. However, when I went to bed, Anne woke up – her cot is next to my bed in Linda's study because sleep is important if you are bipolar, so when Anne was born I moved downstairs with her and have slept there ever since – and she was not only awake, she was angry, she was screaming and screaming. So far she has slept ten hours at a stretch almost from her very first day. I thought: if I pick her up she will do the same every night, wake at half past twelve to be picked up, so I left her there. She screamed. I talked to her, she stopped screaming and listened to my voice for ten seconds perhaps. Then she started again. I tried singing. The same happened: she fell quiet and listened. Perhaps for thirty seconds, then she'd had enough and started again. And crying is self-reinforcing for small children, it is as though they get angry with themselves for crying, and so they cry louder, and then they get angrier and cry even louder. Milk was the key, of course, I knew that, so I went into the kitchen, switched on the light even though we have no curtains to the street and every passer-by would see a podgy forty-five-year-old in his underpants walking around and discovering there were no packets of ready-made milk left. It will have to be powder then, I thought. Usually we have boiled water ready, you just have to mix it up, but not this evening, so I had to heat it – with Anne screaming her head off in the study, you have to remember I didn't pick her up for prevention reasons, besides it is difficult (though not impossible) to mix milk with a child in your arms, so I did it on my own – but when it was hot I had to let it cool down before I could use it. I had two possibilities: either pour the hot water from pan to pan to cool it faster while Anne was still screaming or let it cool while I picked her up and carried her around a bit. I plumped for the latter. She stopped screaming the instant I held her. It is wonderful carrying her around, everyone who has done it knows how nice it is to be close to such a small person, but not at a quarter to one when all your body wants is sleep. We went from room to room, I chatted to her, she wriggled with pleasure now and then, but if we sat down, in front of the TV for example, she began to make disgruntled noises at once, which soon grew into a whine, then it was up onto my feet again. I tried to put her down, of course that didn't work, and we waited until it was possible to drink the milk. I stood over her in the dark, she lay in bed with the feeding bottle in her mouth, I thought, now, now I can take it back, and I did, tiptoed to the bed, lay down – up she started again. All this took me back to the time when we had three small children. It was like this all the time in those days. I had forgotten it or repressed it, and thus far Anne had been so quiet and undemanding that I didn't remember until now. Poor devils, I thought, parents with small children who don't sleep.

Then I was out like a light.

At half past six I took a wide-awake Anne to Linda, who fed her while I went back to sleep. At half past eight I got up, made lunch for the girls, packed some food for them, drove them to the theatre, and as Linda was going to the childcare centre in Ystad with Anne, John came in the car with me. On the way home I dropped in on Geir, who lives, as I have perhaps written, in a hacienda-style house on a hill above us. He has a garden with three hundred different varieties of rose, people used to come out in buses to see them, and three other buildings, an art gallery, a library and an office where we usually sit. He could never have afforded to live somewhere like this, he doesn't earn any money, but, would you believe it, he managed to buy it after seeing it one summer while staying with us. A rose garden, art gallery and hacienda are not so easy to sell, I would imagine, it must have something to do with that, on top of which the prices here are ridiculously low, as you might be aware. Nevertheless, it is such a strange feeling every time I walk through the gate (the property is enclosed by a two-and-a-half-metre-high wall) and he comes out, because I, and I have earned money from my books, live in a house built for agricultural workers, while he, who has barely earned a krona from his, receives me on an estate. He isn't interested in football, knows nothing about it, so the hour or so we sat there was spent talking about anything but. After an hour Linda rang, and I took John and went to pick her up in Ystad, where we were going to buy shrimps as we were having visitors that afternoon. The seafood van wasn't there though. So we went to Kåseberga, a little fishing village around ten kilometres from our place, where there is a very good fish shop in the summer. Linda waited with Anne while John and I went in. I have been to the village in the winter, when it is exposed to the elements – the wind blows non-stop – and utterly deserted, all the shops are closed, all the doors locked. The reason I go there in the winter is Ales Stenar, I don't know if you have seen them? Up on a plateau above the sea there are big stones placed in a circle, like a little Stonehenge – presumably from Viking times, and they must have had an astronomical-ritual function, what, I don't know precisely, and it was, and is, a holy place. The stones are in the shape of a boat, and from there you can see the horizon, all 360 degrees, the whole way around, so from the sea and across the land, and the sky is so high that I feel as if I am standing on a planet and staring into space, and for many years I have thought I must go there at night, you know, one of those icy, clear, starry winter nights. But this day was quite different, the sun was shining, the air was warm, the place was full of tourists in shorts, T-shirts, caps and sunglasses, and the two cafés, the kiosk and the two shops were open. I took a ticket for the queue while John stood in front of the glass counter staring at the various kinds of fish, pointing to some of them and asking what they were called. Fortunately, they had small labels on them, so I could tell him as if this were something I knew everything about. That one is called a blue marlin. Actually it is a tuna fish. When the assistant called out my number I ordered crabs and shrimps. Carrying two bags of seafood, I left the shop with John. The serviettes were blown out of my hand and flew away. The sun glittered on the surface of the sea. A couple of people stared at me as we walked. Pennants fluttered in the wind. Then we drove home. For the next three hours I read a manuscript by a writer who had delivered it three months ago and two days earlier had sent a polite email enquiring whether I could send him a response by Monday, he was going on holiday. Monday is today. I have read the manuscript before, but I hadn't written or rung, and that is something of a disaster because it will become a book and be published in the autumn. On the other hand, it is only 120 pages long. I read until half past two, then I went to bed and dozed for ten minutes, had a hot bath, drove north to pick up the girls, who have their premiere in two days and had accordingly warned me the rehearsal could last longer. When I arrived at the grassy area in front of the barn there was no one around. I parked, opened the door, buzzed down the window, took out my computer, rested my feet on the door window and read more of the manuscript. As I read the last sentence all the children came out. Their group leader shouted at them, or rather she screamed, and they sat down in a circle around her. She gave them a real talking-to. There were only two days left to the premiere. Everyone had to practise at home. And everyone had to listen to their leaders. The way they behaved backstage was unacceptable, I gathered. Also on the stage. People have paid to see you! she shouted. At last, I thought, someone taking them seriously.

The girls got in, we drove home with the windows open, they were happy, full of life. I was also happy. We drove to Ystad, it is almost an hour's drive, to collect their grandmother from the station, she is coming to see the premiere.

At the station they danced for me. Showed me the steps, and I did them too. They laughed, and it was great because they often get so embarrassed when I do things like this in public places.

At home the guests had arrived, and we ate shrimps in the garden during the first half of France v. Nigeria. I hate to miss the start of games. There is something about watching a game from the beginning, it is only that way you can understand the special dynamics, all games are different, as you know, they have their own rhythm and logic. When I managed to get away from the party, which numbered five adults and five children, three of whom were jumping up and down on the trampoline two metres from the table, and the sun shone low on the grass lengthening all the shadows, the second half had been going for two minutes. Nigeria were leading, they sliced their way through the French defence a couple of times with ease, there was enough room between the players. The lead didn't last long, France were getting more and more of a hold, and I was sure they would win. They have one of the strongest midfields in this World Cup, with Matuidi – you wouldn't want to play against him, Fredrik – and Pogba, who is no less of a wall – but both have obvious attacking qualities too, Matuidi in particular is elegant, and then they have little Valbuena on the flank, as well as Benzema, who has been lazy today but showed an explosive turn of speed, played a one-two, was through on his own, got in a good shot, but Enyeama's one-handed save was fantastic, no goal. France were playing well enough to win, I am very confident they have more left in the tank, and somehow I think it is good that Ribéry is not playing, they are more of a team now. If they did have him they would have someone like Robben is for Holland. But I like this French team, who play as a unit, and I hope (but doubt) they will meet Germany in the quarter-finals.

Now it is twenty to ten, the Germany–Algeria match starts in twenty minutes. The *Guardian* wrote that Thomas Müller looks like a dentist and not a footballer, it is true and something of a relief, you get sick of all the tattooed arms and necks, all those shaven temples and designer haircuts, and start noticing and identifying with the ones who look normal and not so cool. My favourite is Diego Godín of Uruguay, he could have been working for a branch of a Scandinavian bank in Montevideo – and of course Di María of Argentina because even his tattoos don't overshadow the fact that he looks like Franz Kafka. But that isn't why he is my favourite player of the tournament. It is because I love his style, his feints, tricks, all the elegant touches he has in his repertoire. He is the opposite of Hulk, he is an anti-Hulk, and he has all the character that Oscar lacks.

Ten minutes left to kick-off. Algeria don't have a chance, but nothing would be better than if they gave Germany a run for their money, shook them, took the game to extra time, and penalties . . . Will that happen? No. But you can live in hope.

More about this, and yesterday's big match, later.

It is eleven o'clock and the second half of Germany v. Algeria has just started. The first half was superb, Algeria played brilliantly, blunting Germany's attack and piercing the German defence surprisingly easily, they had three chances that might well have gone in, Germany one. Interesting how Algeria set up against them, lying deep with the midfield in front, the Germans always searching for space –

Great opportunity for Germany gone begging, they have upped the tempo now, seem more dangerous – and Neuer loses the ball! And grabs it and kicks it up to the lead striker, who almost runs through!

Another great chance for Germany!

Counter-attack! Four Algerians against three Germans!

And denied. I watched for a while, the Germans were holding the ball in front of Algeria's five-man midfield, one or two players moved into the space in the middle, either a forward falling back or a midfield player running up, and if they got the ball it either went back to the defence or straight through the Algerian defenders, but that worked only a couple of times, there simply wasn't the space, Algeria closed everything down. And Germany had no alternatives, apart from long-range shots, they were pegged back and unable to stop Algeria's attacking runs for some strange reason. They simply didn't have control in the middle of the park, they were outplayed, and that with two outstanding defenders like Schweinsteiger and Lahm. But in the second half, which has lasted twelve minutes, everything has opened up, it is no longer positional warfare, it is no longer Germany trying to find ways through and Algeria hitting them on the break, there are enormous wide-open spaces between the players, the game surges back and forth.

A pass between linking players, and out onto the wing, and then a cross, which Algeria clear. Algeria are not Chile or Mexico, there isn't the indefatigable, intense, aggressive pressure, but they are playing with cool heads and clever tactics, or they were, because it is all Germany now and Algeria's shape has gone. What have Germany done? Schürrle has moved to the flank, a lot has happened there. The biggest change is the increase in pace, they are running more, looking for the quick ball through, and it is creating havoc in Algeria's defence, they can barely stem the flow. But they are expert ball players, they need very few passes to break back, so this is still an open contest, even if all your experience tells you Germany will win. If they get one goal, it is over. Now Khedira is on in place of Mustafi, who is injured, that was a wise move, I think, they need a ball winner, someone to open and close space (which I know you don't like as you put down Gustavo and Paulinho in no uncertain terms in your last letter), and he and Özil have always played well together. Algeria break through, the German keeper heads the ball outside the penalty box. Saw in the *Guardian*'s match report that he touched the ball outside the box sixteen times in the first half. Germany's back line is quite far up, and the midfielders are slow, so Neuer's sweeper activities are absolutely vital.

A lot happening now, Algeria have had two breaks, both after passes from Feghouli, who has been Algeria's best player, at least the most creative, but they have been simple build-ups, he won the ball in the middle, played it through to the strikers, the first shot straight at the goalie, the second fluffed his pass. But they are slicing through! This could go either way and there are only thirteen minutes left. Müller dribbles past the wing, passes to Schweinsteiger at the first post, he heads wide. Almost the first time I have seen anyone apart from Schürrle try to dribble past an opponent. If they do, they are away. But they don't have the types, don't have the wingers.

Ooh, ohh, OOF! Double chance for the Germans. Khedira is through on the flank, a cross headed towards goal by Müller, outstanding save, they come again, Schürrle shoots, big chance. Another from the corner afterwards, kicked away by defender. Algerian counter-attack, keeper plucks it out of the air, and ten seconds later Müller dribbles past his man six metres out and shoots wide. Now Algeria are on the attack, the ball is in the box, Germany take control, slow the game down. Seven minutes left.

Everyone is asleep upstairs and the guests are long gone. I saw very little of them, told them I had to work – this is my job this summer, watching football matches and writing letters to you . . .

Another break, the keeper sprints for the ball and gets there just before the Algerian, Feghouli, probably thirty metres from the goal. Germany in attack, a header on target, keeper saves.

. . . and you are left wondering: how can anyone pull off such a magnificent save.

Three minutes left of added time. When will Germany score? They are Germany after all. And Algeria have next to no shape left. They are tired. It is just Germany now.

One minute left. Corner to Germany.

Twenty seconds left. Keeper saves it. Extra time.

Unbelievable that this is 0–0.

1–0 to Germany – Müller through on the flank, Schürrle a

flick of his heel, goal. First minute of extra time. It is deserved, but that doesn't soften the pain.

Shit.

Yesterday I received a wonderful, long, comprehensive, moving letter from you. Doors exist not only in the world, they exist in people too, and open inwards. I asked you a question about a little thing you wrote, you said Tranströmer made life unbearable. What was unbearable? Your answer was like an avalanche – an avalanche of football, everyday life, happiness, excitement and sorrow, which are collective, which belong to everyone, and, as I have said several times in this exchange, not binding, and then down into something else, at a dizzying speed, you mention your ages: beginning when I was twelve, and again when I was sixteen, nineteen, twenty-one, twenty-three and twenty-seven, it is the darkness, the hole, it is death in life – and you mention suicide, which when the pain is too great is the only way out. I know that is how it is, I have seen it, the pain is too great and it is the only way out, but then, and the person in the darkness doesn't know that, it goes, it disappears and life returns – but the person watching knows, and then the meaninglessness is immense. Endure, stay with it, it will pass, it is actually good – no one in the darkness can see that, for there is a gravitation in the darkness, it draws everything into itself and makes it, even the light, dark. I have seen it, though I have never been there myself, so I can't accompany you, I can't understand what it is like, being in the hands of other powers like that. You say the way out was time and work; did you do it all yourself? Or was someone there for you? Did you make a decision – I'm going to get out of this, this is not going to control my life – or did it slowly lose its power over you, by itself, as it were?

Once, a few years ago, I sat backstage somewhere in Denmark, the hall was full, perhaps three hundred people, I was about to be interviewed. I slipped out the back for a smoke. A man I didn't know followed me, we said hello, he asked me if I had thought about who was in the audience. I said no. He said they were cultural types, middle and upper-middle class. Among them were child abusers. Child beaters. Wife beaters. Alcoholics. Now they are sitting there, making themselves comfortable and waiting for you. Have you thought about that? Who is in the audience?

I hadn't thought about it, and have never thought about it since, until now, sitting in my smoke-filled study and writing. Because when we see this sea of people at these football stadiums, we see happiness, all the fans who have painted the colours of their flag on their faces, who wear strange hats and glasses, and at least five times in every match beautiful young women. We see thousands of people in team shirts, singing and jumping or sitting staring vacantly into the distance, some crying, but mostly it is elation, singing and dancing. The sea of faces, the collective, is one body, and everyone is focused on the same thing, the match between the twenty-two players below on the pitch. They all have their own lives, priceless for them, they all have their own qualities and their own histories, which would move us if we allowed them to be told – there is a sister who died when she was six, there is a mother who locked up her children while she drank, there is a brother who became psychotic and took his own life, there is a father who had a neurological disease and suffered a personality change – just to choose a few examples from my circle, which people I happen to know have experienced. On the other hand, all the love stories, all the births of children, all those fantastic evenings and nights when everything seems possible, that is there too. But there is something which is as beautiful as it is frightening in this, how real life – that is, the life we have and find ourselves in – is something we alone have and how we cast ourselves into the collective, where nothing of this is visible or even valid, for there is a rhythm in it, between being alone and being together, between being seen alone and being seen together. I imagine I am thinking this because of a turn of phrase in your letter, at first you describe a togetherness, in the morning with Afonso, afterwards with maybe a hundred people in the bar, but also with everyone at the stadium, everyone in Brazil, everyone in the football-viewing world, I saw what you saw, what everyone saw, Brazil and Chile, and then you are suddenly standing quite alone and telling me something from your life, without adornment or artifice. The movement, from all to one, applies to everyone. Tranströmer triggering this is not a coincidence, is it? Because with him it is the opposite: from one to all. And what do metaphors do if not give the world meaning, by opening it anew? A good metaphor is true in the sense that we recognise it when we read it, although we haven't seen it before. Sometimes it makes you go dizzy. Reading Tranströmer is reading someone who stands all alone. And knowing that that is different from being all alone.

Karl Ove

Botafogo, 30 June

Dear Karl Ove,

On 15 November 1889 Emperor Pedro II handed over power to the military, and thus the Brazilian Republic was born. Slavery had been abolished the previous year, and these two events laid the foundations for modern-day Brazil.

Some years after the establishment of the republic, a preacher and 'crackpot', Antônio Conselheiro, Anthony the Counsellor, wandered around in Bahia's interior. He journeyed from village to town exhorting the inhabitants to build a new society, one based on Christianity and socialism, and after a few years he had collected several thousand followers. He was a utopian in the Jesuitical tradition, and his flock comprised a bizarre mix of every type of outcast in north-east Brazil: vagabonds, loafers, the lame, the disabled, the blind, old, young and even children, and the place these people settled down was, and still is, called Canudos. There, in the heat of the caatinga (an arid landscape of scrub and desert, where at most it might rain once or twice a year) they set about building a society based on their leader's Christian, socialist principles. One for all, all for one. Word of Antônio and his people spread far and wide and many flocked from all over the country to be part of the experiment. In Rio, the capital at the time, the inhabitants shook their heads at 'the lunatics in Canudos', but all the same it was decided to send a contingent of soldiers to put a stop to the experiment. Of the five-hundred-strong force that was dispatched only a few returned, most having succumbed to hunger and heat on their way there through the caatinga, and the rest proving easy prey for Anthony the Counsellor's men. There was a growing sense of unease in the capital. Who were these 'wildmen' out in the wilderness, these people who refused to join the march towards modernity? No one was quite sure. So a new wave of soldiers was sent, thirteen hundred this time, under the rallying cry 'Crush Canudos'! But this fresh force of government soldiers, equipped with heavy artillery, was also beaten back by the poorly armed but deeply devout tramps in Bahia. Several hundred of the thirteen hundred sent survived and, terrified and traumatised, they returned to the capital, where panic began to spread.

What was going on in that 'heart of darkness'? Whatever it was, it had to be stopped, so a third force was sent – we're now in 1897 – 2,350 men, armed to the teeth with the most sophisticated weaponry of the time, and following a two-month siege Canudos was taken by the government troops, and among its defenders, it's said, the last to fall were a boy of seven and a man of seventy.

Canudos grew in time to become a symbol and is today interpreted in different ways depending on whom you speak to. When I interviewed Zizinho, who together with Puskas was one of the best footballers in the world in the early 1950s and captain of the Brazilian team that lost the World Cup final in 1950 at the Maracanã, he described that match as 'our Canudos'. The reason Canudos stays with me is that I can so easily transform myself into a doctor's son in Salvador in 1897. Every day I see my father, the doctor to the poor, return home from his small office on the outskirts of town, hear him speak of the incessant poverty and see for myself, no matter where I go, all the homeless, all the abandoned children, and one day, in the main square in the centre of Salvador, I see the legend himself, Anthony the Counsellor, so charismatic, so eloquent, so persuasive: Join me in the caatinga, we shall build a proper society where everyone is equal, everyone! and beside me are my closest friends, and we're all deeply moved, and it leads us into discussion, for and against, and suddenly one night I feel I've made up my mind, and I pack a small bag, or perhaps it is a stick and a rag bundle, write a letter of explanation of sorts to my mother and father, tell them I love them from the bottom of my heart but that I've decided to join a struggle to change the world, and then head out into the night, joined perhaps by my best friend, who's also just written a similar letter to his parents.

The modern project, that is. This ties up with with my pondering upon 'Are we there yet?' but also with the Enlightenment and what we can contemplate in terms of allowing diversity. You know that I'm a strong believer in the ideals of the Enlightenment – Liberty, Equality, Fraternity/Sorority – and find the steady growth of cultural relativism in Europe today deeply unsettling (and, in my view, indirectly to blame, through the dialectical game being played out, for bolstering right-wing extremism), particularly in England, where the Archbishop of Canterbury a few years ago backed the introduction of sharia law in Britain. In Sweden male genital mutilation is now being carried out on a publicly funded basis in spite of Swedish paediatricians decrying the practice as child abuse. 'The Handshake Case' also follows this new direction, in which the Enlightenment is being eaten away from within: a devout Muslim received compensation because a woman at a job centre shook his hand, thereby violating his religious rights. The Equal Opportunities Commissioner viewed this as discrimination, and thought it more important to defend religious fanaticism than the principle of equality between the sexes (Enlightenment!) that our modern societies, Sweden/ Norway/ Denmark, for example, are based upon.

As I write this, I'm hearing reports (and it is also interesting how the World Cup acts like a drug, an anaesthetic, which makes you forget things like Putin, Ukraine, Assad, Syria and ISIS, for example), fragments of news, from which it is possible to glean that ISIS in Syria and Iraq are gaining ground (what they and Islamic extremists around the world represent is the hardest, bloodiest opposition ever to Modernity and the Enlightenment, there's nothing that can compare, it's not some 'struggle against imperialism' but a war on Modernity and all the values we regard as self-evident, hence their black flag, death as the redeemer, the gateway to paradise, and late last night I read that they have proclaimed a new Caliphate, and that makes me think of our friend Anthony the Counsellor again), and it scares me and I can't understand how they get new recruits, what it is that makes young men across the whole of the Middle East write a letter like I mentioned above and pack a bag – and it's happening where we come from too, right now, young men who yearn to die as martyrs.

Canudos, Karl Ove. Are we there yet? What went wrong?

What you wrote about football simulating real history, real clashes, is true. For the most part. But there are, as you know, situations in footballing history where this simulation suddenly grows into something else and becomes infused with actual conflict. Simulation? Of course. At times, however, with actual history in the background, a history that threatens to come to the fore and imbue the innocent use of flag and jersey with something much more serious, deadly serious, and that's probably all the more reason people – we! – love football the way we do, because deep down inside us we know other, darker inclinations lurk.

With regard to Brazil v. Chile, not least Brazil and the fate that awaits them, we would seem to be in complete agreement. What will Scolari do?

What about Mexico v. Holland? A scandal without a doubt. Robben should have received a yellow card and a telling-off from the referee for diving, and now, having watched a replay of the incident, it strikes me that he and many others probably practise that type of thing. It's so beautiful, reminiscent of a dive in swimming, or rather an actual swimming stroke, the butterfly, in the way he tenses and pushes off, but of course we can't put up with that kind of thing. FIFA has to take steps, do as in ice hockey, stop the game, have the officials go to the halfway line, consult monitors and then make their decision. If goal-line technology can be introduced, then so can that system. Mexico deserved to win but Robben settled it with his corner – it led to 1–1, and his technique and delivery are amazing, probably the best in the world at the moment, the spin, power, precision, a mini-masterpiece every time – and with his dive, which, it has to be said, came after a lovely, typical Robben solo breakthrough.

And what of the Kuper theory? It held true for pretty much the entire match. The main feature of the game was the Mexicans' propensity to attack, and the Dutch found this difficult to deal with, could never create the necessary space for Robben, and the team depended more on the workhorses in defence than the stars in attack, a vulnerable Holland in other words, who looked in trouble. But it was the Mexican trainer's lack of courage that cost them the game. About twenty minutes from the end he abandons the philosophy that has brought his team so far, taking off an attacker and putting on a man-marker. That's what decided the outcome. Mexico had the match in the palm of their hand but relinquished victory thanks to their manager. Maybe he was thinking back to the Spanish game, but it all went wrong, and even though Robben had been rightly cautioned by the referee but escaped any punishment, I'm sure Holland would have won in extra time. Teams that change their philosophy during a game and switch to defending often have problems switching back again.

Costa Rica v. Greece? Not a great match from a footballing point of view, but plenty of drama at the end. Costa Rica got entangled in the Greeks' barbed-wire football. But despite that they scored out of the blue to make it 1–0, just like that, a tiny gap in the wire and a harmless-looking shot that crept inside the post. I thought it was all over then, but the sending-off threw the game wide open, gave the Greeks a way back in and led to their goal. The Costa Ricans were on their knees, but still they managed, exhausted, to take it to penalties, and that for me was the high point: the precision and unwavering composure they showed! And these are Latinos we're talking about, Catholics, emotional people who hug, dance salsa and viva la vida this and viva la vida that, not Andreas Brehme and Lothar Matthäus, the modern game's foremost penalty-takers. Five Costa Ricans did what Brehmer and Matthäus would have done, made the net bulge, and put away each and every penalty, leaving the Greek goalkeeper without a chance, indeed, no goalkeeper in the world could have saved any of those penalties. So good were they. The amateur ethnologist in me is astounded and speechless with admiration. And then, of course, the close-ups of Gekos. I agree with Linda, it's cruel. And with you. This is, after all, what we want.

Best wishes,
Fredrik

Glemmingebro, 1 July

Dear Fredrik,

I agree with everything you say about Mexico v. Holland. Mexico controlled the game, had Holland for the taking through their offensive play. As soon as they tried to play safe and fell back, Holland had the upper hand. And defensive changes in final rounds are always dangerous, at least with a 1–0 lead. Do you remember Argentina v. Germany in 2006? Argentina went ahead, then brought on several defenders, so when Germany scored they had nothing to reply with. It is also odd that there is so much negativity in the Dutch team – remember the terrible final in the previous World Cup when they were so dirty (it takes quite a bit for me to write that), and now Robben's diving – and that is impossible to forgive, however brilliant he has been – yet traditionally they are the talented team everyone wants to win – losing finalists against first Germany, then Argentina in the 70s. Think of all the wonderful players they have had. Van Basten, Cruyff, Neeskens, Gullit, van Nistelrooy, the Milan player with the glasses, what was his name? and van Persie, Robben – anyway now it doesn't matter, I want them to be eliminated or be totally humiliated by Argentina in the semi-final.

I think Brazil will beat Colombia. They aren't Chile, they don't have the aggression or the power, they are more like Brazil and can therefore be beaten on Brazil's premises.

The screw is tightening. Soon only Brazil and Argentina will be left.

Look forward to hearing from you tomorrow! And we mustn't forget that the Sweden v. Norway writers' teams had a match in Oslo last weekend and it wasn't a win home or away but a draw: 0–0.

I suggest they introduce extra time and penalties in those games too. Then I will stop smoking and start running to try and get in the team. If there is one experience I haven't had it is the one you describe in an earlier letter: walking from the centre circle to the spot to take a decisive penalty. Our international games have all the rest: Norway shirts, national anthems, bitter defeats and rousing victories and banquets afterwards. (Where Norway's best players, by the way, have a tradition of not participating if we have lost – I don't have to tell you I have always been a banquet man.)

All the best,
Karl Ove

Botafogo, 1 July

Dear Karl Ove,

I've just printed your last letter but haven't looked at it yet. I'm going to read it later tonight because I've one more thing to add about the pain I described in the letter before last, and it's so clear to me right now that I want to get it down in words. It came to me on the way to Buarque's pitch, where we were going to play football again today.

Afonso is sitting behind the wheel, a cigarette in his mouth. Beside him sits Thiago, his son, who's also a musician: an enormous body, black beard and mournful eyes. I sink into thoughts about our correspondence as the Atlantic comes into view on the left-hand side. We are out of the tunnels, and father and son begin analysing the World Cup and the Brazilian team.

Their voices transform into a soft murmur from the front seats as I began to think about my father. My ex-wife and I lived in Stockholm for two years at the start of the 1990s. My father and his new wife, Lena, had invited us to dinner. They lived in a lovely apartment on Strandvägen, close to the Berwald Concert Hall. We were sitting in their dimly lit dining room, on the wall hung paintings he'd inherited from my grandmother, a large still life of fruit among others. It's late winter 1992, Amanda, just a newborn baby, is in the hall, sleeping in her pram. Out of the blue my father begins telling me about how my grandfather died. He's never said anything about it, neither to me nor my siblings, despite the fact I was almost forty at the time. He tells me about the estate at Hook, 1946, they used to vacation there in the summer, when his father, the doctor from Helsingborg, had some holiday. On this particular day, a hot and sunny day, Grandad was playing tennis with a colleague. My father was, as far as I could gather, seated in the umpire's chair.

That's when it happens. Grandad collapses on the court with the tennis racket in his hand. My father, nineteen years of age and about to start studying medicine in Uppsala in the autumn, realises what's happening. He kneels down, holds his father's head in his arms and tries to shake him into life, screaming, 'You can't die! You can't die, Dad!'

Then he dies, on the tennis court, Nils Ekelund, sixty-two years old.

It's the first time I've heard my father mention it. He was sixty-five at the time. The dining room is dimly lit but I can see his eyes are moist. I find myself crying and, for the first time in over twenty years – I had kept him at arm's length for two decades – feel love for him again, the father who always wanted to be with us when we were little, whether it was to skate, play hockey or football, or go on outings. He's returned to me. I let him back into my life.

How can anyone walk around for decades without talking about something like that, Karl Ove? Live a life? Write a thesis? Attend to a responsible job? Settle down and have three children? Without ever uttering a single word about the greatest source of heartache in their life? In his life. Not once.

And that brings me to my question, or my concluding thought, about pain. This all occurred on a summer's day in 1946, on a country estate in the Småland hills of southern Sweden, and it was there, in that same place, that my mother and I set out on a cross-country ski trip twenty years later, an ice-blue sky above, when the void I spoke of opened up inside me, and brought, in some sense, my childhood to an end. I know he'd never made any mention to me about what had happened twenty years previously. He never talked about it, and that winter holiday was the only time I've ever been to the Hook estate. Never before, never since.

This is a question I presume I'll never get an answer to, all the same, I often ask: could his pain have been transmitted to me non-verbally, triggering what struck me in exactly that spot for the very first time in my life and which has been such torment since?

How, in that case, does such a thing happen? Or is it all mere coincidence, such life-defining sorrow occurring in both a father and son in exactly the same place with a twenty-year interval?

Best wishes,
Fredrik

Glemmingebro, 2 July

Dear Fredrik,

I don't know what your family was like when you were growing up, what the adults talked to the children about, how familiar the tone, how close you became to one another, but I don't regard what you say about your father and his sorrow as strange or incomprehensible. First of all, it was dramatic and life-changing for him, and it is hard to articulate that, it cannot be expressed. He was also very young. From the reaction you describe, he was attached to his father. Perhaps he shut it out to cope, and talking about it would firstly have brought it to the fore again, and secondly perhaps he was unable to do that, as it was shut away. It might also have been too big an issue for him to discuss, there was never an opportunity, you were surrounded by normal everyday events, there was no room or place for it? I have no idea, I am only speculating, but I don't think it is incomprehensible. It may have been to do with his generation, the distance between him and all of you was greater than it is between us and our children? I am not thinking of physical distance, or emotional distance, but what it is possible to talk to your children about, or not. My father told me very little about his life. I never heard about any traumatic events. But after he died and after I published books in which he plays a leading role, I received letters from childhood friends and colleagues, and they told me a lot I didn't know and could never have guessed either. Why hadn't he said anything? I was twenty-nine when he died, so grown-up.

But I assume – from what you write in the letter – you had a better relationship with your father than I did – and a lot of the shock at the withholding of this information you describe lies there. However, Fredrik, in the end he told you. There was a space, he had the opportunity and he told you.

I think, and here I hope you don't consider I am showing a lack of respect, but I think that was a beautiful story. A man losing his father on a tennis court in the 40s, the father a doctor, the son a medical student. And the son telling his son, who is a writer and has distanced himself from his father, one evening over dinner fifty years later. You crying and making up that evening.

Of course an event like that marks a life, it is there even if it isn't mentioned and even if no one else knows. That is why families interest me, for a family is built up around what is said and what isn't, what is done and what isn't, and those who grow up inside are marked by it and then perhaps distance themselves from it, without ever knowing the whole story, without ever knowing everything. Fear, a loathing of life, darkness, these things don't come from nowhere. I reflect a lot on this, naturally enough, as we have four children and there is fear here, and there are grandparents who succumbed. But what the hell, I think almost every single day, what will be will be, and they will be as they will be, they will have their own lives and we can't plan or predict what will rise or what will sink. You coped, and something tells me you wouldn't have been without the experience of fear and depression? It has made you the man you are.

Tell me if I am sticking my nose into matters which have nothing to do with me or I am straying into private territory. It is not my intention, but I can understand if that is the way it is interpreted. Hope not!

It is half past eleven at night, cloudy and hence very dark outside. All the others are asleep. It has been an eventful day; all the driving up and down Österlen's coast bore fruit this evening: the girls had their premiere. I drove them up at four, continued to Simrishamn and bought flowers for them, after which I went to fetch Linda and John, we bought tickets and took a seat. The auditorium was full and I was nervous, how would the little ones do on the big stage? Would they manage? Would they remember their lines, dance steps, songs? Would they suddenly, at the last moment, say no, I can't do it, I'm not going to do it, no way? After all, they are only eight and ten – Heidi is the smallest of them all.

And then there they stood, in the midst of a group of children, singing and dancing. They smiled, they sang, it was going to be fine. And it was. I was so moved afterwards, when the applause had faded and the shouts of bravo died down and I went over to say what great fun it had been, so moved that I couldn't get a word out, I had to give each of them a hug instead, with tears in my eyes.

Now they are asleep. I have spent the rest of the day editing some of the texts we have written for a newspaper article. So far we have written three hundred pages, I managed to reduce them to ninety, then to forty, but it is still quite a way to the four pages it has to be. So much has happened! What has been most important, what can you pick out from the first half of the tournament and say, this was World Cup 2014? The world doesn't look like this, and that is the whole point of this book, we are writing about what happens, everything, big and small, important and unimportant, while it is going on – and then afterwards it will be clear how the story itself turns out. In other words, what we can remember, what stands out. Much of our book will be about what doesn't stand out. Bit strange, but I like the idea.

We have seen an incredible number of goals, for example. Some of them spectacular, some beautiful, some lucky. Which are the first that come to mind? For me there is no doubt. It is Suárez's two goals against England. The way he twists his body and guides the ball into the goal almost without any power for the first, and for the second the way he seems to teeter, at full tilt, as if he is going to take a tumble, but straightens up and then hits a shot that is a goal from the moment he releases his shooting foot: as I wrote that day, what desire there was in that shot.

The reason I remember, of course, is tied up with Suárez's fall from grace, but not only that.

For the first time during this World Cup I got off the sofa, punched the air and shouted JAAA! after a goal. You have probably already guessed. It was Argentina scoring against Switzerland, in the second half of extra time. I reacted with such ecstasy. Oh, that was a frustrating match. Argentina played badly, passes went out of play, to opponents, endless free kicks. I read afterwards that Di María, who, as you know, is my man of the tournament, lost the ball fifty times during the match. Messi can't have been much better; whenever he got the ball there were three men around him, and every single time he tried to dribble his way through. Again it was obvious: the defence is extremely good in one-on-one situations, but as a unit they aren't. The midfield with Mascherano and Gago is incapable of controlling games, incapable of creating anything. Towards the end of the second half I said to Linda and Björn, who also watched the game, that the midfield had to stop moving to the flanks and hitting crosses, Switzerland could cope with them all day, they should try what all the football pundits warn against, run through the middle into the tightest areas, through the box. They can do that, Messi, Lavezzi and Di María (and hopefully soon Agüero). The Argentinians only just managed to keep the ball out of the goal as well; the Swiss had an incredible brace of chances in the final minutes. Neverthless, my Brazilian friend, 1–0 was enough to go through, they are in the quarter-finals, where they will meet your favourite for the competition, Belgium. That, and Germany v. France too!

The World Cup is all about moving on. It doesn't matter if you scrape through by the skin of your teeth with a lamentable lack of creativity or efficacy, like Argentina, or win with style, power and ease, like France.

All the best,
Karl Ove

Botafogo, 2 July

Dear Karl Ove,

That last letter drained me completely, as if I had been assaulted by myself and the scene on the tennis court. Time out. I have a feeling I have been laid bare, like a ball of yarn unrolled, strands going in all directions. Decided to look after myself instead of writing, to take it easy, so I went down to Copacabana, rented a sunlounger, took a swim, perused the newspapers and let my mind wander: Hook Manor House, my father (back in Stockholm in sheltered accommodation, in his wheelchair, with Parkinson's, now eighty-seven years of age but still all together upstairs, and I know he'd be saying hope all is going well with you over in Brazil, and when I get home I'll visit him, push him around Vasa Park in his wheelchair and tell him the same as I've been telling you, how everything is here, really, and all about the World Cup, which I hope and believe he's following to some extent, in spite of being 'forced' into bed at half-past eight every night), Glemmingebro, you and your family's lives, which shine through so strongly and brightly in your beautiful letters, I'm together with you every time you buy ice cream, and actually think the campsite you stopped at was the same place William and I had lunch when we were down to see you.

The pain? No, I didn't make any decision, the pain – as you write – slowly lost its hold over me. The power lay in recovery itself, and in life, the deep concentration on French in Lund and in meeting a woman. It was 2 December 1981, more than thirty years ago, in other words, when I had my last panic attack and have felt well since.

Time? The passage of time? Suddenly I was at Berghof in *The Magic Mountain*, because what Mann is attempting to depict there, I think, is the strange transition from the clarity of the first few days when everything is so defined by its differentness (for me my arrival in Rio), all the tuberculosis patients, Clavdia Chauchat, Lodovico Settembrini, Leo Naphta and the first meals in the dining hall, the high mountains, the surrounding forest and the initial seven days, then suddenly seven weeks have gone by, and time has carried him along, he no longer sees things as clearly because everything is not just different any more, in a way he loses his eye for detail, and all of a sudden seven years have passed and he can never get away from that place, but of course he does, eventually, when he has to go off to war and that takes us there again, Karl Ove, back to Zweig, the fantastic summer of 1914 before everything is destroyed (there was a period in my life when I dreamed of being Hans Castorp, I was seventeen or eighteen, and some friends and I had a small club we called The Power of Words, where we read, among other things, *The Magic Mountain* and were captivated by it, took woollen blankets and deckchairs with us and went to a beech forest outside Helsingør, where we lay in our chairs trying to cough like the TB patients at Berghof . . .) and the reason for Castorp appearing in my lounger now was that eighteen days have passed since I arrived here, and time is flying, the first few days it stood still, was easy to follow, every day an exciting painting filled with newness, but now when I walk up the path leading to Afonso's house I feel I am in a humdrum existence here too, with Afonso, Thiago, football at Buarque's, the newsagent's around the corner, and I marvel at how imperceptibly this strange transition always takes place.

That was it.

As for football? This is the best World Cup ever. It's as if every game, with a couple of exceptions, is better than the last, and in fifty years people will probably talk about 2014 with the same reverence I show for Mexico in 1970 or Spain in 1982. This applies no matter how it goes in the quarter-finals, semi-finals, or in the final, which, as so often, will no doubt turn out to be an anticlimax.

The day before yesterday I discovered the France which you have already discovered and was, like you, beguiled. Pogba. Valbuena. Benzema. This is a new France (it's a pendulum swinging the whole time, the great team of 1998, solid, good morale, with Zidane as their unspoken, but obvious, and modest, leader, a wonderful collective which subsequently falls to pieces and disintegrates into typical French individualism and prima donna antics in 2002, self-indulgence and stupidity, only to be followed by a new great France in 2006, with Zidane at the height of his powers, before the downturn again in 2010 with the puerile behaviour of Anelka and all those others, and the strike in South Africa, where they disgraced themselves in front of the whole world, and back to the present, an impressive unit) under the leadership of Didier Deschamps, and this team seems partly to have been born in the last qualifying game, at Stade de France, where they had a pistol to their heads and just about managed the 3–0 result they needed, otherwise their opponents, Ukraine, would have been here instead. The balance in the team is striking, the way they work for one another and how quickly they turn defence into attack, I could hardly believe my eyes the day before yesterday when they raced up the pitch. Nigeria were good and had several big opportunities, yet still they were never close, since the French created more chances all the time. I was very taken with the man of the match, Valbuena, his body swerves, not unlike Hazard. It must be a nightmare for your average big defender to meet will-o'-the-wisps like that. Pogba was also impressive and can perhaps in time write himself into a French 'Napoleonic' line of midfield generals, Platini–Zidane– ... the difference being that Pogba would appear to be exactly the type of new player Simon Kuper talks about: not a specialist but good at everything, with as much to give offensively as defensively. A clear-cut victory and, unlike you, I hope and believe France will beat Germany on Friday.

Sat at a bar in Ipanema, O Bar dos Marujos, and watched Argentina v. Switzerland, soporific compared to the two matches I've already mentioned. Argentina are still not good enough, all too dependent on Messi (in one sense he reminds me of Maradona, the low centre of gravity, the exquisite left foot, but as a character he's as far from Maradona as you can get, Maradona was passion, humour, conflict, a man of the people, Messi feels like a cool, laid-back Borges, a sort of football scientist who, when he has finished analysing, makes his incision in the body of the opponent), and as for the rest of them only Kafka shone in glimpses, but he's not the one who decides the match, as so often before with this team it's Messi's surgical incision and burst through the middle that settles the game as he slaloms through on his hobbit legs. The pass, like everything he does, is precise, and Di María really only does what you or I would do in the situation, puts the ball in the far corner. This Argentinian side are a huge disappointment to me, Karl Ove, and bear little resemblance to the vintage sides of 1978 or 1986. Can't see this sluggish Argentina team coping against Belgium.

Belgium v. USA, wow! I got to see exactly what I'd hoped and dreamed of, a modern version of total football played by a side with perfect balance between its constituent parts, a team like a perpetual red wave washing over stoutly resistant Americans, thereby exposing their lack of imagination. Belgium could have won 5–1, but triumphed instead with 2–1 after a thriller in extra time, a bizarre but telling result which highlighted their only real weakness: lack of nerve in the box. That is something that, I believe, is related to what I wrote about the Germans. The Belgian team has too little big-match experience. The shirt they wear does not have the history, not in the way the German, Brazilian or for that matter the Argentinian shirt does, and if Belgium don't have a 2–0 lead on Saturday against Argentina, and the scoreboard shows 0–0 with ten minutes left to play, I fear that Messi will, once again, produce his scalpel, and that would be a shame, because Argentina have nothing to offer (neither do Brazil, Karl Ove), and I'm there now. We mustn't allow ourselves to be seduced by a national strip. I hope it will be football as a whole that triumphs in this World Cup, and imagine, just imagine, we have a final on 13 July between Colombia and Belgium. Could there be anything better for the international game than a final like that?

Best wishes,
Fredrik

Glemmingebro, 3 July

Dear Fredrik,

Thank you for your excellent, sun-filled letter! I made a note of something you said at the start, 'Decided to look after myself instead,' and I thought, what the hell, I want to do that too! It's about time! But it has never happened. I don't know any more what I would do. For the last twelve years I haven't had a single whole day when I have stayed in bed or dozed on the beach. I haven't been ill, I haven't had a holiday – apart from the trip to Mauritius I mentioned, but that was with three children, you know what it is like with them, Daddy, Daddy, look look, come on, Daddy, jump in! I am not complaining, that wasn't what I wanted, I wanted more to explain how this life of mine is actually lived, supporting Argentina although they are poor and having no interest in enjoyment. So I am not jealous of you, although I have to admit it sounds rather wonderful, the sun-lounger, the beach, the Atlantic – ALL ALONE! NO CHILDREN! NOT EVEN FOOTBALL MATCHES OR WRITING!

Hans Castorp as a hero; that is only possible in youth. Young people, it has to be said, understand nothing of the world, that is what makes them so fantastic and can bring them to the forest outside Helsingør, where they sit in deckchairs with rugs round their feet pretending they have TB. Young people do pose, that is what youth is about, one minute you are like this, the next you are like that, while the whole world and their whole future lie before them and don't weigh on them yet: everything is possible. Although actually it isn't, because they don't even understand it!

At least I didn't. And neither did you and your friends, judging by what you say you were doing.

It is also a thing of beauty.

I read Mann's *Trollfjellet*, as it is called in Norwegian, when I was on the civilian service course on the coast between Molde and Kristiansund. I was a conscientious objector and interested in literature, those were the camps I was in. The book fascinated me, although I was too young to understand some of the long discussions in it, but I grasped enough, in another way, for the book is still in me. That and *Doctor Faustus*, they are not only masterpieces among Thomas Mann's books but among all those books that came out in the previous century. *The Magic Mountain* is the best book about the First World War; *Doctor Faustus* is the best about the Second World War. In a surprisingly illuminating, though not simplifying, fashion Mann succeeds in giving form to the currents, the ideas and the illusions that existed in that culture and which the war was somehow an extension of or was connected with, without the reader – and this is what is so masterly – having any sense of a zeitgeist, a spirit of the time, because that limits, also with regard to its value and durability, on the contrary the novel is rooted in something which is valid for all eras. Time in *The Magic Mountain*, music in *Doctor Faustus*, they are just paths that lead somewhere else. It can irritate me occasionally that Thomas Mann is never mentioned in the same breath as contemporary German-speaking writers such as Musil or Herman Broch or, for that matter, Virginia Woolf, James Joyce or Marcel Proust. The reason is simple and obvious: Mann narrates, and he uses the novel to do so without challenging the form.

It is not true that I don't give myself breaks. Yesterday I didn't write any letters, only a review of a manuscript, and once it was done I rang Geir and asked if he wanted to join me on a trip to Malmö. He did. I was going to collect a painting I had bought at an auction earlier this spring and which has been in storage ever since. The picture is of a woman and three children in a green field. The light and the colours in it are celestial, ethereal – you will have to see it one day. It was painted by Anna Berger, a Swedish artist, and I wanted to have it, I think, mostly because of the children, I want them to have light and colours around them, even if they don't notice or don't care; it is enough that it is there. So we drove to Malmö, took the road via Lund for variety's sake, chatting the whole time, not a word about football. After collecting the painting, we sat on the terrace of a café in Lille Torget, I ordered a Coke Zero and a coffee, Geir ordered a beer. There we sat watching people passing by. We live in isolated places in Sweden, neither he nor I usually meet anyone outside the family and we have started dressing accordingly, without taking any care at all, so what we looked like – and perhaps also are – was a pair of yokels who had come to town. Big, gawping eyes at all the people, all the life around us. I lived in Malmö for four years, but it was never my town, perhaps because we were living there with three children, who had such a fundamental impact on our our life there, and the times I have been back I haven't had any feelings for the town, I thought only I was glad I didn't live there any longer. But yesterday it was different. When we drove through the town and sat in the café I thought it was wonderful, it was open, unpretentious, you were free of the pressure of beauty – which you have in Stockholm – Malmö is a thoroughly ugly town – though it has something else, and probably more important than beauty, namely life. Malmö is alive.

Nothing happened – as usual, I almost said – we just sat there and chatted and watched, and then we drove home again so that I could see Argentina v. Switzerland. But merely being somewhere with a lot of people has an effect, something opens or else it is then that you realise you were closed before.

You are right about how many remarkably good diminutive players there are in this World Cup, there have not only been Valbuena and Messi but also Shaqiri, from Switzerland, he scored three goals in the same match at the group stage and was technically excellent, he did some sensational things, and he has pace and a powerful shot. But there was something about him I didn't like, his dummies were wasted on me, I didn't like the aura he gave off. This is unfair, I know, it is a bit like saying about a writer that you don't care whether his or her books are exceptionally good if something about their character puts you off, you can't even say what it is, perhaps the way they walk.

But that is one of the things I like about football: you don't have to justify your opinions. You don't have to argue for anything at all. You can leave everything to feelings. Argentina plays shit football? I love them. Germany plays beautiful football? Who cares.

Now it is a few minutes past one. I am calling it a day. We'll be in touch tomorrow!

All the best,
Karl Ove

Botafogo, 3 July

Dear Karl Ove,

Many thanks for your letter. Am struggling to understand how you can submit all these gems of texts considering everything going on around you, the four children, you driving them to and fro, the bouncing on the trampoline outside the window – not least your nerves before the girls' opening night – as well as the need to take Linda's illness into consideration, essay deadlines and then, in the middle of all that, being Mr Publishing Editor as well – while I'm sitting here without any responsibilities of any kind, all on my own, smack in the middle of the most beautiful city in the world, the only sounds I can hear are Mahler's Third on the CD player, an internal flight drowning him out for a few moments every so often, and a subdued discussion in the kitchen between Afonso and Thiago about something I can't quite make out.

Talk about being privileged. Here I sit. Writing to you and deliberating what I'm going to do with the day.

'There was a space, he had the opportunity and he told you.' Exactly. It couldn't be put any better. Also, that he, in order to survive, didn't want to speak of it, since that would only mean reliving the pain. But for me one mystery still remains: that of the place itself. Coincidence or 'necessity'? I'll never know the answer to that. And, as you write, I think I'm richer for the experience, since it's probably the reason I began writing in the first place – to heal the world, to heal myself. To heal (läka, in Swedish) and

285

play (leka), I wonder if there's an etymological thread there, playing (with words, footballs, musical instruments) helps to bring us closer to being whole (non-schizophrenic), and that brings us back to football again: the best goal? Top of the heap, for the time being, are van Persie and James Rodríguez, because both were spectacular strikes, neither of Suárez's two goals were, they had prosaic appeal. In the case of van Persie's and Rodríguez's, we're talking poetry.

Trollfjellet! What a fantastic word! It calls a whole other Nordic magic to mind, Thomas Mann in the Hall of the Mountain King. Nonsensical. But logical all the same. Imagine, we're Scandinavian neighbours, and I'd never have found that out even if I'd sat for weeks on my own trying to figure out what Der Zauberberg could be in Norwegian. So strange how these membranes of foreignness can cause problems and make the difference, which is sacred, so clear.

Football now, and I had so much on my mind to say (or, on the heart, as we say in Swedish). I just want to sit here and write, but the football animal within me has other plans.

(somewhat later in my world)

What a shit afternoon, Karl Ove! Went to Buarque's pitch with Afonso, Thiago and the great, warm-hearted poet Paolo César Feítal. My hopes of revenge were dashed. Crossbar, post, wide and over. Atrocious. Plus I got so fed up with their inability to look around them on the pitch, not just down at their feet and their own dribbling, and cursing and screaming and that irritating

Porra, porra, porra!

that my urge to play deserted me, if you miss a ball, bungle a pass, then expletives rain down upon you. From grown men, Rio's finest musicians! Unbelievable. Almost considered walking off the pitch at one stage, but stayed on and tried to encourage my teammates, vamos a virar, let's turn this around, but they were like sulky little children and

0–6

Karl Ove, and then to sit there afterwards trying to put on a happy face and talk about something else, who'll be on the team sheet for the match against Colombia tomorrow and so on, when you just want to go home, bury yourself in something else and restore some equilibrium. We finally leave, Afonso, Thiago and I, three losers, along with Carlinho (Little Carl), who captained the winning team, happy as Larry in the back seat, coming out with one story after the other, and then we hit traffic just before the tunnel at Rocinha, and Rio is transformed into an urban carbon-dioxide monster, while Carlinho in the back, he thinks life is grand, and he's shaken Garrincha's hand, and so on and so forth, and then, just as we've covered the fifteen kilometres home, comes the real smack in the face: yesterday, as you'll soon read, I was out with some people from SVT (Swedish Television) and as I'm going on about West Germany v. France in 1982, the head of the sports newsdesk says he has a spare ticket for the quarter-final between France and Germany at the Maracanã and I can probably have it, so all day today I've been there, inside the Maracanã in my mind, and then, just as we're going to park on Rua Assunção, I hear the beep of a text message on my little Rio mobile: 'Hi, sorry, but the ticket I thought we had has already been given to someone else. Hope you enjoy the game all the same. All the best. P'

Porra, porra, porra!

So, was there nothing to take from that afternoon then? Well, the following exchange, perhaps. When Feital got into the car, I'd just finished explaining the Amanda mystery (getting good through persistent training) to Thiago and Afonso.

Fredrik: She didn't have any talent but she became good all the same.

Paolo César Feítal: Because she had the gift, o dom.

F: No.

P: Yes, it was there, the gift was there, and she drew it forth, worked at it, the way you described. She roused it as the bear is roused from hibernation. I work all day long writing poetry and lyrics for songs and I discard almost everything. It's work and yet more work, and then suddenly there's the flicker of something. Suddenly, I'll hit upon something. I'm not saying I'm good, but out of the blue something good will come. Villa Lobos had the gift, but without work he would never have amounted to anything. When he writes his music about the topography of Brazil, with the entire Brazilian landscape transformed into words on paper, it's a stroke of genius, but born of – work.

F: What about Mozart?

P: Practised scales day in, day out. Work.

F: Is this not just all words?

P: No, your daughter had the gift, but it lay hidden and she drew it out by hard work and sweat.

He steers the conversation towards language and starts saying how Portuguese is more metaphorical than English, and that when Portuguese tries to synthesise and be tight, like English is, it suffers. He illustrates the metaphorical aspect of the Portuguese language by singing a verse from a poem about a poor man outside the house of a wealthy woman with whom he's fallen in love.

P: Na rua uma poza d'agua, espelho da minha mágoa, transporta o céu para o chão. (On the street a puddle, mirror of my sorrow, transports the sky to the ground.)

I talk about our book, and how both you and I believe in the ancient power of metaphors. Then I tell him about linguistic materialism and how it was born at North American universities and metaphor is its arch enemy. Paolo shoots his head forward from the back seat, between Afonso's and mine in the front, as though someone had attacked him.

P: You can't rationalise feelings, passion! It simply can't be done; it spells death for emotion and passion. This was precisely the basis for Nazism. And there's a lot of it at the heart of capitalism, in a lot of American culture . . .

Afonso, at the wheel, nods in agreement. Followed, of course, by a drag of his cigarette.

F: And now, to Barra!

Laughter in the car. We're out of the tunnels and Barra, Rio's Miami, spreads out in front of us.

The conversation then strays into 'classic' territory, which is on everyone's mind here, at all times: football, and it doesn't take long before we settle on a solution to 'Brazil's problem':

César

Alves   Silva   Luiz   Marcelo

Fernandinho

Paulinho

Hulk   Oscar   Bernard/Willian

Neymar (in a free role)

Last night there was a book launch in Ipanema at the home of the Swedish honorary consul, a fantastic penthouse apartment in one of the high-rises along the beachfront. It had a view of the Atlantic as well as the mountains. Henrik Brandão-Jönsson was promoting his book *Jogo Bonito: Pele, Neymar and Brazil's Beautiful*

Game, a good book dealing primarily with the contemporary situation of Brazilian football. Henrik is on the panel at the SVT studio every day, and is now correspondent for *Dagens Nyheter* and *Sydsvenskan* newspapers, and probably the most influential person in terms of how the domestic Swedish media view Rio and Brazil. And the best informed. He has lived here for over a decade, and is married to a Brazilian lady with whom he has a daughter. Mingling. The buzz of conversation. Small islands of people all around. We wound up on the balcony, Afonso and I, and it was then a feeling crept over me. Jealousy, Karl Ove, that poison we have within. There he stood, the man who'd attended a writing workshop I'd held about ten years ago, and whom I know was strongly influenced by my book *Samba Football*, like a little King of Rio, the entire staff of the SVT sports desk were there, you name them, and many expats living in Rio. A strange feeling, not least because I know I'm probably the European (I might be laying it on thick, but I do actually believe it) who knows most about the history of football in Brazil, but I have the misfortune of having a certain Alex Bellos in the way (an Englishman who's also written a book on the history of football in Brazil, *Futebol, The Brazilian Way of Life*, which blocks both the US and UK markets for me; why turn to a backwater of a country for insight on the topic when we have Bellos?).

Jealousy. And loneliness. And there's ex-footballer Glenn Strömberg. And over there Johanna Fränzén, the sports journalist. And Lotta Schelin, who plays for the women's international team. And . . . No, I won't go over there, to the TV sofa. A glass of red wine. Two glasses. The consul, a voluptuous blonde who, it's whispered, is a multimillionaire and footing the bill for all this. And Henrik, who is introduced and interviewed and gives good, concise answers to all the questions put to him and presents his book really well. He's really grown into his role. I've followed his career with interest and read an early draft of his first book, and he's got something that I don't any more, the courage to leave himself open, to take risks (like when he travels to an away game with a busload of Corinthians' notorious supporter group Os Gaviões da Fiel, The Faithful Hawks, people who don't shrink from theft or murder).

But I'm delighted for him too, seeing him there at that moment, a moment I suspect he'll look back on one day when he's old. Only last autumn we were sitting at one of the most down-at-heel pubs in Möllevången raising a glass because the two of us from Malmö were –and are – the foremost experts in Sweden on Brazilian football.

The serving staff scurry around with sushi-like clumps of food, Henrik has finished speaking and Afonso and I survey the place. Many unfamiliar faces. Then on the other side of the room I see the football reporter Björn Nordling, with his boyish face and happy expression. I'm no mingler, social situations like this always make me nervous, but I make my way through the room, over to the group he's standing with. It includes Chris Härenstam, the commentator, and Patric Hamsch, the head of SVT Sport at the tournament, and I've met Björn before but not the other two. Handshakes all round. Followed by perhaps the funniest and most intense discussion on football I've had during the whole World Cup, and we're all in complete agreement – this is the best World Cup ever. And I make the acquaintance of the beautiful and knowledgeable Johanna Frändén and get the opportunity to pay tribute to Lotta Schelin for her footballing ability, and then Glenn Strömberg comes over to say hello and wonders if we're planning to get a bite to eat, and I know a place nearby, so we go there, to Astor, one of Rio's real hot spots, in Arpoador, and we put away food and put away beer, and a caipirinha, por favor, and Björn Nordling's boyish face and a long conversation with Härenstam on the art of commentating, and then Hamsch says he thinks he can fix me a ticket for Germany–France at the Maracanã, and I'm over the moon, and Glenn S buys rounds for everyone (one of the greats of Swedish football, May 1982, the UEFA Cup Final in Hamburg against Hamburger SV, 3–0 to IFK Göteborg, a team adored by the whole of Sweden at the time, and he, Glenn S, was a giant in midfield, and his career continued with lots of international caps, a World Cup in Italy, and spells abroad with Benfica and Atalanta), and the evening ends with him, Glenn S himself, proposing a toast in my honour.

'I want to raise a glass to you!'

'To me, why?' I ask.

'Because you seem like a knepig kind of guy . . .'

Knepig, Karl Ove, is not a word with positive connotations in my world, a knepig sort is a sly type, one on the lookout to turn things to his advantage.

'Knepig?'

I was a little paf, as we, and the French, say.

'Yes. But maybe I ought to explain. For us in Göteborg this word has a different interpretation, what I mean by it are people who take peculiar routes to get on in life. Skål!'

Then the evening ends, the four of them on their way to their hotel in Ipanema, and I get into a taxi, bursting with joy, because come Friday – my God! – I'll be watching the match of all matches: the quarter-final between France and Germany, and I'll be watching it from a seat inside the stadium.

Best wishes,
Fredrik

Glemmingebro, 4 July

Dear Fredrik,

Nothing worth mentioning has happened here, not even football-wise, as there has been a two-day break, so your letter, lapping like a wave in and out of the social world, constantly interweaving Swedish/Brazilian football and writing, came heaven sent. But the poet in the car, Fredrik: I have never seen what he talks about in such precise terms. Two things, first about your daughter's struggle: 'It was there, the gift was there, and she drew it forth, worked at it, the way you described. She roused it the way the bear is roused from hibernation.' That is exactly how it is. And not just with your daughter, but also with Mozart, as he so rightly says, and actually with everything that is to do with performing or creating something freely: the task, which is hard, is to find it. But there was something else he said which I haven't seen put in exactly that way before and which I also immediately thought is right: 'You can't rationalise feelings, passion! It simply can't be done; it spells death for emotion and passion. This was precisely the basis for Nazism.' That is absolutely true! I have always thought feelings were the problem, you know, the pleasure of the collective, the pleasure of family and belonging, the pleasure of history, being part of something greater, which the mythical also always expresses. I thought it was politicised, but then only that it existed within the framework of politics, never the way Paolo put it, that feelings were being rationalised. Of course that is how it is, I think now. But that wasn't obvious half an hour ago.

I also like what you write about jealousy, the Swedish word is so much better, svartsjuka, black illness, for that is what it is, blackness creeps up on you, and it isn't good, we know that, but it comes anyway and blackens everything. The way the darkness, which everyone knows, but no one will admit to, suddenly becomes light and is gone in the tumult of faces, conversations, eagerness, pleasure, food and drink, which are other words for something greater: community.

The people you spoke to and ate and drank with fill our living room here in Glemminge every evening with their voices. Glen Strömberg is my favourite commentator, not because of his football analysis, which is never about tactics yet always practical, but because of his immense interest in what is happening on the pitch, and his unfailing enthusiasm.

Just over a month ago I travelled round England by train with a PR assistant from the English publishing house responsible for my books. She sat reading, I sat reading – it is always difficult travelling with someone else in these contexts because we don't know each other before the journey starts and we spend all our time together, first on the train, then in the town where the performance is to take place, and at the venue, and the dinner afterwards, only for it all to start again, and often I feel obliged to talk, although actually I want only to occupy myself with my own thoughts and look out of the window or read a book, and so we do talk, until conversation runs out and a new phase of silence ensues – this time, and this is the point, I asked her what she was reading – she was holding an e-reader, so I couldn't see a cover – and she said it was a Swedish book about Brazilian football. For one wild moment I thought it must be yours because there can't be many of them about. But the very next I realised I would have heard about it, either from you or our mutual friend Aage, and she told me the writer's name and the title of the book, *Jogo Bonito*. I said that at Pelikanen we had also published a book about Brazilian football. Really? she said. Yes, I replied, and so we chatted about the two books, then sank back into our individual silences.

That is how it is: it could easily have been your book. But it wasn't. And I think that people outside the book trade don't know how arbitrary such things are, and how big the obstacles to being translated into another language. It isn't the best books that are translated but those which have some hook, something that gives them a potential added value. And then the books the publisher or the agency invests their energies in. As far as foreign literature in Norwegian is concerned, which is what we focus on, very little is translated, publishing houses compete for the same titles, for one reason of course, they are the ones that are talked about and easy to sell. Bolaño, no one was interested in him, in Sweden I think it was the little independent Tranan Bokförlag who published his books until the moment Bolaño became the name on everyone's lips, when he became the big new thing, and what happened? The next book was published by Bonnier. In Norway the house for serious fiction in translation is Solum. They publish only quality, only literature from the very top shelf. But who reads an unknown book from the Czech Republic, Hungary, Poland or for that matter Italy or France, when there are books by Donna Tartt, Salman Rushdie and Orhan Pamuk? Not that they sell a lot either, I have no idea really, I doubt it though, enough to be worth their while, I imagine. A Czech novel is not worthwhile, however good it may be from a literary point of view.

In my case I have been very lucky, as you know, basically because there was a hook, a way of talking about my books which was transferable to other countries, and that set the ball rolling. There are a lot of self-fulfilling prophecies around: when someone says that something is such and such, it becomes such and such. But this someone cannot be anyone at all, it has to be someone with influence. It happened to my books, and here I am now, beside a bookcase of editions from a range of foreign countries. If I had known about that when I began writing as an eighteen-year-old I would have thought, I have done it, this is fantastic, but firstly I never dreamed that anything like this could happen, it was way beyond my horizons, secondly, I don't think like that, everything happens gradually, and what I am looking for doesn't lie there. The fact that it has happened eases all the practical issues, but when it comes to the crunch, being a writer is about only one thing: sitting down behind a desk and looking at an empty page and knowing it has to be filled with something, from nothing. That is where the excitement is, the pleasure, but also the doubt, the uncertainty, the fear of failure. If you don't want that, if you have had your fill and are better off without it, you are no longer a writer. Success has nothing to do with this.

Tonight the two quarter-finals are being played. I received a text yesterday: 'Now it's really starting, and soon it will be over. The semis are too late. The quarter-finals are the last cornucopia.' I know exactly what he meant, and he expressed it so well: the quarter-finals are the last cornucopia. Tonight, Germany v. France, Brazil v. Colombia. I will be surprised if Brazil don't win. Colombia are more their style than Chile, and the result from that game will lift them, in my opinion. As for the Germany v. France game, I have no prediction, it could go either way, neither team is odds on, they are equally matched. But we will soon find out.

Today Anne didn't wake until a quarter past eight, unbelievably, and that was good because I didn't go to sleep until close on two, editing our letters for a newspaper article, which will appear, if they accept it, next Saturday, the day before the final. Had a coffee up at Geir's then, afterwards, I spoke to one of our authors on the phone. He is going to work on his manuscript during the holiday. Then I read your letter and started on a response. Now I have to pick up John, who has had a sleepover at a friend's, and answer emails, which pile up so quickly and then hang around. When I went to fetch the post yesterday I met our neighbour, they are only here in the summer, so we don't know each other very well, but this time we stopped and had a chat for a quarter of an hour, exclusively about the World Cup. How it had gone, who we supported (Germany in his case, mostly because they don't give up, never resort to tricks, are honest, from what I could glean) and who we had an eye on. He talked about the pleasure of discovering new players you had never heard of or seen before. He mentioned Sterling for England, who had impressed him in particular. We were equally enthusiastic, it was as if something flickered into life between us on this otherwise deserted road, and then I said bye and went back to bills and advertising. What else could we have enthused about together? I have no idea, but the thing about the World Cup – not football in general, only this tournament – is that you can talk to everyone about it, strangers and friends alike. And once again I realise something I already know, it isn't important what you say but that you talk. Discussing football, one might object, is discussing nothing, and in nine days' time the competition is over, after that all the intensity, all the outpouring of emotion, all the joy and sorrow will be meaningless, what were we getting het up about? Nothing. One might conclude from all this that it is the very getting-het-up that is the point, not the object of our emotions. In other words, joy, sorrow and passion have a value in themselves.

Anyway, now the France v. Germany game is a local rivalry (I told him I wanted France to win, although actually that did go against my nature, which is to agree with everyone).

I'll write again when the matches are over. More chores await.

Botafogo, 4 July

Dear Karl Ove,

Early morning here in Rua Assunção, and I thought of something I meant to put in my letter to you yesterday. This thing about crying, Karl Ove. Crying and being a man. Thiago Silva and his teammates have been heavily criticised across a range of Brazilian newspapers for crying too much when they sing the national anthem, as well as after the games when they're being interviewed, and for having problems coping with the mental pressure. Only one commentator, albeit an influential one, challenges this reasoning: Tostão, one of the greats from 'the best international team of all time', the winning side from Mexico, 1970. In *Folha de São Paulo* dated 1 July he writes, '. . . as though shedding tears were not compatible with clarity and reason. I believe the opposite is true. What saves this team is the emotional commitment of the players. They're being lifted by the fans and the pressure of playing on home turf.' The longest, and most interesting, conversation on Brazilian football I have ever had was with Tostão, a retired doctor now, who was forced to give up a glittering football career aged twenty-six (recurrent problems with his retina made it impossible for him to continue playing), when I visited him twelve years ago in his Bavarian-style house in Vila Nova, one of Belo Horizonte's better leafy suburbs. When I read his article, I could hear that incredibly high-pitched, almost boy-like voice of his, and thought about masculinity again. It comes in many forms, and Tostão, in my view, was about as far from the Latin American macho ideal as you could get, and his article seems reasonable. Not unlike Pessoa, in which there's no contradiction between reason and emotion. On the contrary, it's as though they are a prerequisite for each other.

But is he right, does crying in this case signify strength? I don't know, Karl Ove, I only know that I too have had my doubts about this Brazilian side for the same reason: how can they play football straight after these enormous outpourings of emotion that the national anthem clearly evokes in them? That's what I've been wondering, and now the match is drawing close, but Afonso isn't worried, he says (for the first time I hear him strumming on the guitar in the background!).

Not yet, he adds.

Best wishes,
Fredrik

Dear Fredrik,

The Germany v. France game has just finished. Germany might have only won by a single goal, but they outclassed France, they completely suffocated France's attack, there was just the one chance on goal, in the last minute of full time, when Neuer easily parried Benzema's shot. There was no excitement, not a hint of France's fantastic periods in the group games, when they were so dynamic, rampaging and inventive. It was tactics that won the day for Germany. And the defence, which was said to be the chink in their armour, tonight it was impressive. All areas were covered, all shots blocked. Germany's weakness was the slowness of the central defenders, who could have been found out as they were so far forward, and this was what France kept trying to do, sending long balls over the defence. When it worked and one of the wingers got through there was never any danger, Germany had as good as total control in the box. It was a masterly performance. Germany played like champions. But they are not invulnerable, viz. Algeria, who succeeded in shaking them in quite a different way. I have no idea how, but the big difference was that Germany took the game to Algeria, who lay deep and counter-attacked while France, because of Germany's early lead, had to attack. Which they did. I assume they were ahead in all the statistics, apart from the only one that counts: goals. It was also interesting that Germany's midfield turned out to be so much better because, on paper, player for player, France are at least as good. But there is something about the German midfield, almost despite who is playing, they are so very mobile, so very good at finding a channel between the midfield and the defence, where they are so dangerous. Had they been behind yesterday, they would have attacked more and, sooner or later, got a goal from a run through the middle or a long-distance shot. The only team, I believe, capable of matching Germany, which has a style Germany will have difficulty coping with, is Holland. Mostly because of Robben, but if they tie him down, there is always van Persie . . . However, they can't meet before the final, and then we will have 1974 all over again, and it will be an enormous anticlimax after all this stupendous South American football.

I wrote this yesterday, before the intense, dramatic game between Brazil and Colombia, which was never really exciting as it was clear from the kick-off that Brazil were going to win. It was a very different team, they had confidence, were aggressive, and they had real pace. And this is typical: when a team puts in a poor performance, critics point to individuals or areas within the team – earlier in this tournament it was evident that Brazil lacked creativity in the middle, a class ball-distributor – whereas when they play well, that perspective disappears completely, which surely says something like: when a team plays well, everyone plays well, not just individuals, but as a unit. Yesterday Brazil had Paulinho and Fernandinho in the centre, both classic battlers, and suddenly there was a wealth of penetration and variety. I saw both games in the living room, the first with Linda and Anne, until the whistle blew for the second half, then Linda was so exhausted – she had been dozing for a while because she hadn't slept properly the night before – and Anne was so stuffed with milk (milk-drunk, what babies become when they have gorged themselves, have milk all over their faces and their eyes are small with contentment and tiredness) that they went to bed.

Heidi came in, sat down and watched for a while although she isn't interested in football, asked who I wanted to win, and I told her I cried when I was thirteen after seeing France lose to Germany, at first she didn't believe me. Did you cry? First of all, they have never seen me cry, and second I don't think crying because of football is in her perceptual world. By the time the Brazil game started everyone was asleep except for Vanja, who was bored and kept popping in to tell me what was going through her mind, only to be ignored by me, let's talk about that afterwards, I'm watching the game now, do you understand, this is important! It isn't, she said, it's just football. And she was right of course. Not much fun if your father goes into the classic 70s Daddy role, be quiet, Dad's world is more important than yours – on the other hand, how often are there World Cup quarter-finals in football? At the next cup the children will be fourteen, twelve, ten and four, and I will be entering my fiftieth year.

Yet, and this is significant, footballers on TV are always older than me. Yes, I know they aren't, but when I watch, it is as if they are, a feeling I never question, this is just how it is. Why? It is obvious. Time doesn't pass in football, faces change and names appear and disappear, but the game is the same and viewers watch in exactly the same way they did when they were twelve. There is no development in football (apart from the increase in tempo, which has happened so slowly it is imperceptible, until you see a game from 1979 and the lack of pace strikes you at once), and there are no advances in football. The players are always in their twenties and always older than the spectators, however old they are. That is how it is, more or less, in my view.

Yesterday the central defenders scored. That gives Brazil hope for their further passage. I don't think Neymar's absence – that was a terrible injury he got, a fractured vertebra in his spine – will prevent them from beating Germany because something else has emerged in this team, an enormous collective energy. Thiago Silva's absence won't be decisive either; they have Dante (what a name for a footballer, and both Dante and Kafka are playing in this World Cup!), he has experience of the Bundesliga and the most important international games. Furthermore, it is not a given that Germany will be in the final. Let us pray to God, us too, Fredrik, even if you are a non-believing Catholic and I am a non-believing Protestant, that Brazil get to the final. There our paths will divide because you want Belgium and I want Argentina to win – and they meet tonight! Then we will find out. Will Argentina raise their game? Will they manage to do what Brazil did yesterday? Or will they continue with their bogged-down style? One thing that has become more and more clear in this World Cup is that the best matches, where play is end to end, where there are goal chances for both teams, where players run so much you wouldn't think it humanly possible, all these matches take place in the evening. All the irritating, disjointed, convoluted, pent-up games interrupted by endless free kicks take place in the midday heat. The exception was Brazil v. Chile, but it wasn't open in the way the evening matches, Algeria v. Germany or Belgium v. America, were.

I am looking forward to reading how yesterday's game looked from the inside, Fredrik. Talk tomorrow!

All the best,
Karl Ove

Botafogo, 5 July

Dear Karl Ove,

It's hot here today, not sure how many degrees exactly, but I could already feel it this morning when I opened the doors on to Afonso's small, paved back yard. Thiago and Afonso woke a few hours after me, they'd been out on the beer last night, at the '98', Afonso's favourite bar in the neighbourhood. I declined to join them. Only water for me last night. Yesterday, just before noon, while I was sitting in my room writing to you, I could hear them in the living room, playing together on acoustic guitars, father and son. It was serene, quite beautiful.

I went to a place nearby, Bar do Italiano, to watch the Germany v. France match. Good food but a bit of an impersonal atmosphere, and when the game got under way I was slightly peeved at the lack of interest displayed by the waiters, bar owner and what few customers there were. People can be rather inward-looking here, and when you're happy to sit chatting indifferently about Flamengo and Botafogo and barely glance at the screen, not even when it's FRANCE against GERMANY in the quarter-finals of the World Cup, then I begin to wonder what kind of people they are.

The match itself? The goal should probably have been disallowed (Hummels' shove/elbow on the French defender) but maybe, Karl Ove, the Germans deserved to win all the same. My impression of the game was that it was a bit of a chess match, with a pawn sacrifice giving results after persistent effort, a pressing game, and just as I had one eye on the screen and was jotting down on the paper in front of me, 'whoever scores the first goal will win', Hummels headed the ball into the net. Löw–Deschamps, 1–0. Why? I'm writing this right after the match without having had time to 'reflect', but I think the German pressure caught the French by surprise, given the heat, and this led to misgivings and doubts about their own tactics. Müller was like a wild animal, his energy was exceptional, and the fact that Löw dared to use that game plan in this heat was a bold move. It could have gone very wrong. The temperature, plus tired legs from the encounter with Algeria, would, had extra time been required, probably have messed things up for them, 'there was never any danger', seriously, Karl Ove, were we watching the same game? When the final score is 1–0, you can't say the losing side were 'outclassed', not when they had two or three chances that nearly resulted in goals, but Germany scored, after which the French could only offer brief, but at times fabulous, waves of attack, and it looked like they'd done their homework on the Algerian match, the exquisite crosses and the long passes opened up the German defence on several occasions, but they didn't make the most of them, partly down to neither Valbuena nor Benzema managing to keep a cool head, but also due to Neuer, who was excellent.

The game on the whole? Not that entertaining, certainly not absorbing and – it has to be said – un-Teutonic. The Germans surprised me, as perhaps they did the French, by playing in the Argentinan/Italian mould, that is to say, in a negative manner (not dirty, they're perfect gentlemen the lot of them), in which they directed their efforts at disrupting the rhythm of the game, preventing the French from putting an attack together, and with Benzema and Valbuena, moody players both, I'll wager, neutralised for long periods, there wasn't much left, even though

Griezmann showed some quality – nutmegs at top speed, my God, that's my type of football right there – they didn't have much more in their locker, and Pogba, in common with Matuidi, didn't seem able to cope with the pressure. It was in the midfield that the Germans won the match, just as you write.

So, I disagree about the opposition being 'outclassed', but it was a great tactical victory from Löw's side. Indicative football triumphed over subjunctive football, and sensing which way it was going halfway through the game, I left Bar do Italiano as I didn't want to sit among uninterested Brazilians and deal with my disappointment, as people used to say. So I watched the second half back in my room, and towards the end of the ninety minutes, when a free kick was followed by a substitution, another free kick, a throw-in, a substitution, a free kick, throw-in and the game was dead, just as Löw wanted, I was struck by that feeling of melancholy that comes when Germany go further in the World Cup, when the machine, the locomotive, call it what you will, has left the platform en route to the next World Cup station.

I also thought about what your friend wrote. About the quarter-finals. Of course, it's like that Sunday every spring, or some time in May, when you go down to the little goals on the pitches at Limhamn and see the first dandelions have shed their blooms, grey, ugly, bare, only the previous Sunday they shone at you, so beautiful and butter-yellow.

Brazil v. Colombia? Watched it at O Bar dos Marujos, where Copacabana and Ipanema intersect, together with Bobo Karlsson, a Swedish journalist and author my own age who has lived in Rio for many years. Bobo calls the bar the sailor bar, and when I arrive it's half-past four in the afternoon, the place is located on a corner, and everyone and everything is draped in green and gold, with only the uniforms of two military policemen standing out from the crowd. On the pavements it looks like a nursing home has disgorged, lots of elderly people dressed in the national colours, children, infants, dogs all decked out in the same colours, and the atmosphere is mildly hysterical even before kick-off, and Bobo, who's also just arrived, has managed to secure a table in the eye of the storm thanks to Geraldo, a friend of his, an elderly black man with a friendly, wrinkled face, who, after spending the entire afternoon in the bar, has an abundance of empty beer bottles on the table in front of him, and I've hardly been there a minute when I have my finger in the air, uma cerveja e uma caipirinha, por favor! And to my left I have Helena Hmelevskij, a Rio resident for almost thirty years, with an apartment in Copa near Posto 6, beautiful, deep, brown eyes, a little gap in her teeth, and sitting a little to my right, her husband, Lars Magnusson, a Steve McQueen lookalike, who works in the oil industry and is wearing a Brazil football top, and directly across from me, Bobo and Geraldo.

The five of us watch the game together, fireworks are going off in the street outside all the time, and when the national anthem is played, everyone sings along, except Bobo and me, while during the match I notice that Lars and Helena are completely Brazilianised, Swedish in appearance but definite converts.

At which point I realise I'm sitting among a gathering of Free Church, devout believers, which makes it impossible for me to say, I support Brazil, but this Brazil, this team has yet to win me over because they don't play jogo bonito, the team is full of wonderful athletes but . . . It's simply not possible. Then Thiago Silva makes it 1–0 with a goal anyone would have put away, a mistake in the Colombian defence. And suddenly I'm not just standing in a Pentecostal congregation but a madhouse too. We order food and more drink, sun-dried beef, fried cassava and another beer, thanks. A caipirinha, perhaps? Really? Ah, why not?! But I do like

Colombia. They play my type of football, Brazil do not. Personally, James Rodríguez is perhaps my player of the tournament, he's my man, and when Cuadrado gets the ball, I almost get the shivers. For me, Colombia exhibit more jogo bonito tendencies than Scolari's Brazil. I'd like to see both teams go further, and as David Luiz scores a superb goal from a free kick and runs towards the corner flag, and the bar erupts once more, I suddenly believe that this Brazil, the one with great morale, the one you think has huge collective strength – quite a different Brazil from that of Pelé, Rivelino, Zico, more like Dunga's, a sweat-and-tears version – can win the World Cup, but I remain seated as Helena, Lars and everyone else in the place dances around, and jot down, 'David Luiz – incredible free kick! His face, religious! Luiz and Silva, both so lovely!'

And by lovely, Karl Ove, I don't mean in the usual aesthetic sense, but how their faces are filled with this intense esprit de corps – one for all and all for one – and as he runs towards the corner flag with a wild look in his eyes, I try to imagine how he must feel right there and then, having in all likelihood just sent Brazil to the semi-finals, and that he hasn't done it for himself but for 190 million people, he's merely a tiny part of the crest of this huge wave, and he knows it, and for the first time during the World Cup I want to talk to William, to tell him that they can go all the way, and if they do I know already that I too will be in tears (but it's only football, as your daughter Vanja would say, as my Marianne would say, and I'm aware of that, still that's how I'll end up).

The match itself? I'm not able to relate it to anything I've ever seen. Football? Yes, perhaps, but to me it looked more like a fierce battle between two Indian tribes deep in the Amazon. All that was missing was Scolari and Pékerman in Indian costume, each with a bow and a quiver full of arrows. Did you see Luiz's seventy-metre sprint? What was that? Pure madness. Everything was thrown out the window early on in that game, tactics, strategy, cool heads – it was, it now occurs to me, the complete opposite of France v. Germany, jungle football juxtaposed with chess.

We went on from Bobo's 'sailor bar' to Lasse and Helena's local, Bodega Cesare, a few streets away. Everything was quiet, the previous hysteria replaced by collective happiness, but then, the news passing like an electric current through the streets, around the blocks and bars, as word emerges of Neymar being 'fora da Copa' (out of the World Cup), and that would probably explain the relative silence that suddenly sets in, and again we find some plastic chairs to sit on, and Helena begins telling us a gripping story about the gold miners in Ouro Preto, about the punishment they could expect – their children were in the mines with them, working their own narrower tunnels, which they had to crawl along – if they were caught with a single gold flake, a single one they tried to hide in their clothes or attempted to conceal in their hair, then they hung them up on a wall right at the very bottom of the mine, one oil lamp left to burn until it went out, and then the poor unfortunate would hang there all night, alone, deep in the mine, until it was time for work again the next day . . .

Before I ask my last question – are we there yet? – which is a recurring theme in our correspondence, Bobo says something that I've so far only sensed but haven't been able to put into words.

'Fredrik, this is the last great party!'

'What do you mean?'

'2018, Russia, Putin. 2022, Qatar. And FIFA's fascism will probably only worsen. This World Cup – right now! – is the last great footballing party ever. In years to come people will look back on this as a high point in the history of football. Nothing is ever going to beat this.'

And then I try to get my last question in but face constant interruption.

'Can I just finish what I was saying?'

'No!'

'Yes, but only if what you're saying is right!'

And then, finally, I launch into my tirade about modernity and our society back home, about the central place of the individual and individualism, and that we probably are there, which is likely not the case here in Brazil yet, although it will be pretty soon, and about loneliness and the loss of that feeling of community, and then I allow Helena to have the last word from her plastic chair.

'I was back home in Sweden last winter, and one day I was out walking in Stockholm. It was cold, there was snow on the ground, and suddenly I see a woman about eighty years old with a walking frame trying to negotiate a snowdrift! On her own, Fredrik. That's what we're teaching our children, what we think is the most important thing they need to learn, to cope by themselves. To manage everything on their own. It's absurd. There are seven billion people in the world today. And we need one another. Sergio, over there . . .'

One of the waiters.

'. . . needs me. I need him. You, Fredrik, need me. I need you. People get that here. They haven't lost sight of it. Sweden and Switzerland are often held up as ideals of some sort, places the rest of the world will one day resemble, but an opposing view has emerged lately, something else . . .'

'Which is?'

'A shift towards the south.'

'In what way?'

'Brian Eno put it well. He's an artist now and had an exhibition here not so long ago. With regard to what we're talking about, he said, it's here the future lies, in Brazil's way of being. Brazil has so much to teach us. I think he's right.'

And I too, Karl Ove, think that she and Eno might be right, and told her as much before settling up and hopping into a taxi back to Lapa.

Best wishes,
Fredrik

PS Come on, Belgium!

Botafogo, Fredrik's place, 6 July

Dear Karl Ove,

Sunday morning here and all is quiet, so very quiet. No sound of internal flights, no dogs barking, just the twittering of birds in the distance and Mahler on the CD player. I'm alone in the house, Thiago and Afonso are each with their respective girlfriends. A place all to myself in the middle of perpetually pulsating Rio de Janeiro! I find myself ruminating on peculiarities particular to Brazilians.

The extent to which people here seem so preoccupied puzzles me at times, this goes for waiters, staff at supermarket check-outs, shop assistants, cab drivers or passengers on buses or on the metro, as though they're present and yet they're not. It's like some sort of abiding absent-mindedness, and yesterday, at a bar in the city centre, the small, stocky waiter didn't look at me once when he was taking my order, didn't say a word, merely communicated via the slightest of facial expressions, which were hard to interpret, and when I told him I'd like to have the risotto with chicken he took an age to look down through the menu as though he'd never heard of the dish, despite the fact it must be one of the most popular, and it's worth mentioning that he was an elderly waiter who must have worked there for years.

His soul wasn't present, it was some place else. Where? Impossible to know for sure. But he put me in mind of a taxi driver I encountered a few years back, in a trip that ended at Ipanema.

'Could I have a receipt, please?'

'Pardon?'

'A receipt for the journey.'

'For how much?'

'The fare plus one real.'

Silence. He rummaged in the glove compartment for the receipt pad and a pen. After a while he leans over, as though about to write and says, 'What day is it today?'

'Tuesday the seventeenth.'

Another pause. Then it comes, in what for me is a prime example of how removed people here sometimes seem to be: 'Which month?'

I got your SMS after congratulating you on Argentina's victory against Belgium. You wrote, 'I know it's not the style of football you like, but they did open well and had control . . .'

No, Karl Ove, the Argentina I saw yesterday was quite different from earlier in the tournament, a team in which Messi really was king once more, not like some inhibited recluse, more like a monarch actively in touch with all his subjects, a beautiful, flowing Argentina that actually, now and again, gave me goose bumps like I had in the summer of 1986, a team that in its structure made me think of Maradona and his generation, a side no football fan could ever forget. The similarity is almost comical: Messi is so like Maradona in his style of play, the sudden body swerves and the magical left foot, a Messi who it's hard (at least for me) to warm to – in the same way as I could with someone so outwardly passionate as Maradona – a Messi who the other day Thiago claimed suffers from some kind of condition, which means when he has the ball now I think as much about that as how his dribbling runs are going to end, he has an unbelievable ability to screen the ball, and I'm equally dumbstruck every time he shakes off the three or four players chasing him, then stops to take a break, and the defenders, who are tired of pursuing him, also stop, and stand there almost stationary and stare, as though hypnotised, at the ball, Messi doesn't need to look, at the level he's at, the ball is merely an extension of his own body.

But the crucial reason for your being off the mark in your text message was that they continued to attack after going 1–0 up. They didn't descend into the Uruguayan/Italian (if we have to pick a team I feel hostile towards, then either of them could fit the bill) mode of play, negative and disruptive, that is to say the 1–0 philosophy. They wanted more, had a spark about them I hadn't previously witnessed, and one of the best things I've seen so far in this tournament was when Higuaín went through alone, his effort hitting the crossbar, and maybe his 'comeback' is the key to what we saw yesterday, a functioning team lit up by an obvious enjoyment of playing, and for the first time I believe in what you've been hoping for (and have thought would come to pass?): that the final will be between los hermanos, as they're called here.

Of course, I 'felt' for the Belgians. For two reasons: they're representative of this fresh, new, offensive football we've seen in the last few years. Attack, attack, attack! And I've taken them to my heart: Hazard, Mertens, Verthongen, Kompany, Fellaini, Lukaku, Origi and Courtois. They're my 'neighbours' now, familiar faces in my world, who play 'my' sort of football on the moules-frites and Trappist beer latitudes, this is a great Belgian side and I'd be willing to put some money on them winning the European Championships in France in 2016, do you fancy having a little bet on it, Karl Ove?, and the explanation for them going out is the same as for Colombia and Chile, the football shirt, that is footballing history, the gap between the four beasts (the four left in the tournament) and countries like Belgium, Colombia and Chile, which is steadily increasing, in spite of the fact that matches between the titans and those knocking on the door of greatness (semi-finals and final) are never walkovers any more, but end 1–0, 2–1, or are decided on penalties, that is to say that the weight of history – which their shirts are steeped in – gets heavier all the time, and that brings us to the second reason: David versus Goliath. We often instinctively cheer on David (Belgium are from a historical perspective David, although not in how they play), like in the other match yesterday, the one between Holland and Costa Rica, where the Dutch deserved to win since they were better, but as I think you've written in your earlier letters, who could support Robben and Sneijder, no matter how well they play? It's out of the question. Holland committed brand hara-kiri in the 2010 final in South Africa with their brutal play, and patching up a reputation is not the easiest thing to do. Neeskens and Cruyff, along with everything they represented, made a big impression on me in my youth, and Gullit and Rijkaard, when they came through, strode right into that orange space in my heart that those players who had gone before had opened in the 1974 World Cup.

That space is now closed, and no matter how much the football player in me might appreciate seeing Robben on the ball, how he controls a pass, his sprints, corner kicks, free kicks, his ability to spot a teammate, it's cold reason that allows me to enjoy his artistry. But it was a fair result. The weight of history decided, and the spot kicks from van Persie, Robben, Sneijder and Kuyt in the shoot-out were all in a day's work for them, because they knew they would win, and the Costa Ricans were happy enough anyway, they had exceeded all expectations, were sated, and it showed in how they took their penalties, and that too is part of the David syndrome, David was content to have fought Goliath for 120 minutes, just like Sweden were content with their semi-final against Brazil in 1994. 'We' never said to 'ourselves', we've got this far, so now we're going to bloody well go the whole way (as, if you recall, the Turks, seemed to do in the semi-final against Brazil in 2002).

Attitude. Psychology. History. We have the four greats left, and let's hope, now that we've come so far, for what would be a fantastic conclusion, a final between Argentina and Brazil, and you should know that you, singular and plural, will have my full support against Holland, just as I know that I/we will have yours against Germany (back in the days when British political influence and capital practically governed the globe, they made it their business to bring the nation state of Uruguay into being, a non-country really, as a wedge between Argentina and Brazil. Why? Because they could already see the economic and political potential in a Brazilgentina, a prospective giant of a country in South America that could one day challenge Britain's domination in world affairs, a fear I think you can still sense emanating from Washington from time to time, not at the moment, the Middle East being the main cause for concern right now, a strong Mercosur, an economically powerful Argenzil could, in the long term, prove a hard nut to crack for a USA who want to hold sway over their own enormous back yard), two sister nations with the greatest rivalry in Latin America, but also much mutual affection, everyone I speak to here expresses feeling and warmth for los hermanos, no swear words, no porra, only respect and goodwill. Whether that will still be the case should there be a new maracanazo (Maracanã fiasco) remains to be seen.

As I've mentioned, it's Sunday here. No matches, and that empty feeling of having a football-free day has crept up on me. Going to take a long walk up towards the Dona Marta favela, and then further perhaps, towards Copacabana, maybe Ipanema.

Best wishes,
Fredrik

Glemmingebro, 6 July

Dear Fredrik,

Today it is sunny and warm, and there is no football on TV, so we plan to go to the beach, for the first time this summer. The problem is that the children don't want to go. Once they are there, they think it is wonderful, and then I say, now remember for next time, so that it won't all be so difficult. Yes, yes, they say. Now it is the next time, and they don't want to go. They'd rather go to Tosselilla, which is the amusement park outside Tosselilla, or the pool in Nybrostrand. Both belong to a kind of 1970s reality, and that is fine, but today I thought we should go somewhere slightly more timeless: the sand, the forest, the sea. The beaches stretch all the way from Ystad up to Simrishamn. The big ones, which have kiosks selling all sorts, are packed now. Then there are the smaller beaches, with no facilities – especially one, which is perhaps the most beautiful place I know, and that is where I want to go. A forest of deciduous trees and pines growing as far as the eye can see on both sides: there everything is open. It is a magical place. I stumbled across it last winter, went there a couple of times this spring but haven't been there this summer yet. It is perfect for the children: they can swim, run along the beach and climb trees. But they don't want to go. For a change, I am going to force them. What kind of world are we living in when children have to be forced to go to the beach?

I will write more today, about last night, which I really enjoyed because of the Argentina v. Belgium match, as Argentina at long last, but also as expected, raised their game and played football of a quality that a number of good individual players always promised, but if there is one lesson we can draw from this World Cup it is that playing as a team has been the most important factor in success; Ronaldo's Portugal is an example of players who didn't, and Holland the possible exception; without Robben they would not have got as far as they did.

Now it is half past three and we have returned from the beach. My prejudices proved to be unfounded, everyone got into the car without a murmur apart from John, whom I had to carry, but strictly speaking that was for the most part because he likes being carried. The landscape down to the sea was magnificent, the corn pure yellow, the sky a clear blue, and the sea a lighter, misty, almost faded blue. The little clearing that was used as a car park was full, but I left our car in the ditch anyway. Somewhat concerned that I might not be able to reverse back up on our return, I walked across the little wooden bridge with the others, over a dirty green stream where the children said they could see frogs, a meadow surrounded by tall oaks and into a forest. Not a sound, the air warm and still, the sunshine filtering through trees and leaves. The girls sang songs from the musical as I walked weighed down with swimming things, food and drink. It is perhaps two kilometres from the car to the sea. Once there, at last, we walked up the sandy slope and could see the beach on both sides, and the gentle blue Baltic, there were nudists everywhere! Many naked old men, some naked old women too. It was a bloody nudist beach, Fredrik. As I assumed they didn't want a clothed family with children in their midst, and stripping off was absolutely out of the question for me, we followed a path in the forest that ran parallel with the beach because I imagined the nudist area would probably have limits. But no. Every time I went out to check, there were naked men roaming around. One by one they stood up with their hands on their hips and stared across, as though they had been posted to keep an eye on the area. We turned and walked back, and I went up onto the dune to scan the horizon. Same there, naked bodies as far as the eye could see. I rejoined the others, they were sweaty and fed up, we sat down and had something to eat and drink, then walked the long way back, got into the car and drove down to the normal beach, which was jam-packed. We all went for a swim, the children laughed and threw themselves into the waves, afterwards we had some buns and lay in the sun a while, so that it wouldn't be difficult the next time, right, Dad, they said, and then we drove back home.

The question is why I got so annoyed, indeed angry. The bloody nudists, why should they have the best beach in Österlen? And why do they strip off at all? I felt like sending a reader's letter to *Ystad Allehånde* about it. Saying words to the effect that of course nudists must have a beach but why precisely this one?

I have not only become bourgeois, I have also developed a not-insignificant degree of narrow-mindedness over the years. That too is the Protestant in me, I think. And it hasn't always been like this. When I was nineteen I went to Greece with a friend, to an island called Antiparos, where there is a nudist beach, and we stayed there for a week. Every morning after breakfast we walked to the beach, undressed, and there we were, naked for the whole day. I didn't like it, but I did it because I believed in it. I was anti-bourgeois, anti-authoritarian, in favour of a natural, hippy-style life and extremely leftist, at the point where it tips into anarchism. I was a pacifist, against NATO, in favour of a basic income, and in the evenings I read Jack Kerouac and aspired to a completely free lifestyle.

Now, twenty-five years later, with a house, car, four children and a large garden with a trampoline in the centre, I am filled with contempt for those idiotic nudists, who think they are so special and so much better than ordinary people.

Well, no, it isn't that bad. But I was irritated.

Jogo bonito people, Fredrik, they don't object to nudism, do they? Tell me if you are getting sick of the endless stream of prejudices I send in your direction, it is done with cordiality and perhaps a little envy – but also the notion that Argentinian-ism, however we choose to interpret it, definitely doesn't include nudism. Knife fights, OK. Gauchos on the pampas, OK. Winning at any price, OK. Cons and tricks, OK. Hand of God, OK. Nudism, not OK.

The most fascinating aspect of the final round yet to be played is the classic status of the teams left. Argentina, Germany, Brazil, Holland. All of them have traditions, all of them have been here before and now they are back, even if they are not the teams who have played the best football, with the possible exception of Germany. There is great strength in that. And that adds a dimension to the matches. Germany v. Holland, the 1974 final. Holland v. Argentina, the 1978 final. Argentina v. Germany, the 1986 and 1990 finals. Brazil v. Germany, the 2002 final.

I was a little nervous before the Argentina–Belgium game began yesterday, but my nerves settled after only a few minutes, there was something assured and confident about their play, they seemed very strong. If Belgium scored, I thought, Argentina would just slot in an equaliser. That was the impression they gave. The goal came after only nine minutes, Messi to Di María, his misjudged ball hit a Belgian player and rebounded towards Higuaín, who just followed it, that is, squared up to it and hit it first time. A goal like that only happens if everything is done right, it is twenty years' experience in three seconds' improvisation: 1–0. Higuaín was brilliant yesterday. He wasn't very good before, but yesterday he was. Did you see his run when he must have passed three Belgians, one of whom, Kompany, was beaten with a little toe-punt of a ball through his legs – and then he was on his own and he shot a hair's breadth too high. He was good at everything he did, especially the way he killed some lofted crosses, the ball died at his feet even when he was under pressure. Messi was unsurpassable yesterday. It didn't matter how difficult the balls he got were, one touch and they were under control. He was dazzling, several notches up from before. He challenged the Belgians every time he had the ball. A second later there were three Belgians around him, and he just went towards them, weaved his way through or got a free kick – which became the tactics for the next eighty minutes. Go for free kicks, go for throw-ins, go for anything that broke up play, and when we have possession, keep it. Belgium never managed to get going, never had the feeling they must have had against the USA, when they attacked in wave after wave. It requires a rhythm, a mood, pressure that builds up, and then wham. It is all one-way traffic. Yesterday there was a wall between them and that feeling. Everything was constantly being interrupted, nothing got going. There was no rhythm, no mood, no pressure. Eventually the solution for them was long balls towards Fellaini in particular and Lukaku, and this produced moments of danger – in the last few minutes they came close, and for the first time I thought they would succeed, and my heart beat faster. But they didn't, and it wasn't because they were poor, it was because they couldn't get their game going, it had been taken from them. Mascherano was fantastic in the middle yesterday, by some distance Argentina's most important player, and the defence was also stellar – they employed man-to-man defensive marking, at which, over the tournament, they have perhaps been the best. Zabaleta, not much gets past him. The central defenders too, incredibly strong in duels, Garay and on this occasion the Manchester City player with the Greek name, Demichelis, criticised in winter and spring, but now he'd had a haircut, I thought that was a good sign, and he played as a centre half, not a defensive midfielder, as so often with City. They controlled everything. The only downside, except for the negative play, which irritated the TV commentators – they said at the end it didn't mean they supported Belgium, and when they say that, it means only one thing, they did support Belgium – but which I was comfortable with, negating another team's play is also an art, was of course that my favourite player, Kafka, had to leave the field with a pulled muscle and will probably miss the rest of the World Cup. Injuries to him and Agüero severely weakened the team.

Holland v. Costa Rica was a strange match. It was incredible that after 120 minutes they should still be 0–0 after the pressure Holland had applied and the chances they'd had, denied by a keeper in the form of his life, and although I know many people disagree with me on this point, the score was fair. Costa Rica didn't have the same level, they played in an incredibly tight, disciplined and controlled way, but had little energy beyond that and have less reason to be in the semi-final than Holland. I don't like this Dutch team, but Robben is playing at an amazingly high level now, and the little cat, Sneijder, is also brilliant – you saw the free kick hit the bar, didn't you, the cat's eyes just before? Argentina v. Holland: hmm. An Argentina weakened in attack, but with Higuaín and Messi in improving form. An efficient Holland – I don't mean in front of goal! I mean in defence, midfield, where they are hard to dislodge – with a van Persie who has used up his quota of mishits and will score at the first sniff of an opportunity.

Germany v. Brazil? I think not having Neymar won't damage their chances hugely, Dante is a worthy replacement for Silva and Luiz is crazy, but also that Germany master all types of play and Löw will know how to keep Brazil quiet. But if Brazil carry on being so crazy, as it seems they are doing – jogo loco – no plan will help, for then they are completely unpredictable.

Time for pancake-making now, then cutting the grass, afterwards I am going to read your letter and perhaps do a bit of writing, though probably not, tomorrow we have guests and there are a lot of practical jobs to be done. Talk soon!

All the best,
Karl Ove

Botafago. 7 July

Dear Karl Ove,

Found myself laughing out loud several times at your last letter, felt like I was there in the pine forest in Österlen the whole time, pictured everything clearly, the image of the naked men as sentries of some kind was hilarious – and jogo loco! Wonderful. David Luiz running towards the corner flag, yes, maybe that's the memory that will stay with me longest from this World Cup, the expression on his face, just thinking of the strange-seeming physics of his free kick again, the trajectory of the ball, his short run-up, the distance to goal, the force with which he struck the ball, and the explanation is quite simple, Karl Ove, we play with the same ball out at Buarque's, it's relatively light, doesn't warp or have the same weight as normal footballs and is a real pleasure to kick.

Yesterday I set out for the favela not far from here, Dona Marta. It was my first time going into a favela on my own – moreover, with a camera in my hand. It may sound daring but I can assure you it's not. The area has been peaceful for some time, as I was well aware. But I wanted to see, with my own eyes, what I call the changes that have taken place, and simply being able to enter the favela is an indication of how far things have come. In 1997, when I visited Rio for the first time, taking a walk up there would have been inconceivable and probably have ended in disaster – in spite of the favela being situated right next to the middle-class district of Botafogo. At that time the favela was ruled by one of the gangs, I think there are around six or seven thousand people living here, under their control. Yet more proof of how excluded the favelas are is the fact that it is impossible to obtain a map of them in spite of the existence of streets, roadways and paths. Twenty per cent of Rio's population are therefore not on the map, the only feature that used to be represented was 'Morro Santa Martha', the name of the actual mountain, until Google Earth changed everything by showing the street names – a real smack in the face for Brazil, highlighting the country's class prejudice and class contempt, a North American multinational giving all the poor in Rio a visible, real address! The funicular to the mountain was only running between stations two to three, so I had to walk up through the narrow alleyways, scarcely a metre wide at some parts, like moving along tunnels, where you have small bars to your left and right and can look straight into people's kitchens and living rooms, and what do you know, the little girl in the house has got an iPad, and look there, they're having feijoada for lunch, and the neighbours are having a delicious-smelling moceca, and everyone has had free Wi-Fi for a number of years and their own local radio station, and on the way I think of all those mothers and grandmothers who have to haul the family shopping up this mountain along these steps, along these Fred-Flintstone-like stone labyrinths, thousands of everyday heroes with a sick baby on one arm and a bag of groceries hanging from the other, and I, no stranger to the physical exertion of sports, am tired after just a few minutes, and generations of women, and of course men – and this is true for several of the favelas in Rio, many of them are on the sides of mountains – have struggled up and down here in the heat every single day of their lives, these are the thoughts that come to mind, but also others, about the gang leader here, who would descend these steps wearing a white blazer back in the 90s, and everyone knew what that meant: that he had killed somebody the evening or night before. Brazil is changing for the better, and what I pass through is a pretty normal Latin American working-class world, no squalor, nobody lying beaten up anywhere, no youths with doped-up eyes, it's a basic, clean, dignified place, with lots of happy children running around all over, on the steps, on the rooftops, playing and chasing after one another and, not least, flying kites, not sitting hunched over smartphones, but playing, playing, playing, and at the top of the mountain, in a small hollow between two peaks, there is an artificial grass pitch full of children playing football and completely enclosed by a large net, which is essential, otherwise a poorly taken free kick could cause the ball to land two hundred metres below on the head of a middle-class woman on her way to the bakery or the hairdresser's, and round me I see reinforced steel sticking up and pink roof tiles, and although it's Sunday some people are working on their houses and rooftop water tanks, and there are small Free Church chapels and churches interspersed here and there: Brazil has seen a strong surge in the last decade in the establishment of Protestant Free Churches – Kaká, Neymar and Luiz are notable followers – especially in shanty towns, as well as Pentecostal denominations and Seventh-Day Adventists, and I came across a number of people this Sunday carrying Bibles, and the election of a South American pope is likely a stroke of genius, the Catholic Church feels threatened by Free Church preachers and is now trying to educate young, charismatic priests to take up the fight for the souls of Brazil's poor. It strikes me now, as I write, that you and I are now closer to these poor people who read and interpret the Bible for themselves, because that's how it was in Sweden, and I suppose in Norway, that was the genius of Luther, the Reformation, the revolution of its time: to give ordinary people access to the Word in Norwegian and Swedish, not only in Latin, and in our part of the world workers' organisations often acted hand in hand with the Free Church and temperance movements. They are the counterpart of Sweden's readers I can see. (It just struck me that, paradoxically, you, the hyper-Protestant, are one hundred per cent behind Pope Francis's Argentina. By the way, I saw a photo of him, dressed in white, his cardinals alongside him, wearing red, watching Argentina on a big screen somewhere inside the Vatican, all of them looking very concentrated, seated in a row, and now, in my mind's eye, you sneak into the image, take a seat by his side, vamos chicos! And the two of you have your eyes glued to your little Messi on the screen, both captivated, unreachable.)

I'm alone, I feel lonely, and the camera only emphasises this feeling of being a gringo. I've been in favelas before a number of times, but always with others, and then I hear Lasse West-man's voice saying, 'All right so go up to the favela and look at the monkeys.' I understand his objections but don't believe the argument – social tourism – holds up. How are we to learn about the world if we don't dare seek out others across class and ethnic divides?

Time for Edson beach. A sunlounger. Read. Take photographs. Have a dip. Then a long walk along the water's edge. On my way I come across a game of football in full swing. A group of Chinese against some Latin Americans. I ask if I can join in, get the OK, and am put on the Chinese team, where I can't communicate with anyone. At least not verbally, so I'm reduced to waving my arms around a lot. And still, as always, we're soon conversing through the Esperanto of the feet, and there's a good atmosphere to the game. I run on to a long goal kick, stretch and connect with a lovely volley that goes just over the bar, and then I land in the sand, relishing the contact I just made, before taking my leave of them shortly after, just another quick visit in a never-ending jam session, and as I'm making my way off the pitch, changing places with another Chinese guy, a player is fouled – at least in his own eyes – and I can't stop myself from shouting 'Robben' loudly enough for everyone to hear, but the Chinese don't understand until after a few seconds when the two syllables penetrate the minds of everyone on the pitch, not just the Chinese, but also the Mexicans and the Colombians, and the meaning blooms in them like a flower, everyone laughs and shouts 'Robben! Robben! Robben!' pointing, like kids in the schoolyard, at the 'fouled' player lying in the sand, and then he too begins to laugh because he knows he's dived, and I think: take that, Arjen, you bastard! (and if you have any pull with the man with the number 266 on his chair, Karl Ove, your friend Francis, please ask him and all the cardinals to kneel and pray to the Man above, a simple appeal from all of us in Copacabana: don't let Robben get a World Cup winner's medal, no cheats should get one of those, it would mean the death of the most beautiful sport of all, amen) while at the same time I am almost mystified at the dynamism in the language of football. We're unable to understand a word each other says but the word 'Robben' opens all doors, all faces.

It's Sunday afternoon, almost five o'clock, the sun is going down behind the high-rise hotels, dusk is descending over Copa, and as I walk along the promenade among thousands of slowly moving people, it's like making my way through a stationary shoal of fish, everything so soft and wonderfully free of aggression, and then once again it hits me, Karl Ove, that this World Cup is almost at an end. There's hardly anyone in a football top to be seen. This is the usual Sunday movement of Copacabana, a Sunday that is sacred to all who reside in Rio, a people who abhor Mondays, everyday life is returning, people are beginning to head home, and the fact there are three matches remaining, the most important matches, is difficult to comprehend: everything is tranquil, mild, the movement of the crowds light and melancholic, as when you're about to lose something, a long-awaited weekend, a carnival – or a World Cup.

Best wishes,
Fredrik

Glemmingebro, 7 July

Dear Frederico,

Another warm, sunny day here in Glemminge. The garden is so green and lush, quiet and full of shadow that it makes me happy just to look. I haven't been in it today, guests are arriving soon, and I spent the morning shopping for food. When I was standing by my car taking the key from my pocket to unlock it there was a vehicle parked by our house a little further away, I wondered if it was a parcel delivery or something, but it was a normal car, so it couldn't have been. When people come to the house, when cars stop outside or there is a knock at the door, I always think, and this is my first thought, someone is going to get me. Something terrible is going to be said or done. I have had that fear lodged in me ever since the first volume of *Min Kamp* came out. It is utterly meaningless, doesn't matter and isn't dramatic, it is just a twenty-second shock whenever someone appears out of the blue. Today a man wearing sunglasses was coming towards me, greeted me, and I suddenly recognised him, it was the *Dagens Nyheter* photographer. We had arranged to do a photo shoot at ten! I had completely forgotten. And now I had to go shopping so that we had some food for the guests. But of course I couldn't possibly send him away, we had made an arrangement, it was made on Friday and was about these letters of ours: *DN* is going to print four pages on Saturday and wanted some shots for it. He suggested going to the football pitch and taking a few photos there. So we did. The pitch is only a few hundred metres away, with golden cornfields on two sides, a hut and a car park on the others. Walking out onto it, I was struck by how small a football pitch actually is, how close the corner flags are to the goal, and that the World Cup pitches are about the same size. Everything looks so big on TV. But it is an area like this they run on. The photographer produced a World Cup ball, he thought it a little silly, a little obvious, but that was the way *DN* wanted it, so it would have to appear in some of the photos. We did some on the reserves bench, that was appropriate, I thought (especially as there was an H on it, assuming it stood for Home?), and then we did some by one goal. I put the ball down on the penalty spot. How bloody difficult can it be? I said. Shoot, he said, and we'll see. I eyed him and felt stupid. Should I shoot? With him watching? OK, suppose I'll have to. I didn't take a run-up, stood quite still and shot. The ball flew towards the corner, hit the underside of the crossbar and went in. It was the perfect penalty! No keeper in the world could have saved it. Wow, he said. I looked at him and said, That would have been a goal in the World Cup too. He chuckled and said the pressure was probably a tiny bit more there. Of course, of course, I said. Obviously. But Fredrik, there was a little pressure on me too, my footballing reputation was on the line, not much of one, granted, but still: I could have made a total prat of myself in front of the photographer, and in fact I was nervous when I shot.

However, I only score like that once in a hundred shots. Once in a hundred shots there. Now it is two years since I last kicked a ball, and it is very likely to be another two before the next time. So in that situation I was more than lucky. The worst of it was I was so proud!

The photographer, whose name is Anders, does reportage, travels to Ukraine, Egypt, trouble spots all over the world. But it's beginning to get tricky, he said, and that is not hard to understand, he has three children. He invited me to an exhibition he was putting on in Malmö in September, and I will try to get along. That is one of the advantages of having a job like this: I meet people outside my life who are exceptionally good at what they do. I suppose I learn nothing from it, but I see things I haven't seen before, and that is the most important reason for me saying yes to invitations, one day I will find a use for it, I think, one day something will come of it. So many strange events I have been to, in remote forests and in the middle of small towns, with the most eccentric event organisers, the weirdest readers and strangest atmospheres. There was one interview in a bookshop inside a Dutch church, on the Belgian border; they had asked me because they used to spend their holidays in Sørland. Once in a little town in north-east Germany I sat in a bookshop talking about one of my books, called *Sterben* in German, and there were so few people, around eight, that after a while we just chatted. They told me their experiences of death; one had a brother who died, another a mother, someone cried and I was so far from home, night had fallen outside, and an hour later the organiser met me in an old 2CV to take me to the ferry, you can imagine, dark sky, dark sea, the throbbing engine of the ferry, the clanking juggernauts driving on board, the few passengers on the gangway, and the light inside the ferry, so harsh and revealing, and all the truck drivers sitting there eating their meaty snacks and drinking beer, some TVs are on, a tiny tax-free shop is empty, and then, next day, the morning in Trelleborg, the bus to Malmö, and back home. The evening in the provincial east German bookshop, strangers sitting and grieving and telling me about 'their' deaths; how had that come about, how I had ended up there? Me, who never talks to anyone and definitely not strangers abroad? The division between home and away is so sharp that these moments, of which there are many, simply vanish the instant I set foot in my house, home erases everything. It is a sort of shadow life I lead. Small Dutch, Belgian or German towns, old-fashioned freezing-cold hotels where you are allowed to smoke in the rooms, but there is no mini-bar, breakfasts reading the local papers, I usually look at the obituaries, it is the most evocative section I can imagine, foreign names of foreign people who spent their lives here, in this rain-drenched, grey European landscape. What was it like? At dinner, after the event, I might be sitting next to someone who once arranged a concert with Lou Reed and tells me he is the biggest arsehole he has ever met, worse people don't exist, do you know what he did? Do you know what he said? No, by the way I know someone just as bad, Willy de Ville. Then there is someone else who has also met Lou Reed and describes him as even worse. This in a town whose name I have long forgotten, on the border between Holland and Germany, in a little cellar restaurant as the rain beats down on the cobblestones outside. Everyone there was foreign, and the town was the size of Arendal or Ystad. Again, how had I ended up there? Another memory of a tour: the book fair in Frankfurt, it must be seven or eight years ago, I was having dinner with Norwegian publishers and the minister of culture, Trond Giske. They laughed at his jokes in a way I thought existed only in films, you know, the sycophantic laughter – a bit like Elvis's comeback film in ... it must have been 68: everyone around him laughing themselves silly whenever he said anything. I saw it. I didn't believe it was true, it was so transparent, but no, they were laughing. And then I noticed Giske humming while he was eating. I have never witnessed anything like it before. A third thing I can tell you about the dinner, which I hadn't planned to write about today, and have no idea what made me think of it, was that there were topics that had to be brought up, influence that had to be won for causes. I was in a taxi with two women, and they were discussing what they were going to say, one of them had in fact made notes on a slip of paper, I think. During the dinner she said her piece. Giske interrupted her and asked jokingly if she had rehearsed it. Everyone laughed, she was embarrassed, and the dinner continued. Why had he said that? Did he think what she said was boring? Did he think it was too obvious? Did he want to get a laugh? Or when I was at a college outside Minneapolis in Minnesota, presumably because there was a Norwegian link, I was driven there by someone who was interested in Norway, it was a long drive, he ran and assisted Scandinavian companies to establish themselves in the area, I gathered, until conversation dried up and we drove through these American fields, me almost out of my mind with unease, he had volunteered his help, probably hoping for a cosy chat with a Norwegian. At the college, which was in a beautiful location and well maintained in that special American way, I was supposed to talk in a room resembling a canteen. Sixty people were there, more or less, they were young, many of them men, they had muscular upper bodies and somewhat vacant eyes; they played American football or ice hockey and must have been told to turn out, what do I know. I spoke about death, as I usually do, and afterwards some of them came over, polite and well mannered, and said it had been an interesting talk. I am not kidding! Such meetings with people I would never have met in normal life naturally enough, some of them total wackos – people who have created some work of art they want to hand over or poems or letters they have written – some of them forced to attend to get some intellectual nutrition as part of their training day – some local-culture honchos or cultural idealists or Norway-friends or God knows what, but most just your standard readers who have come out one evening to listen to a talk – recent years have been full of these talks, but sitting here now and thinking about them – not quite sure why – I feel they are so weird it is almost as though they happened to someone else. I never talk about this with anyone, not even Linda, these are experiences that are mine alone, and in many ways they resemble dreams. They are so lacking in context and clarity, you meet some people one evening, after a few hours they are the people you know best and treat them as friends, the rest of the table is full of complete strangers, then the same happens again the next night. In some way all the meetings and places must be stored inside me, but I don't know how. I hope that one day these experiences will come out in my writing – not that any of this happens on book tours, of course, because they are a different matter – but the atmospheres in these towns, the feeling they communicate, not least that they are the centre for everyone who lives there and for the history of which they are a part, such as in the Flanders area, where those I had just met and were already 'friends' ordered huge amounts of meat, there were several kilos on the table, as well as chips and mayonnaise, they said we were only a few kilometres behind the Front now, and then they talked about the war, which was the First World War, for an hour at least. The flooding darkness outside, and the rain, and the small group of drunken youths hanging around in front of a bar and smoking, the freezing-cold hotel, which was as far from a chain hotel as it is possible to be. Or the chapel where I once did a reading in Germany, which was attached to a palace, with drawings from the *Odyssey* on the wall, early Middle Ages, and where the stage was just below where Charlemagne had sat – someone told me there had been no wall there, so those in attendance saw him against the background of the setting sun, and where I, after answering some questions, sat down in the hall to listen to the next performance, an actor on the German TV programme *Derrick*, who read from the *Odyssey*, when I was so tired I dozed off, he must have read for an hour and I slept right through. The next day I went round the palace, mostly on my own and into a cordoned-off colonnade, a coffin with burning candles and flowers: it was the Schlossherr who had died a few days earlier. No one around, only this coffin and the burning candles. This was the area where the brothers Grimm collected their fairy tales, not far from the forest where the Romans were driven back, which Tacitus describes in *Germania*. I was completely overwhelmed by the intensity, the feeling of being at the heart of something. I don't know of what, Germany, Europe, history, literature, death. Then I left and went to a café, I was drinking a coffee, perhaps even with a beer, as a coach full of tourists parked, and when the door opened the passengers clambering out shouted to each other, joked and fooled around in a language I recognised: it was a coach full of pensioners from Stavanger.

The contrast with the USA could not have been greater. Even in the most peripheral places in Europe it feels as if we have something in common, it is somehow home, but the USA is foreign. There things are different. There it is something else which counts. I went to Los Angeles for the first time this spring, but was struck by how different it is, the atmosphere, the buildings, the structure, actually everything, and it didn't evoke any of the notions I had, all the clichés of Los Angeles were gone as I walked along Santa Monica Beach, with the Pacific straight ahead. So open, so ... well, as I walked I didn't have a care in the world. Why don't we live there? I thought. Why do we live in Sweden? It is lovely and warm here! Palm trees and sand, the smell of sea, and nothing of the compact skyscraper-America, more like Spain, except that it didn't seem Spanish at all.

The USA is exciting also because it is so primitive in many ways, yet this is where hi-tech is developed, this is where the leading academics and writers, film-makers and artists are to be found. The army culture, the weapon culture, illiteracy, every-thing is about the visual image now. I spoke to some writers there, they taught writing at universities and said the students being accepted now had read hardly any contemporary litera-ture, the biggest names, they had no knowledge of literary history and they saw writing as a potential career. I answered that wasn't necessarily a decline, presumably they could do other things, but the writers looked at me and said no, it is a decline. There is a big cultural decline in America. This is sort of tangen-tial to what you write about, that things are getting better. From a material standpoint, and this has always been the priority, the most important area, perhaps things are improving. From a cul-tural standpoint I am not sure they are. It is normal for the older generation to perceive decline in what is actually only change, but what happens when the number of people who can read drops and drops? The American writers were amazed by the situation in Scandinavia, where so many people read literature and where literature is supported by the state – much more in Norway than in Sweden, it has to be said, but much more in Sweden than in the USA. Can we say this is just what is hap-pening, and that it is no loss, based on the logic that literature will die of its own accord because it is losing ground, and then it is no loss because what people don't want has no value? People, that is you and me, Fredrik, and our neighbours and our neigh-bours' neighbours, those who live in Rio and those who live in Glemminge, Paris and Malmö, Stavanger and Bergen, in the USA and China. Is literature important? Is it dying, will it disappear to be replaced by the visual, is it a loss or is it just a change and not necessarily a deterioration? Are those of us who think litera-ture is important elitist? Are we talking on behalf of our own dying mother?

Last night Geir came down to collect his son, who had been

playing with my daughter all afternoon, we sat in my office chatting for an hour and drinking coffee. We started off talking about what music meant to us. Geir said we had made two mistakes in our lives. One is that we haven't learned languages. You speak Spanish, French and Portuguese, Fredrik, as well as English and Swedish (and for all I know a couple more) – while Geir and I speak Norwegian and English. Languages not only open worlds, so the theory goes, but also something inside ourselves. You have access to something else when you speak another language. I believe that is true. The second mistake, according to Geir, was that we never built up a relationship with music – pop music, yes, but that is like reading The Phantom or Donald Duck, it has a limited effect on our emotional lives. Geir thought that music, real music, opens up parts of ourselves that otherwise lie dormant. I disagreed because what we have, our inner life, our emotional life, what used to be called the soul, finds its way up to consciousness anyway or into the nervous system or wherever it is we feel what we feel. I find it in art and literature, I said to Geir. Music would elicit the same, nothing else. He disagreed, and there we sat, stuck on a point that could neither be confirmed nor denied, it was all hypothetical, and we went on to discuss another subject. Last winter I listened to a lot of Wagner, but the distance is too great, and it is too late to bridge the gap, that was how I felt.

My favourite quote about music is what Rilke wrote somewhere. He describes how music lifts you up – only to put you down again somewhere else.

This 'somewhere else', this is what music does and what I am excluded from. But I don't think you are, not from what I have read in your letters, where music is always present or thereabouts – do you play Mahler when you write?

Incidentally, it was interesting to read what you wrote about

France v. Germany the other day. Where I saw Germany outclass, control and tactically outplay France, and a French team totally devoid of the qualities they had manifested earlier, you saw an even game in which France gradually became the dominant team playing well for periods and creating scoring opportunities. Is this about feelings? About my feeling that they wouldn't score, that they were light years away, while you felt the opposite, that a goal could materialise any minute, and therefore you interpreted the game as attacking while I interpreted it as defensive? I don't know. After the Argentina game I was sure you would be negative because they played as cynically as one might have expected, wasting time, but you reacted positively and seemed to be praising the football they played. I assume that must have something to do with the fact that they never went defensive, but kept trying to break Holland down when the opportunity arose, not at any price admittedly with Messi and Higuaín lurking, and the absolutely sensational qualities they showed us in glimpses. Anyway, Robben is the player of the tournament so far, as his whole team stands or falls on his work rate, to an even greater degree than Argentina with Messi, I think. But I still can't stand him, and the spectacular runs he makes mean nothing because he does them. It is unfair, illogical, irrational, however, unlike all the other judgements I make when I write, I don't need to justify this one. It is football, I can say what I want, it is my privilege as a spectator. It is very prejudiced. Why don't I like the best player in the tournament? I think it is something to do with the way he walks, his arms out to the side, and his face. In other words, his body language says something I don't like to see. Strange that his body language prevents me and many others from appreciating what he actually does on the pitch, which is exceptional, however, it is the reality. I think something is becoming apparent here: how important appearance is, how important body language is, all those things in a player that appeal to emotion, and how taboo it is to say so or acknowledge it. We are, in our own opinions, rational beings: we think, judge, analyse everything with a certain objectivity. For that, appearance is irrelevant. But it might be the opposite. Appearance and body language mean such a lot, trump analysis without our realising it, because we rationalise feelings, rationalise impulses, make them into arguments: Robben cheats, he dives, we don't like him. But Maradona cheated and dived, and we like him, don't we?

It is quite true that van Persie's and Rodríguez's goals are the most pleasing to the eye because they are spectacular while Suárez's two are 'prosaically beautiful', as you wrote a few letters ago. That is precisely why I like Suárez's because, first and foremost, these goals are efficient, the beauty of them lies in his doing what is necessary to put the ball in the net and nothing else – but with a vertiginously high tariff of difficulty, I have to add, this is no volley at an open goal we are talking about here – and that is why I place van Persie's and Rodríguez's goals below, although objectively they are clearly more attractive and actually should not have been possible: if we had given the ball to Blind ten times and he had crossed to van Persie running through the middle ten times there might have been one goal, but never with the original's perfection, and that is why we admire it, it shouldn't have been possible, but at exactly that moment, under those circumstances, it happened anyway. Ditto, Rodríguez's goal. Difficult to copy (but less impossible because there was only one player involved, no interaction, so – a bit like Zlatan's scissors kick against England), and in that sense Tim Cahill's volley, from a forty-metre pass, is more spectacular than Rodríguez's chested volley. But all these are circus goals! Suárez's were football goals.

Having said that, how much insight and feeling and intuition lie behind Neymar's uncomplicated shot on goal, you know, when he received a pass on the ground at the edge of the penalty box and just flicked the ball on, no power, no beauty, but in such a way that the keeper could only stand and stare? There was a lot of Maradona about that goal – not that Maradona ever scored any like that, I don't know if he did, but a natural lack of complication was as vital to his game as the spectacular: a case in point would be the way he slid round Shilton in the 86 World Cup, as I have mentioned. I have seen it many times, and what he does is merely run past him with the ball. No feint, no nothing. He glides past and puts the ball in the net. When I saw the clip again today it was in slow motion, and the unbelievable thing about that unending slalom run, beating England player after England player and leaving them in the dust, is that it was all improvised, spontaneous decisions, and what Maradona did was to read the opponent's anticipation of his next move and do the opposite. If they thought he would go left, he went right, if they thought forward, he went back, and what presence of mind that requires! What concentration, what composure! It is the opposite of mechanical, it is the opposite of learned, and that, but only that, is related to art. Again I am thinking of your friend in the car, who talked about Mozart's scale exercises as the basis for freedom and lightness of touch. Surely this is what all creativity is about, freeing yourself from what is expected, which, first of all, has to be mastered.

I cannot believe that I am actually comparing Maradona's game to art. Oh, is there a more embarrassing or more stupid cliché? Football is football, full stop. And football is excess, something extra, something no one needs, it is superfluous – and that, my Brazilian friend, is all that a Protestant longs for but cannot allow himself. That was why Protestant football was invented – it is the kind of football that deals in efficiency, graft, pain and suffering for the result, in other words, a game where the excess is reduced to a minimum and where nothing is superfluous. Everyone who plays football like this and everyone who puts the collective first knows that they are eclipsed by dribblers and feinters, that those are the great footballers – everyone knows that, even if not everyone will admit it – but whatever eclipses is decadent, this is about morality basically, and a footballer who feints and dribbles and does overhead kicks and nutmegs and performs tricks is an immoral footballer.

Now it is a quarter past one in the morning, all the guests went to bed long ago, the shrimps and crabs, the raspberries and ice cream, were eaten long ago, and I am so tired I can barely distinguish the letters on the screen. Tomorrow it is decided. May Brazil beat Germany.

All the best,
Karlovaldo

Botafogo, 8 July

Dear Karl Ove,

Yesterday a large dark cloud appeared in the World Cup sky, our – your and my – 'heaven' and our dream of a final between Brazil and Argentina, and that cloud says a lot about my naivety. We were on our way to Buarque's pitch, the weather was overcast and not too warm, and Feital was in the back seat going on about the history of bossa nova and samba, two different histories, according to him, that can be summed up as 'bossa' being more middle class, since it originated in Ipanema, while samba has more folksy roots and was born in 'os morros' (the hills) here in Rio and Bahia (there's disagreement apparently concerning which samba can lay claim to being older, that of Rio or Bahia). He was at the same time careful to emphasise that the two styles are independent of one another, and not in opposition, and then he told the story of Noel Rossa, the brilliant samba exponent who gave up his medical studies and plunged himself into the bohemian lifestyle up on Morro Estácio in the middle of Rio, where he began making music with the people in the favela, playing on plates, beer cans, refrigerators, whatever was around, simplicity, symptomatic of the aesthetic here, you take what you can find, rhythm being foremost, not melody, and by 1936 he'd created and collected over three hundred samba songs, but, and this was the point of his whole argument: there was no contradiction in this, merely different genres weaving in and out of one another, and then Afonso chimed in to mention how bossa was influenced by jazz, and I told them that we, in Sweden, and perhaps in the rest of Europe, would like to think it was more

black or white

either/or

at which point they both piped up to say that it's nearly always both one and the other

here in Brazil, and from there it wasn't far to who they really are, and they both smiled and said in unison,

We're mongrels (viralatas) here,

all mixed race, everything's always intermingled, and then Afonso told us that he was descended from an Englishman, George John Dodsworth, who left his home shores long ago, probably on account of having done something stupid in England, some trouble he had to flee, and once here he met a black woman, Maria Leocadia, and thus their family line came into being. Mongrels, Karl Ove. And when people like Feital and Afonso say so, they say it with pride.

But what about this 'cloud', you're asking yourself? When we arrived at Politheama, Buarque's football pitch, and Afonso parked the car, I told them about the dream you and I had of a final between Brazil and Argentina. They both visibly tensed, and for the first time I saw something in their faces resembling deep anxiety, not of a sporting nature, but with regard to the situation which could arise in Rio on Sunday in the case of a possible Argentinian victory, and it was then I realised how naïve I'd been. The World Cup has been fantastic, even from the general public's point of view, but they told me that there are 90,000 Argentinians living in Rio and if they, together with the travelling support, were to celebrate victory in what was seen as too provocative a manner – which Afonso assumed they would – then 'os dos morros descer' (the people from the mountains, the favelas, would descend on the city), and things may turn nasty. Really nasty, he said. And then, Karl Ove, we'd find ourselves in a situation where simulation would develop into something real, and as I tried picturing it, I understood Afonso and Feital's concern, and perhaps the jeers and contempt from the 1920s and 30s would again be heard in the mouths of the white 'European' Argentinians mocking 'los macacos', the monkeys, as the Brazilian national team was called when they went to Buenos Aires and were pelted with hard pears and bananas.

But we haven't got to that. Not yet. And today I'm heading off to Campo Grande, to my oldest friend in Rio, the poet Reynaldo Valinho Alvarez, who I first became acquainted with in the early 1990s.

Reynaldo was among the 221,000 crowd at the Maracanã on 16 July 1950, and the silence on leaving the stadium and walking to the bus taking him home to Lapa, he's told me, was not of this world. You could hear the leaves rustling on the ground, and on the drive home you could have heard a pin drop, so I'm saying a silent prayer, Karl Ove, that I don't experience a similar episode with him in Campo Grande today.

Got your meandering letter just a while ago. Went out and read it at a newly opened restaurant nearby. Ate a bloody filet mignon with peas and palm hearts in butter, along with a couple of small, dark, slightly sweet beers. Liked the dreamy, melancholy odyssey you depicted, the hotel rooms, obituaries, the 'contextless' bookshop in east Germany, the encounters with people you know you'll never see again.

I found the part about the USA slightly alarming, and it made me think of how I act as an 'intellectual': I didn't want to take in the information about the decline in that part of the world, about becoming an author as a planned career path, for example, or the impending death of literature in favour of the visual image, and I think it has to do with the fact that I'm a profoundly optimistic person (I react instinctively to all those declarations you make, bloody hell, Karl Ovaldo!, about 'having missed the bus' and 'it's too late', and you not yet fifty with every opportunity to do things, not only quit smoking but start training with Glemminge-bro's reserves, where you'd have no problem fitting in, I'm sure of that, but to do whatever you want), and at the moment I want to safeguard my positivity, the world is improving, the Third World can't be said to exist any more when Angola is giving economic support to Portugal, when there are iPads and Wi-Fi in Dona Marta, and then you come along with, that's all well and good but culturally things are going backwards.

I don't know if that's the case but thought your USA report made for uncomfortable reading.

With reference to France v. Germany, no! It was a tactical knockout by Löw, I already wrote that. Daring to push high up the pitch in that heat caused the French to lose their rhythm. A stroke of genius which, as I said, would probably have been to their detriment had there been a need for extra time. What I took exception to was the word 'outclassed', Germany v. Saudi Arabia 8–0 in 2002 was an example of a team being outclassed, the second half of Holland v. Spain in this tournament was another example; 1–0 with two or three huge chances for La France never means a team is 'outclassed', not unless you want to divest the word of all meaning, but I think I know what you're getting at: the Germans controlled pretty much the entire game, and that, Karl Ove, I'm willing to agree with, as well as you being correct in that I watched the match with 'karma' and justice for 1982 foremost in my mind. Absolument!

As regards doing what's appropriate and efficient, the spectacular and the prosaic aren't at odds with one another, Suárez's goal, like van Persie's and Rodríguez's, these were all born under the little star of expediency, what was spectacular about van Persie's was his body, flying horizontally through the air, and in Rodríguez's case, the in-off-the-post syndrome, the chest control, his torso leaned slightly back, which put a spin on the ball, the turn, the volley, all logical, all in one movement, natural enough if he wants to score there and then, a thing of beauty, of course, but it's the off-the-post element that elevates it to the spectacular.

So there is no real contradiction, only in an aesthetic sense. And that windmill you're tilting at is long gone from football, and the boys and girls who want to be Garrincha, Nacka Skoglund or George Best are now already being singled out and dissuaded at junior level. Everything for the team, everything in the service of being efficient is the paradigm that has applied for a long time, players who pull the defender every which way because it is fun, as Garrincha did, don't exist any more, players like Nacka, who would chat to the spectators or smile to them and laugh, don't exist any more, players like Leônidas da Silva, the Black Diamond, who could pull down his shorts and expose his rear to the crowd, don't exist any more. Everything is done to serve expediency, everything Pelé did was, everything Maradona did was, all Messi does is, and as Maradona reaches the end of that fantastic dribble and was one on one with Shilton, he finishes it with the outside of his foot precisely because it was the only thing possible in the situation. (And now, of course, while I give this little sermon, an example of the opposite comes to mind: 1) Some of Shaqiri's dribbles were the only instances in this World Cup I've witnessed that could be termed non-expedient, Griezmann's exquisite nutmeg while running at full speed adheres to the same aforementioned rule, and should someone, contrary to expectation, perform an overhead kick during this World Cup – of the sort Leônidas da Silva did customarily and for the fun of it – then that too would in all likelihood be to serve a purpose. While we're on the subject, Zlatan's scissors kick against England was incidentally in the same vein, it was the only thing he could do in that situation if he wanted to score, so the distinction between moral and non-moral players isn't to be found there, it takes place on other levels (for or against the collective, hence the immorality of Ronaldo when at a press conference he said that Portugal have a pretty average team ...), not in what you describe, because what you're talking about depends on which half of the pitch you find yourself, in attack or defence, 2) the quarter-final of the 1990 World Cup in Naples between Cameroon and England, Cameroon led with approximately ten minutes remaining, when Omam Biyik was one on one with Shilton, and what did he do, our leggy friend Omam, yes, instead of going around Shilton, which he could easily have done, he had the speed, he tried to hammer it past him – and failed, he chose the spectacular rather than what was expedient, and a few minutes later Lineker, an over-expedient player, equalised and England won in extra time, and Africa have yet to make the semi-finals of the World Cup, why? You can only speculate, but in Biyik's case I think it was about choosing risk and dancing on the edge ahead of going for the safer option, something I think every person can recognise in their own lives, but which I think, in Biyik's case went deeper and was more culturally conditioned.)

That, Karl Ove, was an immoral act. Not scoring from an overhead kick when it's the only thing you can do because the goalie has all the other angles covered.

Best wishes,
Fredrik

Glemmingebro, 8 July

Dear Fredrik,

The pope being Argentinian, which I had completely forgotten, changes a lot of my arguments, indeed it makes some of them untenable; on the other hand, the previous pope was German, so perhaps we shouldn't place too much importance on this. But when you describe the pope and the cardinals watching football on TV I react with a strong sense that this is wrong. TV and the pope don't belong together, two unequal worlds collide. Do not imagine I am joking, I mean this. Not rationally, but emotionally: the form of TV and all it represents are irreconcilable with the form of the pope and all it represents. I think this is interesting, I mean that such a strong emotion can spring up – don't get me wrong, I have no axe to grind here, the pope has to be allowed to do what he wants – it is about what religion is, what it means to believe in God and, in that event, what the human relationship with the divine is – because it has to signify something. What I often think, walking around here, back and forth between the houses, day in, day out, is that being human is so small, so random, so improvised, so arbitrary, somehow hastily assembled, because we cut ourselves on tin cans as we open them, we forget where we leave our car key and can spend a whole morning looking for it, we miss the bus, sometimes we run after it banging on the door while the driver sits inside in the warm (it happens mostly in winter) shaking his head, probably gloating. Children miss their footing on the trampoline, hit themselves in the face on the iron frame and break a tooth. We spill coffee on the computer keyboard, we say stupid things to people we don't like and regret it for days afterwards, we forget the oven plate is on and boil the pan dry, we put too much salt in our food so that it is nigh on impossible to eat, we cut our hands as we tie up a rose bush blown over in the winter storms or we notice too late that the weed we are pulling up is a nettle. This is only a tiny selection of all the foolishness that happens everywhere every single day. We can raise it a notch and think about all the foolishness that results in a fatality – the man wearing a mummy troll outfit who was knocked down by a car and died, people who fall and hit their heads on the edge of the bath and die, in winter people who walk onto the smooth coastal rocks to see the enormous waves and are swept into the sea and drown. People who saw down trees and are killed under the weight. The tractors that turn over and crush the driver. People who go to sleep drunk and suffocate on their own vomit. People who have a hand in water and are holding some kind of electrical apparatus. People who stumble down cellar stairs and die. Yes, you know where I am going. The world is material, it consists of more or less hard surfaces, with more or less jagged edges, and we humans move around and never have complete control of our actions, unforeseen accidents happen all the time, some with a fatal outcome. Not to mention all the misunderstandings that arise and all the vague and downright incorrect knowledge people possess. That is how it is. That is our world. Religion, in this light, is a fantastic discovery, the greatest in the history of mankind, because there we erect a magnificent sky above all this smallness and misery, and then we say this is the real, the essential and the true existence or reality. There, in this perfect space, are the perfect creatures, the holy beings, the divine principles. We believe this or we don't believe this. But whatever our attitude, churches were built, holy places, in other words, a kind of holy zone in the midst of trivial reality. There everything was different. The priests' attire magnificent, you didn't see the like elsewhere. The songs and the music magnificent. The language, the invocation or the interpretation of God magnificent, and as far away from reality as you could get. The incense magnificent. The lights magnificent. No weapons. No arguing. No loud voices. No stumbling. No making of food. Only devotion, solemnity. It was in these holy edifices that human life was made solemn, through the rituals of baptism, marriage and burial. It didn't matter whether the man had fallen into the slurry pit and drowned in excreta, when he was buried it was with dignity, piety, solemnity, his life was sacred, our lives were sacred, humanity was immense, not small. All this was based on something being demonstrated in a particular place everyone attended at particular times. Whether the priest wanked over the bathroom sink or had worms and pulled down his trousers to scratch his arse as soon as he was alone in a room made no difference, because no one saw. Some probably thought when the priest was giving a sermon that he shits too, but it wasn't said aloud, it wasn't seen and wasn't present in the holiness, wasn't a part of it. The technology we have now means that human foolishness, which previously was private and was seen by one or two or maybe twenty people who happened to be there, and human smallness, which was bound by time and place, have become boundless, are everywhere, and what has been lost, and no one wants back, is grandness and dignity. The pope has probably watched TV since the 50s, and enjoyed it, but when he does so openly, not covertly, in the full glare of publicity, his picture is disseminated by press agencies and printed in newspapers and shown on webpages all over the world, and there is no longer any pope, he is no longer a representative of the divine on earth, everything has got mixed up and holiness has dissolved into all the constituent parts of the small and the foolish. The fact that no one reacts, or at least very few, to this is due to there being other places, other zones which have taken over the role the church used to have, a sky beneath whose vaults human life has become something big.

As yesterday I was foolish enough to compare football to art, today I will be even more foolish and compare football and religion. Because on a football pitch, like the one we will see in exactly forty-nine minutes, when Brazil and Germany kick off, almost everything from human life has been removed, what is left are rules, rituals and predetermined patterns of behaviour, where as good as all doubt and ambivalence have been erased: when a goal is scored that is all that exists, the goal-scorer's happiness is total, he screams as loudly as he can and wheels away with his arms in the air while all his teammates are shouting and running after him. When do you see such elation in real life? Not even when a child is born do you see such comprehensive and systematic unalloyed joy. Football is a theatre, a place where the normal world has no place, it is a zone of concentrated meaning. If someone in the street threw a melon in the air, jumped up backwards and kicked it, upside down in the air, like Zlatan did against England, no one would admire the acrobatics, no one would acclaim the acrobat or appreciate the performance, because it was worthless. What a footballer can do has value only on the field, not outside. Actually football matches are worthless, of course, in the same way that pouring water onto a child's head is actually worthless. It has value because it takes place in a resticted area where we say that such actions have value. The difference, one might object, is that acts and rituals in church do in fact have a value whereas acts in football stadiums do not. They have only a kind of pseudo-value, a substitute for fighting, war, in other words entertainment. But the structure is the same, and that was what became so clear when the pope was watching football on TV as you described, Fredrik. Accordingly I will close with a prayer:

> Dear God,
> Let Brazil win against Germany tonight,
> May the match be good, may the match be even,
> You can let Germany lead,
> But don't let them win!
> Let Brazil win so that they reach the final,
> Let them meet Argentina there
> And let Argentina win the cup.
> For thine is the kingdom,
> And the power, and the glory, for ever,
> Amen.

All the best,
Karlos Blasfémios Días

Dear Fredrik,

The game has just finished. Brazil lost 7–1. In a semi-final with
home advantage. If I were twelve now, I would be weeping. One
of the hardest things to witness is loss of face, it is sad, shaming,
you want to look away. I wonder how it is for you now, among
your Brazilian friends, wonder what people are saying and doing
and what it was like to see the match there. We watched it in the
living room, Linda and I with our friends Fredrik and Karin, and
their son Olle. Brazil applied the pressure in the first five minutes, but made several mistakes, lost the ball going forward, and
then Germany scored, it wasn't an opportunity, it was a corner,
and Müller was standing unmarked five metres from the goal as
Luiz charged towards him in vain: the ball landed at his feet:
1–0. It is scarcely possible to make a bigger defensive error, and
they made it in the opening of the most important game in
Brazilian football for sixty years. Only six minutes had gone,
so all the time in the world for Brazil to equalise. We saw in
the quarter-final what Germany can do with such a lead, so it
wouldn't be easy, but it wasn't impossible. However, Brazil completely lost their grip, suddenly their desire was so strong that
they forgot everything they knew about team organisation,
everything to do with tactics, to do with guile and a cool head, they
had only the desire and attacked one on one; Luiz wanted to
win the match on his own, so he moved forward or to the flanks,
and when the Germans broke, there was no one there to mark

them, only poor Dante and Maicon, and Marcel on the turn, more and more outplayed and helpless as time went on, in the end they were running around the Germans like headless chickens. No formation, not even the defensive midfield held to meet the Germans, they weren't working together, they were all desire. It wasn't panic, it was just too much desire, hot heads, too little structure and no collective unit. And it was striking, as this was precisely the impression the team made – you saw them enter the field, in a line with their hands on each other's shoulder, like one single organism. They held Neymar's shirt during the national anthem. And the national anthem: solidarity, unity, brotherhood, collective. While the Germans, who came in separately and have no visible emotional bond between them, I mean, they aren't as demonstrative as Brazil but turn out to be the real unit, playing for one another, keeping their positions and doing the job as per instructions.

After the game Bastian Schweinsteiger walking across the grass bare-chested with a Brazilian shirt slung casually over his shoulder and a broad grin on his face. The team in a line, arms around one another's shoulders, they bowed to the stadium, and it seemed indecent, as though celebrating a victory didn't belong here because this wasn't a victory but something else. Further away, Oscar couldn't stop crying, on Thiago's shoulder.

A collapse on this scale has never happened before at this level. But, watching, I thought it was strange it didn't happen more often. Why did Brazil lose 7–1 to Germany when Ghana didn't? Isn't Brazil better than Ghana? Ghana had a grip on Germany, they spread alarm through Germany's ranks, and, with a bit of luck, could have beaten them. And Ghana is an African team without Brazil's great championship experience. The difference is absolutely vital: Ghana knew Germany was the best team in the world, and they adapted their play accordingly. Keep your positions whatever happens, don't push forward with all you have, stay back, control, balance, there will always be a goal-scoring opportunity. Brazil never had this attitude. They never considered Germany a better team and it never occurred to them that the sole chance of winning was to lie in wait, deny their midfield space, keep it tight and be physical, run and run. Brazil thought they could dominate the game, outplay Germany, that was their whole game plan, and it was reinforced when they went behind, they wanted to attack, they would soon regain control, and that, my friend in Brazil, is known as hubris. Brazil was proud and, as in all tragedies, that was what leads to the protagonist's downfall.

The qualities I thought spoke in Brazil's favour – emotional intensity, religiosity, the almost insane will to win – I imagined this irrationality and unpredictability, along with enormous pressure, would unsettle the German side, they wouldn't be able to defend against this because their game is so rational and sensible. Seldom has anyone been so utterly wrong. That was what did for Brazil, and now we know for all time: in football reason trumps emotion in an absolutely devastating way.

The thing is, Brazil had too much at stake. They were playing for 200 million Brazilians, they were playing to restore the 1950 World Cup, they were playing for God, they were playing to show the world, they were playing for Neymar, whereas the Germans were only playing for themselves, this match, this team, this evening. They played for the next tackle, the next pass, the next counter-attack, the next corner. This situation reminds me of something Geir wrote about in his book *Baghdad Indigo*, about the peace-lovers who went to Baghdad wanting to stop the invasion with their own bodies, all of them had lofty ideals, they wanted to save the world, but when the bombs began to fall everything disintegrated and everyone, almost down to the last man, fled. The ideals were worthless, they couldn't be translated into action, they didn't create a bond between people, by which I mean horizontally – and horizontality, that is working together, acting together, interpersonal links – no, everything was vertical, going from the individual up to the abstract ideal, it was that – peace on earth – they acted upon, and it wasn't strong enough, it couldn't keep them there and they bolted. Whereas the US Marines, with whom Geir also spent some time, were an expression of the diametrically opposed attitude, they didn't fight for ideals, not for the fatherland nor against a dictatorship, but for their comrades, the soldier at their sides, and the bond, which isn't idealistic but in touch with reality, concrete, physical, held. All the time there are things to be done, and it is these things, one by one, each of them small, which hold them there and make them carry out whatever has to be carried out, and which, in the larger view, serve the collective. Of course it is a big jump to this evening's match, it was only football after all, not war, but I can't stop thinking about it, the difference in unity through word and deed and how the bonds that create action cannot be abstract or idealistic, they must be related to the situation, what is going on in the here and now.

This match will also make this World Cup one of the most memorable. The reigning world champions were knocked out after the opening rounds. The smaller nations matched the level of the bigger nations almost the whole way. And the host nation, the multiple holders of the world championship, lost 7–1 in the semi-final. It was a sensation, but not a game I like to dwell on, such as the already much-mentioned semi-final of 1982 between France and West Germany, that one had everything a football match can have, and the difference is of course that it was a contest between two well-matched opponents, the more evenly matched teams are, the better the game, is surely a kind of principle, while what we saw this evening was a lamb to the slaughter, cold steel held to its throat, the incision precise and pitiless in the face of the imminent suffering. It was Brazil against Germany.

I am looking forward to reading about your description of it, and what you think about it, Fredrik. Tonight it is Argentina v. Holland, and both teams are capable of upsetting Germany, as Ghana did, perhaps also of beating them, because even if Germany played their best game in this tournament so far, they won so well because the game followed a certain logic, a certain arc, not because they are – generally, I mean – so much better. And that is part of what makes football so fascinating, every match takes on a life of its own, as the cliché goes, and sometimes what has never happened before, happens. We can never know when it will, only that it will – in fifty years or tomorrow. Then Holland, a mediocre team with three stellar exceptions, can win, and Argentina, organic-cynical football with one genius, can win.

Knowing you as I do, Fredrik, I believe you think Germany should win after what happened yesterday, they are already the moral winners, as people say, of the World Cup, after their fantastic performance. However, I have misread your reactions countless times already this month. I have no idea what you think about this result.

I will write more later today, but I will have the children, and Anne, so it will be glimpses here and there, I imagine. Talk soon!

Karl Ove

Botafogo, 9 July

Dear Karl Ove,

There was a game of football played here yesterday. It was a semi-final in the World Cup between Germany and Brazil. Around midday I took a taxi over to see Denise, the daughter of the poet Reynaldo Valinho Alvarez, who has moved from Ipanema to Campo Grande, one of the largest suburbs in Rio, where together with his other daughter Ula he cares for his ailing wife, who suffers from Shy-Drager syndrome, a very serious form of Parkinson's. Denise drove. There were traffic jams the whole way. We talked about our children. About Denise's job. A slow but pleasant car journey. It seemed a lot of people were looking forward to this match. Many of them were dressed in Brazilian colours, and Denise herself was wearing a pretty yellow blouse. When we arrived in Campo Grande, I met my old friend Reynaldo, and it was a warm reunion. Then we – he, Ula, Denise and I – ate in a kitchen illuminated by a neon tube, a ready-made meal we heated in the microwave, then they wanted to watch the game, so we made our way into Maria José's bedroom-cum-sickroom, where she lay, looking lean and unable to communicate, but I was so happy to see her and gave her a big, long hug. The illness prevents her from speaking, which is terrible and also means she requires round-the-clock care, but I felt such warmth seeing her narrow eyes and the denim skirt and Brazilian top they had dressed her in, so beautiful, and so we sat beside her as the match kicked off, and when the Germans went into the lead,

I remember Reynaldo saying something to the effect that if Hitler could see this German team he'd commit suicide again, while Maria José lay there completely still, the drip bag, the dimly lit room, the stuffy air and Denise half-leaning back on a bed behind us, and my poet friend Reynaldo in a Neymar shirt with 10 on the back, so old and small, but youthful all the same, and one of them is called Dante but he looks like Jimi Hendrix, Denise says, laughing, before remarking that Fred looks like he's perched on the edge of an armchair waiting for the ball, and when the other team makes it 2–0, Maria José begins to cough and a nurse comes running in, and as they increase their lead to 3–0, the respirator is connected up, and then the ball goes into the Brazilian net again, and again, and then it's half-time and Ula brings me a caipirinha, and it goes down well, and apparently it's 5–0 now, prompting Reynaldo to say that in the 1938 World Cup in France, a tournament he remembers since he was born in 1931, Brazil beat Poland 6–5 in Strasbourg, but it was a different type of game, both teams scoring freely, one after another, so it could be hard for Brazil to turn this around in the second half, and Denise calls Scolari porquería, dirt, and apparently Fred is only in the team because he's dating Scolari's daughter or some-thing, how can that be right, she says, and then in the second half they, and I, sitting with my writing pad making notes, start to laugh and talk about other things, and as the sixth German goal goes in, the nurse turns the respirator up to maximum, and I then ask Reynaldo if this could lead to social unrest in Brazil, I hope so, he replies – him, my friend, usually the epitome of calm, diplomacy and level-headedness! – and it seems like the Brazil-ians are having problems finding each other with the ball, while the Germans are pinging it around as though it were on a string, is Hulk on the pitch, I wonder aloud, nobody knows, is Oscar still on or has he been substituted, no one appears to know that either, and Reynaldo has lived through sixteen World Cups, but has never seen anything like this, and then César and Luiz cry when they're being interviewed afterwards and are trying to explain what's happened, while Scolari, with his harsh gaucho features, says it was down to some minor technicalities, and I send Afonso in Botafogo a text, saying Scolari should be exiled to St Helena, where the English sent Napoleon after Waterloo, and Afonso responds saying the players ought to be sent to Afghanistan, and after the game there's an unexpected sense of cheerfulness in the house, and the kitchen, and Ula says it's hard to be Brazilian because there are always so many emotions involved, it's all up and down and here and there, how are you supposed to deal with everything, she says, and then the rain lashes down, a real downpour, the tears of 200 million people, I reflect, and Denise and I need to get back to Rio, and it's so dark and quiet everywhere, the whole of Campo Grande seems like it's been evacuated, and I spot a restaurant that's open but empty of customers, hundreds of vacant seats, and the rain pours, and at times Denise has problems keeping the car on the road and everywhere we pass is dark and quiet, the road a channel of darkness, silence and rain, and I say something about the Brazilian team being a vergonha, a disgrace, and she smiles and laughs and I notice her yellow blouse and her breasts and Marianne is so far away, oh dear, and fantasies emerge from the darkness, the longing to get away, into a woman's arms to forget this nightmare of a night, and I fight the thoughts, and as we near Recreio and Barra, she puts on samba music and begins to sing along to lyrics about, I don't know what, finding it hard to believe what's happened, and as we enter Rio, a city I like a lot, a city named after a river, which my friend Reynaldo has written many a fine poem about, it's so wet and dark, and in the bars only a few people are to be seen, and as Denise drops me off on Rua Assunção, we smile

and laugh the way you do after seeing something you have difficulty believing was real, and then I sit down and write this,
and a half an hour later I hear the key in the door and in walks
my bearded friend, my host, with a rueful look, after having
been at his mother's place and watched the match together with
her and one of his sisters, and it's eleven at night and he wonders
if I want to go for a beer, and I answer no, I had four caipirinhas and two beers at Reynaldo's in Campo Grande and need to
write a letter to that Norwegian, you know, and then he disappears alone into the darkness, and I continue to write, but after
about thirty minutes I think, Jesus, I have to to be there with
him, and turn off the laptop and go out into the night, and after
a while we're both propping up a bar in the middle of Rio,
engaged in no-frills drinking, straight cachaça and beer chasers.
Then they pull the shutters down and we wander slowly home to
Rua Assunção 174, along the footpath in the darkness, take a
right in towards the house, the beautiful red house, and boa
noite, Afonso, and boa noite, Frederico and Boa noite, Brazil.

Glemmingebro, 9 July

Dear Fredrik,

Quite often I wonder if there is something wrong with me. I can watch a game on TV, get sucked in and be absolutely spellbound, filled with the excitement and tension of the game, and then when I read a newspaper article about the match the following day, it says it was boring, nothing happened, a lousy game of football, nothing more. Yesterday it happened again. I watched Argentina v. Holland, and it was a fantastic contest because it was so even, both sides played almost perfect defensive games, neutralised each other's forwards for the whole ninety minutes, tried to lever the defence open, to penetrate, to score, and it could have happened. At any moment, but it didn't. After 120 minutes it was still 0–0. And we are talking notorious goal-scorers here, who can rip open a defence, such as Messi, Robben and van Persie. They failed, they neither scored goals nor opened defences, the match was trench warfare, a stalemate. One goal in a match, there is an imbalance which has to be redressed, and as soon as it is, the match picks up speed, opens, then it becomes what people call 'entertaining'. The other semi-final, Brazil v. Germany, had eight goals, some beautiful, one of them spectacular (Schürrle brings the ball down and fires it into the corner), and it must have been one of the most 'entertaining' matches ever, but for me Argentina v. Holland was a much better game, it was so full of tension, so full of missed opportunities, and in it was the 'destructive' element, stopping and spoiling, versus the constructive, creating and developing, negative versus positive, death versus life. Oh, deny life any space! Oh, try to penetrate death and cheat it! This is the game for me, this is football. A player like Messi, who comes into his own in games like these, in my opinion, attempting the impossible and doing what can't be done. Why? Because it increases the value of the magic exponentially. Imagine if he had managed to wriggle past the four Dutch players he was surrounded by whenever he received the ball, burst through, send the keeper the wrong way and make it 1–0! It would have been a magnificent feat, the goal would have emblazoned World Cup history. But, and this is the point, it is just as magnificent when it doesn't happen. When he gets bogged down. When he is stopped, time after time, and in the end he sulks. That can happen, we hope it will happen, but it doesn't. That is why the magic is magical because it is impossible. To score seven goals in a semi-final, just rolling them in because there is no resistance, that isn't magic from a football perspective, but it is magic from a human perspective, it is a tragedy, and it unfolded before our eyes, in Brazil, with Brazil, and it enriched this World Cup, it was an unforgettable match, I will always remember it. But viewed as a football game, Argentina v. Holland was better by light years. And it is equally as unique as Germany v. Brazil because, as far as I know, it was the first semi-final in history to finish 0–0. That is, it finished 4–2 on penalties of course, to Argentina.

So it will be a different final from the one we had hoped for, not Brazil v. Argentina but Germany v. Argentina, and there can be no doubt that Germany are the overwhelming favourites. This will be hugely interesting because Argentina's strength in this tournament has been their man-to-man marking. Zabaleta, Demichelis, Garay and Rocco have proved to be extremely difficult to get past, and they are quick to recover and tackle or block a shot if someone does. Argentina have let in three goals in the whole competition, and yesterday Holland didn't have a single shot on target. Not one! Demichelis, so criticised this season at Manchester City, was absolutely outstanding. But Argentina can expect to encounter a combination game, not forwards who dribble past, but an utterly brilliant midfield combining, and in every conceivable way. This is probably the only way to score against this Argentinian side. Yesterday their midfield was good too, they have raised the bar over recent games, after Gigo was replaced by Biglia. Mascherano was the best player on the pitch, in a different league. When he was injured, after a clash of heads with a Dutch player, and staggered around for some seconds, apparently losing consciousness, he seemed to crumple and would have sunk to the ground like a sack some metres away if another Dutch player hadn't grabbed him, then I was sure: first, he would be substituted and, second, Argentina would lose. But he struggled to his feet, ran back out onto the field, presumably still dizzy and groggy, because he hit a couple of rare stray passes before he was back to his old self. If, Fredrik, Brazil had had Mascherano and Zabaleta they would never have collapsed against Germany. But, and it is a big but, their attack was not impressive yesterday. Of course, it was like that because they played with such caution, even when Lavezzi, who was really good in the first half, wriggled past on the right flank, it happened at least three times, only Higuaín followed and maximum one other player, not in numbers, and they were never really dangerous. But with a quarter of an hour left they changed the attack, it was a risk, Agüero came on, but nothing happened, nothing opened up. If Di María had played it would have been a different matter, he has the desire and the ability to break through and would have troubled Holland much more as Messi constantly tied up so many players.

But they won!

They are in the final!

There is so much I'd like to say about subjects you have brought up in your letters over the last few days, and I will do that tonight after everyone has gone to bed. We still have guests here, they have a poor host in me, and today they are going to look after our children, take them to an amusement park while a nanny I have hired will keep an eye on Anne, I have an urgent manuscript to see to, the writer has sent me several emails, and they are getting less and less polite, shorter and shorter, he wants an answer, that is easy to understand, so I'd better get down to reading it and then write to him. This afternoon the girls have a performance, I will drive them there and back, and either Linda or I will clean up afterwards and perhaps also sit in the kiosk – we have two jobs and do one each – and the deadline is approaching for my fate essay, which I have neglected over recent weeks, hoping when I resumed it would all be crystal clear.

France, such an uplifting side, fell to Germany by allowing itself to be controlled, Brazil fell to its own failings, one has to say, by underestimating the Germans and overestimating itself, Portugal was found out by them and crushed: in this World Cup Germany have won in so many different ways and are bound to have a plan for how they are going to beat Argentina. But this is football, and even if Germany are obviously the better team, it is still open: what if Messi has one of his moments of genius after two minutes and Argentina lead 1–0?

All the best,
Karl Ove

Botafogo, 10 July

Congratulations, Karl Ove!

Yesterday I woke up early, as though stirred from sleep by the tremendous silence and sorrow, as though the misery of millions of people had condensed the atmosphere and roused me extra-early, just so I could experience the hush. There wasn't a sound to be heard, even though it was a 'normal' weekday. Not a dog, not a child, nothing, nada. Then, all of a sudden, the silence is shattered by the noise of an argument between a man and woman next door. A despairing male voice shouting something about cinco anos, five years, and I figure the row will escalate and really take off, but after twenty seconds or so it ebbs away and is swallowed up by the silence that has inundated Botafogo like an ocean.

Then, a little later, around eight, I take a walk down to the newsagent's, the people I pass wearing empty expressions, eyes downcast, and there's something else that I can't put my finger on at first, only sense, before I realise that all the yellow from yesterday is gone, all the signs and bunting in the colours of Brazil are no longer to be seen, everything now is in dun and neutral colours, not unlike at home in chromophobic Sweden, but then I hear the noise of a jackhammer – people at work! – and catch sight of a street cleaner sweeping up a pile of leaves, a taxi moving at full speed, a bus thundering inexorably on, and so the great machinery has restarted, and this excruciating day, a day no Brazilian wants to start, live through, be forced to be a part of, now lies rolled out in front of them, and there's no way back, all they can do is step out into this warmth, this sunshine and stand face to face with that bizarre, historic defeat, try to hold their heads high, go to work and ignore the temptation to throw themselves in front of the metro, to take that extra stride off the pavement in front of the bus, and arriving at the newsagent's I see the newspaper placards with the headlines splashed in bold lettering: VERGONHA (disgrace) VEXAME (outrage) HUMIL-HAÇÃO (humiliation) VÁ PRO INFERNO VOCÊ, FELIPÃO (Go to Hell, Felipão!) and in *Extra*, a Rio paper, there's a huge photograph on the front page with the goalie Moacyr Barbosa face down and Ghiggia's shot creeping in at the post in the 1950 final, with the headline CONGRATULATIONS, directed towards the Brazilian players in that match (most of them are dead now, but just to illustrate how long the pain of defeat from that game lasted. I can tell you that I was at the Maracanã in 2000, a few days after Barbosa passed away, and saw a banner on the far side of the pitch which read, Barbosa, it wasn't your fault! – fifty years after the actual match, and when, in 2001, I interviewed Zizinho, the captain of that team, he was still angry and bitter at the polit-icians who'd ruined the squad's build-up to the game, over half a century earlier! Life became a real hell for a lot of the players on that team, and I can easily picture many of the current squad having to deal with something similar, not least when you com-pare the scorelines, losing by one goal in an evenly contested World Cup final as opposed to behaving like a bewildered youth team in a World Cup semi-final and being beaten 7–1, and I can only imagine many of them are relieved today that they play their club football overseas, and I wouldn't swap places with Fred, no matter how much he earns at Fluminense here in Rio, his journey through hell has only just begun and might not end, if the Barbosa rule holds true, until he dies, in let's say, fifty or sixty years' time, so cruel can football be here). The players from 1950 can quit the pillory of shame they've been tied to since then, because now the players from yesterday will be bound to it, for the humiliation they've subjected the Brazilian people to, which defies, according to all the newspapers – every one! – all description, and in Brazil's biggest sporting daily, *Lance*, the players' average score for their performance is an incomprehensible 1.8 (Felipão 0.7) out of 10, a first in the history of the newspaper. A score of around 3.0 is usually the worst, and only ever awarded in the case of a downright appalling performance.

Thought your match analysis was brilliant and don't have much to add, except maybe to further emphasise the psychological pressure, which I was fearful of prior to the tournament, that this young team wouldn't have the mental strength to bear the expectation of 190 million people, and so it turned out, there was no leader on the pitch, and what helped them to victory over Colombia, and came to such beautiful expression in Luiz's face, boomeranged after the score went to 3–0, and hit each of them in turn. A historic meltdown on every level – the greatest champions, the ones we all immediately associate with a love of football, the host nation – where Sweden's defeat in 1958, with a final score of 2–5, now means 'we' can leave our pillory and make way for Brazil. Scolari had built a house of cards around Neymar, and when he was injured it collapsed, despite, as you write, Germany not being impossible to stop, both Ghana and Algeria had the better of them at times, but perhaps yesterday's loss has uncovered a deeper truth about Brazilian football: a lack of humility. The Germans have built a fantastic team and started from the ground up (a focus on young players with immigrant backgrounds) since change, both social and sporting, was what was intended. Brazil put its trust in fossils like Parreira and

Scolari, who have both won the World Cup previously with a similar football philosophy, solidity at the back (defence first) and then counter-attacks thereafter. It worked in the USA in 1994, it paid off in Japan/South Korea in 2002, but now it was almost comical to see how far behind Brazilian football has fallen, and I can name eight or nine teams off the top of my head who played more attractive football in this World Cup (Colombia, Belgium, France, Ghana, Chile, Mexico, Germany, Holland and perhaps Argentina). The CBF, the Brazilian Football Confederation, made it their priority to win the World Cup at any cost and gambled everything on what they regarded as a safe bet, Scolari/Parreira. In return, they got, to put it bluntly, shit football that is anathema to very many Brazilians, and fortunately, you'd have to add, was not capable of winning the World Cup.

Argentina–Holland? A wrestling match between two of the greats, a contest in which they grappled in a clinch for about ten or fifteen minutes, before they seemed to agree to back away, lick their wounds and recover their strength, a Karl Ove match, I thought, he loves these physical contests, this digging and sniffing around, this wild-boar football, where they probe for holes in thick defensive walls and where the play never really gets going, never turns into two teams storming up and down the pitch switching attack and defence, but instead gets bogged down in a kind of trench warfare in the middle, each team searching for fresh movement, fresh cracks for Robben or Messi to exploit. Not my type of football, Karl Ove, but seeing as we're corresponding with one another, and I'm trying to understand your way of thinking and your perspectives on football, I attempted to look at it from your point of view and suddenly saw, for example, the greatness of a Mascherano, and I have in fact a favourite here that I don't need your help to like, Lavezzi, who for me was

Argentina's greatest asset in the first half, although I nodded off at the start of the second! I had difficulty staying awake and following the changes in movement, and the whole time I feared Robben would slip through and settle it, at the same time as I was waiting for some magic from Messi, with whom my fascination only increases as this World Cup goes on, and the difference between him and Maradona was so obvious yesterday, Diego decided games like this on his own (the quarter-final against Brazil in Florence in 1990, his change of direction, break from the middle, ending in the pass to Caniggia), Messi doesn't do that, isn't at that level, doesn't have that power, but should he settle the final by a fortunate stroke of genius, he'll be up there, in footballing Valhalla, among the greats. I can sometimes sit watching him, just him, in a Barcelona or Argentina shirt, when the ball is elsewhere and I ought really to be following the game, but I like to look at him walking around the pitch during a match that may be a real back and forth thriller, an intense affair, it satisfies my deep need for otherness, as well as which I enjoy the sight of his face, that slightly absent, cold, pre-occupied look – what the hell is he thinking about? That's what I wonder.

One of the last, but certainly not the least, pieces of action in that game was Mascherano's block in the dying seconds. Absolutely outstanding, he's behind Robben, the fastest player in the world, who has the ball at his feet, yet Mascherano succeeds in a way that defies all physical and physiological laws, in stretching out a toe in the last hundredth of a second, and if Argentina become world champions, it was that moment that will have proved decisive, because the ball would have gone in otherwise, and that brings us to the intrinsic injustice in all judgement of football: that tackle will be forgotten, and if Messi seals victory in the final with a lovely, mazy run, that's what will be talked about, not what laid the groundwork for it, sadly.

Once again, congratulations, Karl Ove!

Best wishes,
Fredrik

PS Any defenders in this tournament that you've taken a shine to, anyone you wish you could be, if you could swap body, age and nationality?

Glemmingebro, 10 July

Dear Fredrik,

I love this World Cup, the way it has developed. It was good to read about how you tried to give yesterday's game a chance, assuming as you did, correctly, it was one after my heart. How you tried to see what I was seeing at the same time across the Atlantic. I was reminded of the earlier exchange we had, about energy and efficiency, where I wrote about Protestant and Catholic football – and you said all the examples I gave were about efficiency – when Maradona slid past Shilton it was because it was the only way it could be done. And that is right. But efficiency is relative: it wouldn't have occurred to anyone else to dribble from the midfield, past England player after England player, all the way to the goal, glide past the keeper and put the ball in the net. Yes, I agree, every single feint and glide are what it takes to beat an opponent, that is efficiency at the highest level, but he doesn't do it because it is efficient. Had he been thinking of efficiency, I mean, as a term or concept, as was the case with, in fact especially with, Drillo – analysing the statistics of every game so that you know when and how goal chances appear and then drawing up a game plan based on them (for Drillo it was counter-attacks, so-called breakdowns, when the opposing side loses the ball: full speed ahead. It means that the most dangerous moment for a team is when they have possession because they can lose it, the team is out of kilter, and the counter-attack follows. Better therefore, in Drillo's reasoning, to hit a long cross. Instead of a small, nippy, dribbling winger, Drillo put in the team's tallest player. He nodded down the cross, and the ball was suddenly loose close to the opposition goal, and there was a chance of a shot, while at your own end there was no threat. Drillo was an extremely attack-minded coach – that hasn't come across in Sweden – he hated back passes and side passes, the ball had to go forward because that was where the goal was. The reason for zealous defensive work, with first a number 5 on the line, then a number 4 on the line, was of course to prevent goals – which was efficient, Norway was an extremely difficult opponent to score against – but also to regain possession and counter-attack. Against England at Ullevaal, I remember, the ball was in the net after a three-man counter-attack, bang, bang, bang, goal. From way back in our own half. Drillo probably enjoyed Chile and Mexico, and Holland. The principle of holding on to the ball, which is how Spain won the last World Cup, requires exceptionally good players, something Norway has never had. The only way to make progress was by nurturing efficient play in this way) – in this light, seeing efficiency in this way, isn't this what Maradona was doing? It couldn't be planned, couldn't be drummed in, it sprang into life there and then, in Maradona's head, and the route to goal he chose was the most difficult imaginable. It is the same with Messi, he keeps trying all the time, he goes to where the action is at its thickest and most impossible. Incidentally, I am in total agreement with your comparison of the two, Messi is streets away from Maradona – there is something monotonous about his game (as there is about Robben's), it is the same runs and dribbles all the time, you recognise them, while Maradona was the complete player in a different way and a better director of play than Messi. My God though, Messi is not bad!

The best defenders in the tournament? Ones I have taken a

shine to? You are forcing me onto the defensive again! Yesterday, I think Demichelis of Argentina was brilliant. Made no mistakes, won all the duels, van Persie was kept in check by him and Garay. On the other hand, Vlaar played the game of his life, he was incredible, but then there is that aura thing again, and the type of player – he is more of a slugger. The Argentinians are also supple, elegant, good on the ball, and, as I can choose freely, they are my choice.

It has been a stressful day today. First of all, I wrote the letter about the Argentina game, then I had to edit the article that is going to press on Saturday. After the Brazil game *Dagens Nyheter* sent me an email with STOP in the title, saying it would be a dereliction of duty to publish a letter about the Brazil World Cup in which there is no mention of their team's dramatic collapse, so one section will have to be cut and something new added. Had to pick up Linda from the station at three, was almost there when she phoned to say she would be half an hour late, and that was no good because I had to drive the girls to the theatre for half past, so I turned, dropped in on our guests and asked if they could look after Anne for an hour, they could, and then I drove to Brantevik, dropped off the girls, went back home, took Anne, who slept for an hour, then I started on this letter, and when she woke we stayed together in her room for two hours. She is so happy, today she lay laughing for probably ten minutes, I leaned forward, letting my hair hang over her face, she grabbed it with her small hands and I lifted my head until her grip loosened. Linda, John and our guests were at the theatre, they came home at around ten, by then Anne had fallen asleep. So here I am again, sitting in this exceptionally messy study, thick with smoke and a faint smell of acrid, rotting food, while the others are asleep, writing letters, the night dense outside. It felt like August in town, both because of the darkness, which is drawing in earlier every evening, and something in the air – it can't be autumn, can it? The summer has hardly begun!

But it fits. Something will soon be over. The summer, the letters to and from you, the 2014 football World Cup in Brazil.

Thirty-two teams were reduced to sixteen, sixteen to eight, eight to four, and four to two. Argentina haven't played the best football, haven't scored the most attractive goals or the most, but they have succeeded in making it through to meet Germany, who, on the other hand, have played the best football and have scored the most goals, if not the most attractive, then at least many attractive goals.

This fits too. The team with the majestic football meets the team limping through. And it is important that there is one team from South America and one from Europe.

Now there are probably a thousand tiny threads running through these letters. Some have been taken up; some haven't. I will pick up some, but not now because I am so tired my head is exploding. It is only twelve o'clock, but there have been many late nights with football and writing after the games, so I am rounding off here and I wish you a good night in six hours, from the darkness and silence of Glemmingebro.

Karl Ove

Botafogo, 11 July

Dear Karl Ove,

A quiet day yesterday. Wrote a letter to you, ran a few errands and was able to confirm that daily life had once again begun for many Brazilians, that people's repression mechanisms had swung into operation, and myself I notice how everything is beginning to slip away, drift off, as though I'm preparing to bid farewell to Rio and Brazil. My thoughts have turned to suitcases, gifts, checking flight schedules but also to which friends I want and need to see again before it's time for me to set off.

You ghost into taking your leave of people and of a place after being there for a while, and when it happens, the final handshake, you're already in Kastrup or in Sveagatan, as if your soul had taken an earlier flight. As Afonso, Thiago and I drove out to Buarque's yesterday, there was a mute, melancholic atmosphere in the car. Suddenly the weight of the 7–1 scoreline was perceptible. All was quiet and we had no Feital in the back seat to regale us with his intense commentaries on everything under the sun. The silence was eventually broken, and we began talking about Argentina v. Holland. I told them how much you love the Argentinian team.

Afonso turned to me and said, 'Does he know anything about football, this Norwegian guy?'

'Muito! Lots! He's very good at analysing games.'

'But, Fredrik, stopping other teams from playing, that's not football. There are many coaches who favour that style in Brazil today. Coaches who aim for a draw, and if they win 1-0, they're in seventh heaven. For me it's not football. That's just the way it is. I like 3-2.'

'Me too! But I like 4-3 even more, I love games that end 4-3,' I said.

And at this point I want to refer to your letter, which is interesting, because our different football philosophies are now crystallised and mutually opposed. It's amusing how you – the drummer! – bang the drum for your Argentina and the philosophy you identify there (negative versus positive . . . death versus life . . . this is the game for me, this is football), you as Sauron's vassal! And that is the style of play that appeals to you, in the same way as jogo bonito – Gandalf! – is what speaks to me, completely different worlds, but the difference isn't to be found between 1-0 and 7-1, Karl Ove, because I too want a contest. I want 4-3, 4-2, 3-2, scorelines like that, granted if Malmö or Sweden are playing then it's quite a different matter, then of course I like the opposing team to be outclassed, but in general I am for the contest, as long as it's between two teams actually playing, not between what I, and many along with me, call dödgrävarfotboll, gravedigger football. Argentina are, for me, a mixture of extremes and not simply 'destructive'. Great matches from past World Cups that I remember and have loved for this reason are, to pick a few: England v. West Germany 1966 (4-2), Portugal v. North Korea 1966 (5-3), Italy v. West Germany 1970 (4-3), West Germany v. France 1982 (3-3), Italy v. Brazil 1982 (3-2), Argentina v. West Germany 1986 (3-2), England v. Cameroon 1990 (3-2). In games like those you have everything: beauty, excitement, creativity, fabulous goals and negativity. All wonderfully chaotic and nobody, absolutely nobody, can tell how it's going to end.

Studies in elegance, in which one team is outclassed, such as Sweden v. Brazil in 1958 (2-5), Brazil v. Italy in 1970 (4-1), France v.

Brazil in 1998 (3–0) or – why not? – Germany v. Brazil in 2014 (7–1), fall under another, aesthetic law. The struggle to win, the contest element, is jettisoned, and you enjoy football as art alone, that is, the application of one team's superior skill. We meet, in other words, at that one word, contest, but I want ebb and flow, intense waves of movement up and down the pitch where both teams give everything, you're fascinated by attritional warfare and the question of how a human wall can be breached. Looking at the history of football, I think you can be said to belong to a small but vocal minority, with ideological bastions in Italy, Uruguay, Greece and, to a certain extent, Argentina. Perhaps this is where Brazilian football has lost its way, in the wake of the 1986 World Cup in Mexico. Telê Santana, one of the most popular coaches and captains of his country ever, and the very personification of jogo bonito, led the fantastic Zico generation to two World Cups, in 1982 (lost against Italy) and in 1986 (lost on penalties against Platini's France), after which the CBF drew the conclusion that Brazil would never win the World Cup again by playing beautifully, and consequently took the choice to go down the Lazaroni–Parreira–Dunga–Scolari road.

And the CBF was proved right in the short term but wrong in the long term. Brazil won in 1994 with result-focused football. They won in 2002 (Scolari) with the same style of play, albeit spiced up by three 'magicians' – Ronaldinho, Ronaldo and Rivaldo – but where has it got them? How are things today? They lag behind and are in deep crisis. Brazilian football has lost its soul, Argentinian football hasn't. They've stuck to what they're good at, the combination of the 'destructive' (Mascherano) and individual brilliance (Maradona/Messi), and that's why I believe your Argentina have a good chance on Sunday, because they're in harmony with their football soul, while the Brazilians were like junior players, all at odds and bereft of an internal compass. If

Mascherano can tear the superb German midfield to pieces and Messi find the crack in the German wall and take an early lead, I think your team will be world champions.

Our correspondence is nearing an end. Which means it is time to reflect, and when I was in Manolo I got to thinking about my childhood hero, Bosse Larsson. He broke through as a seventeen-year-old in 1963, the same year we moved to Malmö, and he was the reason I switched allegiance from Hammarby to Malmö at the age of nine. Bosse Larsson was the Thomas Müller of Sweden back then. He could do everything, he set out as a midfielder before converting into a striker, the most dangerous in the country in front of goal (on three occasions he figured at the top of the Allsvenske top-scorer list) and finally became perhaps Sweden's best centre half ever (three World Cups, 1970, 1974 and 1978). King Bosse, he was known as. In 1965 'we' won Allsvenskan and Bosse was top scorer.

Bosse Larsson was the embodiment of the Swedish working class, Sandemose from top to toe – do not think you are anything special; be loyal, humble, always put the collective first, and when he scored he would, more often than not, just turn and jog back to the centre circle without making any big deal about it, as though he'd simply slotted a metal disc into place at Kockum's Shipyard, where his father still worked (the complete opposite to Zlatan in that sense, and in the difference between them there lies a whole social and cultural history, I fancy). For many of my generation, and those before, he's bigger than Zlatan.

In 1965, when I was twelve, I was top scorer in a junior tournament organised by Malmö FF. At the last league game of the year, when the senior team were to be awarded their gold medals, there was also to be a prize-giving ceremony for us, and just before we were to go out onto the pitch, the club chairman came into our dressing room. He looked around. Then he came over to me and said, Are you the next Bosse Larsson? That was a big moment for me.

Many years later I was sitting in my taxi outside Kramer, a dance club and restaurant on Malmö's main square, late one autumn evening. An older couple opened the door, got in and gave me an address. I began to drive, swung down Hamngatan on to Norra Vallgatan, past the Savoy Hotel, and then I glanced in the rear-view mirror: Bosse Larsson, in my taxi. I was speechless, wanted to say so much about all the joy he'd given me watching him play in my childhood and teens, but couldn't get a word out, just continued driving in the autumn darkness down Amiralsgatan, Nobeltorget, through Rosengård and into Röda Höja, finally pulling in at the turnaround on his street, and as he was about to pay I'd finally settled on what to say/do: the fare is on me, for all the great times you've given me at Malmö Stadium.

And that was that. And I can still feel the warmth of his hand in the palm of my own. Bosse, one of Sweden's footballing greats, and he lived there and still does.

Best wishes,
Fredrik

Glemmingebro, 11 July

Dear Fredrik,

When I read that you had driven Bosse Larsson, and had thanked him, shivers ran down my spine. Not because I was thinking about what you felt but because I was thinking about what he felt, the sudden certainty, so unexpected, in the darkness of the night that what he had done had given so much pleasure and had had such importance for so many. We have written a lot about all the footballers we have seen since we were children, and it is striking how brightly they still shine in our memories. Once I was hitchhiking through Germany. A lorry driver who picked me up couldn't speak English, I couldn't speak German, and there we sat, high above the tarmac looking into the illuminated darkness racing towards us without saying a word. Then, I don't recall how it started, we exchanged names of footballers. The first was Rune Bratseth, the Norwegian defensive genius (I know, the two entities are mutually exclusive for you – genius and defence!) who played many seasons for Werder Bremen. It was me who said his name, I think, because I remember the driver brightening up and repeating it several times. Then he said a name, so I said Ja! Ja! And maybe the club, and then I said a name, and he said Ja! Ja! It isn't only what they did on the pitch we connect with footballers, but also the era they were part of, and when I initiate similar conversations late at night in a pub somewhere, people always respond enthusiastically, it can become a sport naming Liverpool's 1978 team, for example, or

Brann or Start or Barcelona. You don't see that glow of pleasure with writers' names! Norwegian writers from the 1960s don't exactly evoke the same nostalgia and feeling of community.

I am a little embarrassed at the thought that you mentioned my attitude to Argentina in the car with your Brazilian friends. It is not that I have anything against attacking football – my favourite player from the outset of this World Cup was Ángel Di María, and a more attacking brain than his would be hard to find – and I have already touched on my all-time favourite match, the semi in 82, which had the lot, also pace, openings, chances and six goals (wasn't it?). In my view, all those who dismiss matches like the one yesterday as boring, anti-football, death and so on or, like your friends, who don't see it as football at all, they are blind to an essential part of the game, and occasionally that irritates me. What is fantastic about football is that you can watch it at any level, and there is always something interesting to see. A Division 7 match in Bergen, if you see it from the beginning, it sucks you in as well, there are various dramas and all sorts of characters emerge. Even junior matches can do the same. There has to be an interest right from the kick-off though. Last winter I paid to see all the matches in the Premier League at home, and I did this because I was so curious to see Ole Gunnar Solskjær, who became the manager at Cardiff. This sounds very patriotic, I know, but I remember what a big thing it was when Solskjær was bought by Manchester United for a pittance, as a squad player, what do I know what they were thinking, but for a Norwegian this was big, at least when you were my age – latter half of my twenties – at that time I even watched United's summer practice matches. Solskjær came on, played well and he had a fantastic first season. He was quick then and banging in goals. Since then I have always followed him. So now too. I saw almost all the Cardiff games. They were relegated, as you know, and played worse and worse. Nevertheless, when you follow a team you begin to get a handle on the players, they go from being anonymous to players you associate with certain things. Medel, by the way, he played defensive midfield, but he wasn't good, at any rate not compared with what he has produced for Chile at this World Cup, as a defender he has been one of the team's most important and best players. What makes a good team? Why didn't Solskjær succeed? Or Moyes at United? Why was his season such a fiasco? I am sure that the same team under van Gaal will be fantastic. It isn't just tactics, nor is it simply having good players, it is about building a team and getting everyone to function optimally in relation to one another, as much psychology as playing qualities. It was what Eggen did in Rosenborg in the 90s, when they were not only in the Champions League every year, but they also beat the big Italian and Spanish teams. It is the best Norwegian team ever, but not one of the players was good enough to turn out for Real Madrid or Milan. It is elementary but fascinating how players who are worse, man for man, can raise their performances as a unit and beat the best. The collective as opposed to artistry, but watching Rosenborg's sometimes extremely fast games was just as entertaining as watching PSG's games, for example, in this year's Champions League. I like seeing circus artists performing tricks, but that is not the essence or soul of football for me. It is never one player, it is all of them.

The logical conclusion of this is that I should be with Germany on Sunday. They must have one of the World Cup's best teams in this tournament. But I won't be – as I have mentioned before, one of the pleasures of watching football is that you don't have to justify your sympathies or antipathies.

Last night I slept well for the first time in at least two weeks. Usually I need eight hours' sleep for the day not to be ruined, but during these World Cup weeks I have been surviving on five or six, until this morning, when I was woken at half past nine (after carrying Anne to Linda, semi-comatose, at six) by a text, it was a friend I had promised to give a car seat to. I jumped out of bed, got the seat and drove down with it. Then it was back home, pack swimming things and try to get all the children in the car: we were going to Tosselilla, the amusement park here in Skåne. Three families, nine children, sun and heat, water slides of all shapes and sizes. As the girls had friends with them I had to take care of John, so we waded around in the water, went down a slide in a rubber ring, shot water cannons and ate ice creams, before all of us went to the fairground part, where he drove a dodgem and showed what an aggressive motorist he was. Got back at five, cooked and started on a letter to you. Four days to the deadline for the essay, which is still half-finished, one day to my manuscript promise. Girls to the theatre for the day's performance, barbecue with friends tomorrow evening. New guests coming here on Sunday – the final – and then next week a German, an English and a French journalist, respectively. Over the last few weeks I have smoked two packets a day, that is forty cigarettes, Fredrik, and not good at all. As you might know, I agreed to run the New York Marathon with our mutual friend Aage, we shook hands on it, that is two years ago now, but perhaps it is what you need – even though it is pathetic doing it at my age (not for Aage, he has always trained and played and cycled and run, but for me). Christ, yes, you are right, the opportunity is still there. I haven't missed all the buses. But the biggest and most important ones, I think they leave when you are forty-five. The crucial decisions in life have already been taken. I can't imagine that I am going to experience a new spring of any kind. Nevertheless, sometimes things happen. Last winter I was so tired that suddenly I couldn't move. Well, I managed to get up from bed and go down to the kitchen, but getting into the car and driving to the shop for milk and bread, for that I had to make an ENORMOUS effort. I always want to work, so I did, but very little. Go and get the post? I didn't have the energy. Pay bills? Impossible. In brief, it was like being stuck under ice. Having a shower and getting dressed became large, complicated operations. It was all I could do to be normal with the children and get them to school and make them food and so on, and that was because I had to. I thought I was ill, so I went to the doctor to have a full check-up. I have never been to the doctor in my life, I find the idea very off-putting. Well, once I went to satisfy Linda, who told me to have some moles checked, and because of the potential serious-ness, I did go – but never otherwise. Now I was sitting on a bench with my chest bared. At first he wanted to chat with me, so we chatted. I told him how I felt, no energy. He asked me about my habits. When I said I smoked thirty a day, I saw something click in his head. He had a theory. He took out a chart and drew a – football pitch! Thing was, with normal lung capacity you can run all over the pitch while someone with COPD can only move in the penalty box. That was what he said, honest to God. When I was small we used to say goal-hangers were 'fishing'. He just 'fishes', we said, in other words, they stood around waiting for the ball near the goal (we didn't play the offside rule when we were small). OK, I said. So have I got COPD? We don't know yet, he said. He took out a little instrument I was supposed to blow into. This instrument showed the age of my lungs. I had to blow as hard as I could and the real age of my lungs would appear on the computer. Jesus, I got really nervous then, Fredrik! I stood up and blew, and my mouth was so open there was hardly any pres-sure, my lungs emptied immediately – hhhhhhaaaaaaaa – and then there was nothing left, I had no more air and began to cough. I had blown so softly that now I was sure I had COPD. The doctor looked at his screen. Do you know what? he said, looking up at me earnestly. Do you know what age it says? I shook my head. Thought of saying eighty but said nothing. Twenty, he said. You have the lungs of a twenty-year-old. Over the next few days I told everyone I knew. I have been smoking since I was sixteen, and rarely fewer than twenty a day, at least for the last twenty years. And then this. The X-rays were fine too – lung cancer was his second theory – and there was nothing wrong with my heart either. So what was wrong? And what should I do? I could barely lift my arms. Could barely shuffle from the house to my study, where I am sitting now. The doctor, who knew a little more than I gave him credit for, had also suggested I should start taking walks. But there are two things I will never do, I would rather put a pistol to my head and pull the trigger, and they are: a) family therapy and b) walks. So, naturally enough, I didn't. What I did do, and it helped in an amazingly short time, was to start painting. I drove to Ystad, went into a painting shop and bought oils, canvas, thinner, brushes. I came home, sat down and painted. I have never done it before, I have only liked paintings, but now there I was, no idea what I was doing, no idea whether you could mix colours, no idea whether you could superimpose one layer over another, no idea what turpentine was for, but I didn't give a shit, to express myself in a way I don't really like, I am becoming more and more narrow-minded year by year, I just painted. And I became hooked. At the peak I painted eighteen hours a day. After only a week I began to feel better, and after two everything was fine again, at least as regards energy. Then I stopped, I didn't have the time, but ever since then I have thought I am going to do it, going to find time, because it is fantastically obsessive and challenging, and a very special feeling, seeing the colours in front of you, changing them, building with them in a way, layers and strata and contrasts and light – even if my paintings are a real mess. I have mentioned this to only a couple of friends, and when they ask me what I paint, I have to tell them the truth, I paint exactly what a pensioner in Österlen would, yellow corn, blue sky, perhaps a tree in the far distance, which is easier to do than a tree close up of course.

So that is at least one completely new thing I have started over recent years. But it won't take me to Buenos Aires, and there is nothing young and new about it – at any rate not what I paint – it is more of an act of resignation, something you do when you have also started to wear slippers and a cardigan indoors because you are so sensitive to the cold – on the other hand, the obsession, just wanting to do this hour after hour, that reminds me of writing at its best. Well, not best in the sense of quality, but as something which characterises this state, the best writing state, when you write and write and don't want to do anything else. You recognise it. It is like writing but also like playing football. You don't want it to stop; you just want to go on. Watching football is quite different, it is not obsessive in the same way, it is more something you do to relax and be entertained.

Twenty to ten, it is still light outside, the children are up, woozy from the sun and sleepy after a long day in the amusement park.

A few years ago, before moving out here, we were driving around and I saw a signpost. Sommerland Sjælland, it said. Sjæl, soul. Soul land, I thought, that sounds nice. I'd like to go there.

All the best,
Karl Ove

Botafogo, 12 July

Dear Karl Ove,

Genius and defence? No, Karl Ove. No, no, no! I had the privilege of seeing Franz Beckenbauer play, perhaps the greatest defender ever, in the flesh. It's true I focus on attackers and attacking play more, but in your letters you've taught me quite a bit about defending and reminded me of that art; like you, I was mightily impressed when Mascherano stopped Robben, and Thiago Silva, if you remember, when there were four Colombians against two defenders, and he stuck a leg out to make such a precise tackle – to dare to do that, to 'sell yourself' in that way, and get away with it. What you said about Di María is also noted. Solskjær was big, even in my world, and I always loved it when he came on for United towards the end of a match, his boyish face, nimble movement and you knew he was likely to tuck the ball away even if he came on in the eighty-second minute. This despite the fact I've never followed an English team and am often annoyed at Scandinavian men in their Arsenal and United tops putting so much emotion and aggression into their affiliation with a team from an island in the Atlantic/North Sea, I really don't get it, what's that all about? I bring it up in company sometimes, after all, we live in a different country and have our own teams, but no, then someone in all seriousness pipes up about Crystal Palace, then someone else about Hull and Newcastle, and then they're off again, and a fresh round of beers; I liked Beckham a lot, and I've always enjoyed watching Giggs, I'm really fascinated by him, and back in 1998 when I was writing a piece about the different financial structures of Barcelona, United and Malmö, I was standing in the car park at United's training ground waiting for Jesper Blomqvist, whom I was going to interview, and it was taking a while, and then Beckham came out with his bag over his shoulder on the way to his car, and I was surprised at how he looked, so slight, so normal, he was smaller than me and looked like a youth team player, but that's more to do with the iconic status the media confer upon footballers, they give them an aura, making them unreal, and when you see them in real life, it's – well – unreal, since we don't actually want them down here on earth with us mere mortals, so Solskjær was big here too! As were Rosenberg, and sometimes I think about how they succeeded where Swedish teams have not, in spite of our football history being 'weightier' and better than yours, and how Malmö FF's ambition ought to be to 'do a Rosenborg': win the Swedish league ten years in a row and get into the group stages of the Champions League each year.

And now, my friend, as they say on *Monty Python*, for something completely different, a question you don't need to answer if you don't want to, a question I've been mulling over ever since that Sunday one winter, prior to us playing a game on the pitches at Limhamn, when we exchanged books, you giving me volumes one and two of *Min Kamp* and my giving you *Torget* and a few others.

When I read Marcel Proust's *À la recherche du temps perdu*, I was about fifty or sixty pages through volume one, *Du côté de chez Swann*, when I got the feeling that this wasn't possible, how can this torrent of detail exist without drowning the narrative, without killing off the main thread of the story? A feeling hit me in almost exactly the same way approximately fifty or sixty pages into your first volume: how is it possible that he, the friend I play football with, can succeed in maintaining such a vivid story and prevent it from drowning in all the detail? I still don't understand it, and that brings me to my question (which by the way you don't have to answer, I know an expert in card tricks, Lennart Green, world champion in close-up card magic, no less, and he would never dream of publicly revealing his techniques), a little way into his first volume, Marcel Proust writes,

Chercher? Pas seulement: créer (Seek? More than that: create)

and I've pondered these two sentences a great deal, what it looks like in there, deep within ourselves, where memory meets the will to narrate (language) and what it looks like, what is it that happens when an incident is brought to life by language, and words lead us from the truth (what really occurred) towards 'the lie', that which we as writers believe to be the truth and therefore recount, but which our siblings/parents/nearest and dearest can suddenly inform us didn't take place, because you weren't in Uppsala that morning, Fredrik, you were in Gällivare then, or we never ate potato cakes at home or, as some friends of mine told me about a detail in one of my books, that petrol station you wrote about has never existed, there's never been a petrol station on that spot, even though I have a strong memory of it having been there, right there, I filled the tank of my parents' old scooter and was so nervous I dropped the pump and the petrol went everywhere, things like that?

I have, I see now, actually two questions, the first of a mnemonic nature: how are you able to recall so much? (Do you have an extra head with an extra brain/hard disk, which you can connect/hook up to and/or mnemonic aids like songs or rhymes to help?) The other is ethical: what's your view of the part where the potato cakes are placed on the table, even though you've never been served potato cakes at home?

Best wishes,
Fredrik

PS Speaking of Maradona's solo run in 1986, there's a story from the Argentinian dressing room afterwards, from in the showers, to be exact. Jorge Valdano (whose great passion outside football is literature and who has edited a very nice anthology with twenty-four stories about football, *Cuentos de fútbol*, for which he wrote the foreword) says to Maradona, 'Diego, why didn't you pass the ball, I was completely unmarked and running beside you the whole time?'

Whereupon el pibo de oro, the golden boy, replies, 'I know. I saw you the entire time but never thought I was in a position to pass . . .'

Glemmingebro, 13 July

Dear Fredrik,

I laughed out loud when I read your Maradona story. Also because it is so true: he must have seen all the potential passes at every moment, that was where a lot of his greatness lay. Footballers, like other people, usually have one talent, a gift, are good at something special – keeping a cool head in front of the goal and putting the ball where there is the greatest chance it will go in, dribbling, crossing, tackling, heading. Maradona, though, must be the greatest footballing talent there has ever been. Did you read Lineker's description of Maradona warming up? He was manipulating the ball with his feet the way others did with their hands. He had kicked it high into the air, it landed exactly on his foot, not just once but ten times consecutively. Lineker and his teammates had tried to do the same in training later, no one even got close. Twice consecutively, maybe three times, but ten? He had total ball control – what is unique about him is that he also had a complete overview of the game and was ice-cold in front of goal – and that is funny because if you watch the sequence starting in midfield you also see that he is so busy, he has hardly tricked his way past one player before he is on to the next, and then he speeds up, another player comes and then another, and after they are left behind he is by the goal and has to concentrate on the tasks awaiting him there.

When I was growing up English football was the big thing simply because it was all that was shown on TV. Every Saturday we had the pools – the matches selected were published in the newspapers a few days before (was it Wednesday?) – and if you were a football fan it was a fixed ritual. Norwegian matches weren't broadcast, only a few minutes on the TV sports round-up every Sunday, when three were chosen, and we always hoped it would be Start – consequently our familiarity with John Toshack was the same as with Helge Skuseth, West Bromwich with Mjøndalen. Many of my values were established then; in a world where almost everything was hard to access, where you had to make an effort to get hold of a record or watch a team, that obviously increases the value radically, makes it exclusive; watching your team play was not an everyday event. When I was thirteen we moved to Tveit outside Kristiansand, and my neighbour, one year younger than me, was as interested in football as I was.

They had their own little pitch with a goal down by the river, which flooded sometimes in the spring and autumn. We gathered there, a group of friends, and played from dawn to dusk. When we grew older we also began to go to matches together; we realised that if we arrived long before kick-off there were no guards by the fence in the forest, so we climbed over, hid for a while and strolled over to the stands just below the small TV tower and got the best places without paying. We also started going in supporters' coaches to some of the away games. So for me seeing Norwegian football on TV has always been unusual, I associate football with England, when that was how the world was divided.

As far as writing is concerned, what you do and how, I remember a conversation I had a long time ago with the woman who is the editor of our book, Cathrine Sandnes. I had published my first book, and after the interview we walked down to my hotel together. Cathrine is a Norwegian martial arts champion, so she has experience of being a top sportswoman, and we talked about the odd phenomenon of 'being in form'. You know it yourself. Suddenly everything goes your way when you play. You can do things you haven't done before. It flows. Everything goes well. Then suddenly it stops. The flow dries up, you can't do anything any more, there is a block, you are 'out of form'. What sort of phenomenon is this? It doesn't apply only to football, it applies to all areas of life where you have to perform, also to writing. You can sit and toil away and nothing works, there is a block, there is no flow, just resistance, and the text is lifeless, stiff, artificial, jagged. Then all of a sudden it can loosen up. All of a sudden it flows. All of a sudden nothing is difficult, the text is alive, everything is possible. Is this the same phenomenon? I believe so. My writing now is about finding my way to the flow zones. Once I am there it takes care of itself, I don't need to do anything. But it is the getting there which is difficult, that is where the challenge lies. All the doubt, all the self-contempt, all the shame and all the self-criticism has to be broken down, you have to work through it, and then, if it happens, and you can never know if it will, you just have to write. Then what you describe happens, a text can be weighed down with detail and still be alive. Usually I remember little of what I see and experience, I am poor at noticing things and registering them, but when I write, and I am in the zone where everything is easy, it transpires that I have noticed things and registered them after all, but with something else, not consciousness. And I think that is the same for a footballer in form: what happens, only happens without thinking. As soon as you start thinking about it – what shall I do or not do? – a striker who hasn't scored for some games is a classic example – then you freeze, and once you freeze it will only get worse. This is also about getting in as many hours as you can so that in the end it can be done blindfold, knowing how it has to be done without having to think about it. Musicians are my favourite example, they don't think about what they do, they have done it so many times that the instrument is a part of them and they are that music – the music of football, the music of writing that we want to reach.

This issue is also relevant for today because Messi is obviously out of form. We thought it couldn't happen after his previous seasons, where absolutely everything went his way. But then he met some resistance. He has had a semi-decent season, only. How is that possible? He has the same skill as before, he has the same ball sense and footballing intelligence – but he has lost the flow, the zone where everything goes of its own accord. It was obvious in the very first match for Argentina – you saw it live – he got bogged down, never managed to free himself, and if he did, it was in areas of the pitch where he was no danger – up until he scored, of course. And scoring four goals in the opening group matches meant it wasn't so obvious. But against Holland he was poor – I mean, as poor as a player of his class can be – he ran less than he usually does, and when he did it wasn't the Duracell-bunny speed he is known for, the speed no one can stop. Maradona said he looked tired, but you can't be tired in a final. We will see. He is not in form, but he is Messi . . .

I fear an early German goal, like they have scored in their last two games, but this is Argentina and I would guess they will start off deep. They have seen Ghana and Algeria successfully keep Germany in check, and they are a much better outfit than both of them. On the other hand, this is dangerous too, of course. Di María, who brings so much to this team, was in training yesterday, the latest rumours suggest he will be on the bench. I have a feeling that Sabella will take a gamble and put him on in the last half an hour. I am also keen to know whether Agüero will start (he wasn't very good when he came on against Holland, but that was after an injury, he has had a few days' rest) or whether he will put Higuaín up front, with Messi in behind him and Lavezzi and Palacio on the flanks.

I hope these pre-match musings aren't smashed by a German offensive in the opening minutes that results in an early one- or two-goal lead. On the other hand, the opposite image, an early Argentinian goal, will lead to immense German pressure which I cannot see any team withstanding. In other words, I fear Germany whatever happens.

Now it is a quarter past two, so roughly eight hours to the final. The girls are at the theatre, the performance starts at three, Linda, John and Anne are indoors, I am in my study in the garden and writing and listening to Bonnie 'Prince' Billy. Cloudy and quite cold; it rained all yesterday and a bit this morning. Our guests have left – the son, Olle, supported Argentina and had played for Hammerby himself. The father, Fredrik, is not very interested in football, but he laughed in disbelief when Germany scored the fourth and fifth goals against Brazil, fascinated by the drama and the collapse; the mother, Karin, has played football herself and was the person who said to me that joy on the football pitch is so unconfined that you never see the same off the pitch – as I wrote to you some letters ago. They don't have TV where they are going now, an old house in the border area with Norway, quite far up – and would have to knock on their neighbour's door and ask if they can see it there. This is how it will be in all of Norway and Sweden today, the match will be relayed to millions of TV screens, many will have a vaguely festive mood – I certainly will – and not just here on the edge of the world, but in almost every country.

All the best,
Karl Ove

Botafogo, 13 July

Dear Karl Ove,

Last night the Brazilian fiasco was, as you yourself saw, complete. I was at a bar called Botequin Esquina Botafogo, it was desolate, a few Germans, some Argentinians, and the Brazilians who were there weren't wearing any yellow, as though ashamed of their team and not wanting to be associated with them. Can't recall ever having seen such a disorganised Brazilian national side, there appeared to be a complete lack of coherence, and strangest of all, and something I'd already noticed in the game against Germany, was the lack of technique, how comfortable the Germans and Dutch, each and every one, were controlling the ball, how much more assured in their passing game they were generally – and it pains me to write – how much better their ball sense was, the one thing that's always been the hallmark of Brazilian football.

I was rooting for Holland, and for the first time during this World Cup I could sit and enjoy Robben and van Persie's exquisite runs and razor-sharp passes without any emotional resistance. Me an opportunist, you say? Far from it. I only want this to hurt, really hurt, so that as many people as possible in this country realise that Brazilian football at national level, and as a whole, has hit rock bottom where things can only improve. There's probably more talent here than anywhere in the world, but the organisation (CBF is by the way a private company, and like any other company run on private capital seems to view profit

399

generation as its main aim, as opposed to securing the development of Brazilian football and caring for its future) is seriously deficient, corrupt, and the appointment of Scolari was based mostly on his enthusiasm, his ability to lift the morale of the players by jumping around and gesticulating on the sideline, which narrowly got them to the semi-final, but when it got really serious his tactical knowledge wasn't sufficient, and neither was his footballing philosophy. Nor the player material he had to work with for that matter, and yesterday's display demonstrated that neither Silva nor Luiz is good enough.

So yet another shameful day here, Karl Ove, and as Holland made it 3–0 after yet one more exquisite attack, I noted it with pleasure, since 3–0 smarts a lot more than 2–0. A team has been outclassed at 3–0, and now they find themselves at the lowest level where the 'Hegelian' turning point can come. Being a romantic and prone to daydreams, I'm hoping that reassessment will mean a return to the beautiful approach of Brazilian football: jogo bonito.

Otherwise, it was a quiet day. Bought two copies of Min Kamp for Claudio and Afonso. I met Lennart ('Ipanema left-wingers against the workers on the right' if you recall) in Lapa, by a place known as the Selarón Steps, a stairway connecting the bohemian quarter of Lapa with Santa Teresa, a large district covering several hills in the centre of Rio, which was previously jungle and was where the slaves moved after being freed to set up their own small communities. Santa Teresa is still an exciting place, with winding streets and alleyways, old rambling buildings, apartment blocks, abandoned haunted houses, huge villas in baroque and rococo style and favelas interspersed in between, a real adventure to wander through and easy to lose your way in. The steps were tiled by a Chilean artist, Selarón, who's considered a bit of an eccentric. He moved into one of the houses along the steps and began painting tiles with different motifs from Brazilian history, not least its footballing history. He used what he had to hand, and today it's one of Rio's most popular tourist attractions, with thousands of visitors walking up and down, sitting and having their photographs taken there.

Although Selarón is Chilean, whenever I think of him it always puts me in mind of a typical Brazilian trait I admire, that of using whatever you've got, an aesthetic that crops up in relation to many things, not least cafés and art.

Lennart and I ascended the long stairway and continued uphill to Arnaudo, a café specialising in food from north-east Brazil. We drank beer and discussed the World Cup over a meal of sun-dried meat and bean stew. It has, in spite of the home team's catastrophic showing, and no matter what happens today, been a success from start to finish in terms of organisation, games and goals, as well as the spectator experience.

In the evening Denise and I went out to dance in Lapa, which I haven't done once since I've been here. But unfortunately I didn't get the opportunity to rectify that. Lapa, as so often before, was crowded with people, Argentinians and Germans in their respective kits, Brazilians relinquishing their own, and there were long queues outside all the dance places, so we sat at an open-air restaurant instead, drank water and caipirinhas, both of us tired, me from the World Cup, her from the latest drive to Campo Grande to witness Brazil being demolished by the Dutch, and we talked about our lives, and she told me about a piece she's doing on the working conditions of female engineers and women employed in other jobs on Brazilian oil platforms in the Atlantic. After that, we took a taxi and shared a lively discussion with the driver on the way. He was wearing the new German kit, the black and red one (the German team has become unusually popular here due to their exuberance and the attitude they display, and the fact that their away strip is the same as Flamengo's, Brazil's most popular team, os rubros negros, the black and red, means they'll receive tremendous support at the Maracanã). Reynaldo, Denise, Ula and Denise's son Gabriel are all diehard Flamengo supporters, and there was little doubt which team both her and our taxi driver would be supporting in the final: Germany. And me? The last thing I said as I was dropped off on Rua Assunção, Karl Ove, was, 'Estou com Messi!' I'm supporting Messi! Whereupon they both laughed, before disappearing into the darkness.

Best wishes,
Fredrik

Glemmingebro, the night of 13/14 July

Dear Fredrik,

And so the 2014 World Cup was over, and Germany were the new world champions. I didn't see the victory ceremony, I switched off the TV as the referee blew for full time and it was clear that Germany had won the final 1–0. Now it is half past one in the morning and I don't feel so consumed any more. It was a worthy final between easily the best two teams in the tournament. Argentina could equally well have won – Higuaín was through on his own, Messi was through on his own and Palacio was through on his own, furthermore Higuaín had a goal disallowed. Germany also had their chances, if not as big and clear cut. The match was more or less as imagined: Argentina played deep with little distance between their midfield and defence, counter-attacked whenever they broke, Messi and Lavezzi and Higuaín in the first half, Agüero replacing Lavezzi in the second. Germany, for their part, pushed upfield, kept possession, controlled the play, but showed themselves to be vulnerable at the back, some-times it took the Argentinians only two passes to race through. The Germans also struggled at the top end, their tight passing game was constantly being broken up, sucked in as it were, by the Argentinian defence, and there were only half-chances. The Argentines are very adept at man-to-man marking, as I have said before, and it has never been as clear as tonight, encounter-ing a team which has danced through the World Cup and outplayed all their opponents at some stage. Tonight they didn't, but Argentina were gradually weakened, sapped by Germany's offensive play, in the last part of the second half Argentina mounted hardly any attacks – except for Palacio's run through – and in extra time they only defended. What Schürrle did towards the end of the second half of extra time – broke free on the flank, raced down the sideline, crossed to Götze, who was unmarked in front of goal and, in the most exquisite, elegant and rapid fashion, like a predator, chested the ball and volleyed past the keeper – this would not have happened in normal time, Schürrle would have been stopped, and, if not, Götze would have been hemmed in. Overall in the tournament, Germany were best, while the classic limp to the final, of which perhaps Italy are usually the prime exponents, didn't quite work this time.

It was a good final, always exciting and intense, and not without dramatic incident, such as when Neuer kneed Higuaín in the head – after the ball was punched away – or when Agüero put his fist into Schweinsteiger's face, causing it to bleed. By the way, Schweinsteiger was impressive tonight, he played with enormous authority and was perhaps the leader you were looking for in this team. His darting runs failed time after time, but he was everywhere, won balls everywhere and sprayed passes continuously, set a rhythm for the Germans and, next to the two Argentinian midfielders, was the best player on the pitch, from my point of view. What do you think? Schürrle was also good; he has had a fantastic championship.

And we have too!

Look forward to hearing from you tomorrow.

All the best,
Karl Ove

Botafogo, 14 July

Dear Karl Ove,

Yesterday was beautiful weather, twenty-nine degrees, a clear blue sky, the big day, the day of plenty never is the first, the best day is a day of craving thirst, to quote Karin Boye. Wasn't quite sure where to go and ended up roaming. Decided to head in the direction of the Maracanã but took the wrong train, however, when I got out I could still make out thousands of supporters winding like a giant snake towards the temple in the distance. I made for the Tijuca district to find a place to watch the game with the Argentinians, as my sympathies had tipped towards them. So I wanted to see the game with los hermanos. But by the Maracanã and in Tijuca I find I'm out of luck, there's no big screen at Alzirão any longer because, I'm told, they only use it when Brazil play, so I'm left standing there, dejected, wondering what my next move will be, the game is starting soon and I'm wandering about through deserted streets with high-rises and car parks when by chance a taxi comes driving along, so I hop in and say, 'O Sambódromo,' and he turns out to be a nice sort who doesn't dislike Argentinians, 'We're Latin Americans, we need to stick together,' he says, and is against any talk of trouble after the game, and makes me think of a driver I met a couple of days previously, who described Argentinians as a stinking shower who'd invaded their city, pissed and shat pretty much everywhere and parked wherever they felt like parking, but not this guy, he's open and warm, and I take to him, would have liked to speak longer but am aware we'll only ever spend about ten minutes in each another's company. The Sambadrome is completely empty, just Argentinian cars and tents, not a soul to be seen, no bar anywhere. What the hell am I to do now? 'Lapa,' he says, and we drive there instead. I'm back in good old Lapa and find a large bar with a terrazza, which is almost full except for one small table for me, thank you very much! And I order a large Quilmes, Argentina's best beer, in honour of you and Argentina, and there are little clusters of Argentinians around, but mostly Brazilians and a small number of Germans, and Santa Teresa can be seen in the background with its beautiful gardens and the lovely white aqueduct rising up, and now the World Cup final is under way, and it's the best 0–0 game I've seen, but I feel a little like a hostage since the people around me are so clearly and primitively anti-Argentinian, and I sit with my Quilmes, and as Lavezzi tears up the wing I get carried away and forget to hide which side I'm rooting for but soon compose myself, I don't want to land in trouble, and the Germans roll the ball to one another à la Löw, the Argentinians position themselves in the trenches, and then Messi, suddenly, like greased lightning, fantastic to see, more happens in ten minutes than during the entire 1990 final, and Zabaleta, my God, and it's still early days and not going to be easy for the Germans, the Argentinians have enormous garra, courage, and when Higuaín is left one on one with Neuer after Kroos's misplaced header, I can't believe my eyes, in a World Cup final! – but Higuaín puts it wide and that's scandalous because if you're a striker you've one job, and that's not to win the ball and hit beautiful diagonal passes, but to put it away when the chance presents itself, the pickpocket's predicament, you get one opportunity on a bus ride and you need to be alert when someone's handbag or back pocket slips open, a momentous miss which he'll have to live with for the rest of his life, but the game is going the way the Argentinians want it to, the Germans may have 63 per cent of possession to their 37 per cent, but they're being held to the middle of the park, and you don't often score from there, but now and again the Germans get in behind them, down to the byline, all textbook stuff, and there's something awe-inspiring about this elegant machine, how all the cogs in the gearwheel are so well oiled, and how everyone knows where to be all the time, but real goal chances are thin on the ground, Mascherano, the warrior, and Sabella, the man with the bordello-owner eyes, have this game of chess progressing the way they want, and the Argentinian counter-attacks are lightning-fast, and as Higuaín puts the ball in the net after just such a break, there's cheering from a minority on the premises, but when the goal's ruled offside, the rest of the bar cheer even louder, and the Brazilians, following the logic of my enemy's enemy is my friend, shout Alemanha, and Kramer is substituted for Schürrle, and Messi spots Higuaín, hits a beautiful pass, but a German leg intercepts, and I suddenly understand why Müller is so good, what it's down to, his fantastic physical make-up, he's capable of pushing himself more than everyone else, is stronger than everyone else, a monster who looks like a dentist, and Romero makes a great save from a shot by Schürrle, and now the Germans increase the pressure and I'm bursting to go to the toilet but don't want to be standing at a urinal when a goal is scored in the final, and now, Jesus, what was that? A header against the upright! by a bearded German player whom up until now I hadn't noticed, Hummel-Bummel or something, and there's no way of knowing which way this is going to go, and Lavezzi is taken off for Agüero, whose marriage to Maradona's daughter is apparently over, and now Diego himself can't stand his former son-in-law and is making his preference for Tévez clearly known, and every time Agüero gets the ball I'm reminded of that little family drama, and the Argentinians have neutralised the German midfield, the best in the world, and when the Germans attack it's rarely dangerous, but when they counter, in the Argentinian way, then things happen, football, like life, is ironic by nature, and Neuer almost does a Schumacher on Higuaín, but no action is taken, which after all was also the case with Schumacher, and I'm thinking what a scandal, but all around me they accept it because Argentina have to lose, that's just how it is, Argentina can't win, and then the opportunist writer in me thinks how I want to experience it, to get the chance to write about 100,000 Argentinians celebrating winning the World Cup in the heart of Rio, and Mascherano is shown a yellow card, and then Agüero, and now their Janus face comes out, I think, the real brutality, and Demichelis, your friend, performs an audacious backward header, and the Germans appear tired, tired of banging their head against this blue human wall, and Löw's eyes are serious, questioning, does he have an ace up his sleeve, I ask myself, or is this it? And where is Messi, I wonder, yes, there he is, strolling in the middle of the pitch in a World Cup final while everyone around him runs, then he loses the ball and I make a note: Maradona never did that, never, not like that, and Higuaín is taken off – my oh my! How is it possible to miss a chance like that, you should have controlled the ball, that's what the real art of scoring is all about, getting it under control and slotting it coolly to either side of the keeper, whether it's the World Cup final or the final of the Malmö Cup, why this idiotic shot? – and Palacio comes on and Perez is substituted for Gago and they're just names to me, not people, and off goes Klose and on comes Götze, has he grown a little beard? Perhaps Das Wunderkind wants to show that he's a man, it's a fantastic final, the best since 1986, and now it's extra time and Romero makes a great save from a Schürrle shot after another textbook attack and a precise pass from the Zahnarzt, and then the ball comes to Palacio in the middle of the area, he controls it with his chest, is this it!? But no, he manages a lob, the ball goes wide and time ticks on towards penalties and we don't want that in a World Cup final, and now I'd say both you and I are longing for the same thing, a golden Messi incision in the white, German anatomy, but then, while I'm waiting for that, Schürrle gets the ball out on the left and knocks it in, and here comes Das Wunderkind, and it is like a fairy tale, Mario Götze enters football history in an unforgettable way, and here comes the ball and it's beautiful, great art, and if the Argentines had been paying more attention, they would have seen that it was not the cross that is the problem, but one of the centre backs, Demichelis(?), who isn't marking Götze, and Götze chests the ball to take the spin off it and lets it drop for a left-footed volley that Romero stands no chance of stopping and the net and the ball and the fantastic camera shot that captures everything, even Götze's face in the hundredth of a second it takes before he understands what he's done and then realises the linesman is not raising his little flag to all those millions sitting watching on screens, to decide a World Cup final in such a magnificent fashion, it happens, but it's never happened before, not as magnificently, and the only negative thing you can say is that in the case of Götzinho he'll never, and he's only twenty-two, do anything in his football career ever to rival this, to settle a World Cup final at the Maracanã in Brazil with a dream goal in extra time, and Dilma lifts her hand to her mouth, and beside her Merkel jumps up clenching both fists, and Müller's face is burning with joy as he races over the pitch and then it's over and if I have to find one word it would be

Justice

because over the tournament Germany have been the best team, you can't say otherwise, a great team, wonderful, one which plays attractive football as a strong unit, a physical and technical team, and if one player goes off another comes on who's just as good, and yes, Schweinsteiger was fantastic, Karl Ove, but the secret is that Khedira, Schürrle, Götze and Podolski started on the bench, and no one player is bigger than another, as we say in Sweden, but I feel sorry for the Argentinians sitting a few feet away from me, who are now being openly mocked, and it's all sexual swear words, se fuderon! You lot were fucked, eh! And I don't understand that, is it Catholic collateral? Isn't fucking the nicest thing you can do? And I leave the bar, want to get to Copa, hurry to the metro, descend the steps, get into one of the empty carriages, then up to Cardoal Arcoverde station, and there they are in their thousands, coming off trains and going up escalators, but everything is so quiet, no racket, no songs, thousands of Argentinians who aren't crying but are walking with heads held high, as they should, because your chicos played an amazing game, a close-to-perfect Karl Ove game, and if Tévez had been leading the line they would have won, and on Copa dusk has fallen, and people crowd everywhere, at first I can't even locate the ocean and there are military police in all the streets and there's a German and an Argentinian with an arm around each another and beers in their other hands, and now suddenly a disturbance, a big gang of Argentinians coming down a narrow street, jumping and singing and throwing beer cans at Brazilians giving them the finger from the windows above, and out on Avenida Atlântica tens of thousands of people move this way and that, and waves break in the background, beautiful and white against the dark Atlantic, and the match is warm in everyone's memory, Götze's superb goal, Higuaín's incredible miss, and then the sounds of jeering again, groups of young Brazilians taunting Argentinians a few metres away, jumping, singing, The whore that bore you! And an Argentinian forms a ring with the finger and thumb of one hand and puts his other forefinger in and out seven times, and if this had been at home, in our part of the world, it would have ended in a melee, but here it's more a threatening dance, as though they're simulating violence and hatred, not engaging directly in it, a little like a samba dance, a simulation of the sexual act, but always, always on the right side of the line, then I walk on, become enveloped by and become one with the enormous crowd and feel how everything seems to fade out in the arms of this vast beach, as if Copacabana itself had a voice that whispered brotherhood not hatred, and suddenly new games are being played on the sand beneath the floodlights, Argentinians, Germans, Brazilians gathered around the ball in the twilight, and the huge breakers, and not a hint of trouble, not a fist raised, no police intervention that I can see, and there's an Argentinian arm in arm with a Brazilian girl and there are three Germans sitting on a bench with two sweet Brazilian girls, and I think about how somewhere in Germany, Brazil or Argentina, Darmstadt, Rio or Rosário perhaps, in twenty-six years, a twenty-five-year-old will ask his parents during Sunday dinner the kind of thing you ask when you wonder about where you came from: How did the two of you actually meet? And then the parents will smile, maybe exchange a coy glance, then the mother or father will say, Well, you see, they'd played the World Cup final in Rio, at the Maracanã, and after the game everyone went to Copacabana, to the beach there, and then all of a sudden I saw your mother/father come walking towards me and . . . and two Swedes in Swedish tops and three sad Indian girls from Ecuador playing pan pipes and everyone stops to look and the music is so beautiful I get goose bumps, and further down at one of the bars dancing is under way, and the jeering feels like it's evaporating and the German supporters, happy of course but many of them calm too, so Nordic, looking a little out of place walking along so sedately in their white kits that it makes you want to shout at them, Jesus, you're world champions! Dance! Sing! And cries of Alemanha here and Alemanha there, as they're congratulated no matter where they go by Brazilians, and there of course, I think as I catch sight of him, he comes, the pirate on stilts, looking like Johnny Depp and swaying back and forth in the half-light of the dusk, as though to bring to an end the World Cup he officially opened for me exactly one month ago at the tunnel between Botafogo and Copacabana, are we there yet, Karl Ove?

Best wishes,
Fredrik

WORLD CUP STATISTICS

	P	W	D	L	GD	Pts
Brazil	3	2	1	0	+5	7
Mexico	3	2	1	0	+3	7
Croatia	3	1	0	2	0	3
Cameroon	3	0	0	3	−8	0

12 June	Brazil –	Croatia	3–1	Arena de São Paulo
	Neymar 29', 71' pen.	Marcelo 11' OG		Attendance: 62,103
	Oscar 90+1'			

13 June	Mexico –	Cameroon	1–0	Arena das Dunas
	Peralta 61'			Attendance: 39,216

17 June	Brazil –	Mexico	0–0	Estádio Castelão
				Attendance: 60,342

18 June	Cameroon –	Croatia	0–4	Arena Amazônia
		Olić 11'		Attendance: 39,982
		Perišić 48'		
		Mandžukić 61', 73'		

23 June	Cameroon –	Brazil	1–4	Estádio Nacional
	Matip 26'	Neymar 17', 35'		de Brasília
		Fred 49'		Attendance: 69,112
		Fernandinho 84'		

23 June	Croatia –	Mexico	1–3	Arena Pernambuco
	Perišić 87'	Marquez 72'		Attendance: 41,212
		Guardado 75'		
		Hernández 82'		

	P	W	D	L	GD	Pts
Netherlands	3	3	0	0	+7	9
Chile	3	2	0	1	+2	6
Spain	3	1	0	2	−3	3
Australia	3	0	0	3	−6	0

13 June	Spain — Alonso 27' pen.	Netherlands 1–5 van Persie 44', 72' Robben 53', 80' de Vrij 65'	Arena Fonte Nova Attendance: 48,173
13 June	Chile — Sánchez 12' Valdivia 14' Beausejour 90+2'	Australia 3–1 Cahill 35'	Arena Pantanal Attendance: 40,275
18 June	Spain —	Chile 0–2 Vargas 20' Aránguiz 43'	Estádio do Maracanã Attendance: 74,101
23 June	Australia — Cahill 21' Jedinak 54' pen.	Netherlands 2–3 Robben 20' van Persie 58' Depay 68'	Estádio Beira-Rio Attendance: 42,877
23 June	Australia —	Spain 0–3 Villa 36' Torres 69' Mata 82'	Arena da Baixada Attendance: 39,375
23 June	Netherlands – Fer 77' Depay 90+2'	Chile 2–0	Arena de São Paulo Attendance: 62,966

	P	W	D	L	GD	Pts
Colombia	3	3	0	0	+7	9
Greece	3	1	1	1	+2	4
Ivory Coast	3	1	0	2	−1	3
Japan	3	0	1	2	−4	1

14 June	Colombia Armero 5' Gutiérrez 58' Rodríguez 90+3'	–	Greece	3–0	Estádio Mineirão Attendance: 57,174
14 June	Ivory Coast Bony 64' Gervinho 66'	–	Japan Honda 16'	2–1	Arena Pernambuco Attendance: 40,267
19 June	Colombia Rodríguez 64' Quintero 70'	–	Ivory Coast Gervinho 73'	2–1	Estádio Nacional de Brasília Attendance: 68,748
19 June	Japan	–	Greece	0–0	Arena das Dunas Attendance: 39,485
24 June	Japan Okazaki 45+1'	–	Colombia Cuadrado 18' pen. Martinez 55', 82' Rodríguez 89'	1–4	Arena Pantanal Attendance: 40,340
2 4 June	Greece Samaris 42' Samaras 90+3' pen.	–	Ivory Coast Bony 74'	2–1	Estádio Castelão Attendance: 59,095

	P	W	D	L	GD	Pts
Costa Rica	3	2	1	0	+3	7
Uruguay	3	2	0	1	+0	6
Italy	3	1	0	2	−1	3
England	3	0	1	2	−2	1

14 June	Uruguay – Cavani 24' pen.	Costa Rica Campbell 54' Duarte 57' Urena 84'	1–3	Estadio Castelão Attendance: 58,679
14 June	England – Sturridge 37'	Italy Marchisio 35' Balotelli 50'	1–2	Arena Amazônia Attendance: 39,800
19 June	Uruguay – Suárez 39', 85'	England Rooney 75'	2–1	Arena de São Paulo Attendance: 62,575
20 June	Italy –	Costa Rica Ruiz 44'	0–1	Arena Pernambuco Attendance: 40,285
24 June	Italy –	Uruguay Godin 81'	0–1	Arena das Dunas Attendance: 39,706
24 June	Costa Rica –	England	0–0	Estádio Mineirão Attendance: 57,823

	P	W	D	L	GD	Pts
France	3	2	1	0	+6	7
Switzerland	3	2	0	1	+1	6
Ecuador	3	1	1	1	0	4
Honduras	3	0	0	3	−7	0

15 June	Switzerland Mehmedi 48' Seferovic 90+3'	–	Ecuador E Valencia 22'	2–1	Estádio Nacional de Brasília Attendance: 68,351
15 June	France Benzema 45' pen. Valladares 48' OG	–	Honduras	3–0	Estádio Beira-Rio Attendance: 43,012
20 June	Switzerland Dzemaili 81' Xhaka 87'	–	France Giroud 17' Matuidi 18' Valbuena 40' Benzema 67' Sissoko 73'	2–5	Arena Fonte Nova Attendance: 51,003
20 June	Honduras Costly 31'	–	Ecuador E Valencia 34', 65'	1–2	Arena de Baixada Attendance: 39,224
25 June	Honduras	–	Switzerland Shaqiri 6', 31', 71'	0–3	Arena Amazônia Attendance: 40,322
25 June	Ecuador	–	France	0–0	Estádio do Maracanã Attendance: 73,749

	P	W	D	L	GD	Pts
Argentina	3	3	0	0	+3	9
Nigeria	3	1	1	1	0	4
Bosnia	3	1	0	2	0	3
Iran	3	0	1	2	−3	1

15 June	Argentina – Kolašinac 3' OG Messi 65'	Bosnia 2–1 Ibišević 84'	Estádio do Maracanã Attendance: 74,738
16 June	Iran –	Nigeria 0–0	Arena da Baixada Attendance: 39,081
21 June	Argentina – Messi 90+1'	Iran 1–0	Estádio Mineirão Attendance: 57,698
21 June	Nigeria – Odemwingie 29	Bosnia 1–0	Arena Pantanal Attendance: 40,499
25 June	Nigeria – Musa 4', 47'	Argentina 2–3 Messi 3', 45+1' Rojo 50	Estádio Beira-Rio Attendance: 43,285
25 June	Bosnia – Džeko 23' Pjanić 59' Vršajević 83'	Iran 3–1 Ghoochanne- jhad 82'	Arena Fonte Nova Attendance: 48,011

	P	W	D	L	GD	Pts
Germany	3	2	1	0	+5	7
USA	3	1	1	1	0	4
Portugal	3	1	1	1	−3	4
Ghana	3	0	1	2	−2	1

16 June	Germany Müller 12' pen., 45+1', 78' Hummels 32'	–	Portugal	4–0	Arena Fonte Nova Attendance: 51,081
16 June	Ghana A Ayew 82'	–	USA Dempsey 1' Brooks 86'	1–2	Arena das Dunas Attendance: 39,760
21 June	Germany Götze 51' Klose 71'	–	Ghana A Ayew 54' Gyan 63'	2–2	Estádio Castelão Attendance: 59,621
22 June	USA Jones 64' Dempsey 81'	–	Portugal Nani 5' Varela 90+5'	2–2	Arena Amazônia Attendance: 40,123
26 June	USA	–	Germany Müller 55'	0–1	Arena Pernambuco Attendance: 41,876
26 June	Portugal Boye 31' OG Ronaldo 80'	–	Ghana Gyan 57'	2–1	Estádio Nacional de Brasília Attendance: 67,450

	P	W	D	L	GD	Pts
Belgium	3	3	0	0	+3	9
Algeria	3	1	1	1	+1	4
Russia	3	0	2	1	−1	2
South Korea	3	0	1	2	−3	1

17 June   Belgium   –   Algeria   2–1   Estádio Mineirão
Fellaini 70'   Feghouli 25' pen.   Attendance: 56,800
Mertens 80'

17 June   Russia   –   South Korea   1–1   Arena Pantanal
Kerzjakov 74'   Lee Keun-Ho 68'   Attendance: 37,603

22 June   Belgium   –   Russia   1–0   Estádio do Maracanã
Origi 88'   Attendance: 73,819

22 June   South Korea   –   Algeria   2–4   Estádio Beira-Rio
Son Heung-min 50'   Slimani 26'   Attendance: 42,732
Koo Já-cheol 72'   Halliche 28'
Djabou 38'
Brahimi 62'

26 June   South Korea   –   Belgium   0–1   Arena de São Paulo
Vertonghen 78'   Attendance: 61,397

26 June   Algeria   –   Russia   1–1   Arena da Baixada
Slimani 60'   Kokorin 6'   Attendance: 39,311

28 June, Belo Horizonte

Brazil   1
Chile   1
Brazil win 4–3
on penalties

28 June, Rio de Janeiro

Colombia   2
Uruguay   0

4 July, Fortaleza

Brazil   2
Colombia   1

30 June, Brasília

France   2
Nigeria   0

8 July, Belo Horizonte

Brazil   1
Germany   7

30 June, Porto Alegre

Germany   2
Algeria   1
After extra time

4 July, Rio de Janeiro

France   0
Germany   1

FINAL

13 July, Rio de Janeiro

Germany   1
Argentina   0
After extra time

29 June, Fortaleza

Netherlands   2
Mexico   1

THIRD PLACE
PLAY-OFF

12 July, Brasília

Brazil   0
Netherlands   3

29 June, Recife

Costa Rica   1
Greece   1
Costa Rica win 5–3
on penalties

5 July, Salvador

Netherlands   0
Costa Rica   0
Netherlands win 4–3
on penalties

9 July, São Paulo

Netherlands   0
Argentina   0
Argentina win 2–4
on penalties

1 July, São Paulo

Argentina   1
Switzerland   0
After extra time

5 July, Brasília

Argentina   1
Belgium   0

1 July, Salvador

Belgium   2
USA   1
After extra time

28 June	Brazil	–	Chile	1–1	Estádio Mineirão
	Luiz 18'		Sánchez 32'		Attendance: 57,714
	Brazil win 4–3 on penalties				
	Luiz		Aránguiz		
	Marcelo		Diaz		
	Neymar				

28 June	Colombia	–	Uruguay	2–0	Estádio do Maracanã
	Rodríguez 28', 50'				Attendance: 73,804

29 June	Netherlands	–	Mexico	2–1	Estádio Castelão
	Sneijder 88'		Dos Santos 48'		Attendance: 58,817
	Huntelaar 90+4' pen.				

29 June	Costa Rica	–	Greece	1–1	Arena Pernambuco
	Ruiz 52'		Sokratis 90+1'		Attendance: 41,242
	Costa Rica win 6–4 on penalties				
	Borges		Mitroglou		
	Ruiz		Christodoulopoulos		
	González		Holebas		
	Campbell				
	Umana				

30 June	France	–	Nigeria	2–0	Estádio Nacional de
	Pogba 79'				Brasília
	Yobo 90+2' OG				Attendance: 67,882

30 June	Germany	–	Algeria	2–1	Estádio Beira-Rio
	Schürrle 92'		Djabou 120+1'		Attendance: 43,063
	Özil 120'				
	After extra time				

1 July	Argentina	–	Switzerland	1–0	Arena de São Paulo
	Di María 118'				Attendance: 63,225
	After extra time				

1 July	Belgium	–	USA	2–1	Arena Fonte Nova
	de Bruyne 93'		Green 107'		Attendance: 51,227
	Lukaku 105'				
	After extra time				

QUARTER-FINALS

4 July	Brazil Thiago Silva 7' David Luiz 69'	–	Colombia Rodríguez 80' pen.	2–1	Estádio Castelão Attendance: 60,342
4 July	France	–	Germany Hummels 13'	0–1	Estádio do Maracanã Attendance: 74,240
5 July	Netherlands Netherlands win 4–3 on penalties van Persie Robben Sneijder Kuyt	–	Costa Rica Borges González Bolaños	0–0	Arena Fonte Nova Attendance: 51,179
5 July	Argentina Higuaín 8'	–	Belgium	1–0	Estadio Nacional de Brasília Attendance: 68,551

SEMI-FINALS

8 July	Brazil Oscar 90'	–	Germany Müller 11' Klose 23' Kroos 24', 26' Khedira 29' Schürrle 69', 79'	1–7	Estádio Mineirão Attendance: 58,141
9 July	Netherlands Argentina win 2–4 on penalties Robben Kuyt	–	Argentina Messi Garay Agüero Rodríguez	0–0	Arena de São Paulo Attendance: 63,267

THIRD PLACE PLAY-OFF

12 July	Brazil	–	Netherlands van Persie 3' pen. Blind 17' Wijnaldum 90+1'	0–3	Estádio Nacional de Brasília Attendance: 68,034

FINAL

13 July	Germany Götze 113' After extra time	–	Argentina	1–0	Estádio do Maracanã Attendance: 74,738

TOP SCORERS

1. James Rodríguez, Colombia: 6 goals
2. Thomas Müller, Germany: 5 goals
3. Lionel Messi, Argentina; Neymar Jr, Brazil; Robin van Persie, Netherlands: 4 goals

ALL-STAR TEAM

Goalkeeper: Neuer, Germany
Defenders: de Vrij, Netherlands; Thiago Silva, Brazil; Hummels, Germany; Rojo,
   Argentina
Midfielders: Rodríguez, Colombia; Lahm, Germany; Kroos, Germany; Oscar, Brazil
Forwards: Müller, Germany; Robben, Netherlands

Golden Ball (best player): Lionel Messi, Argentina
Golden Boot (top scorer): James Rodríguez, Colombia
Golden Glove (best goalkeeper): Manuel Neuer, Germany
Young Player Award: Paul Pogba, France
FIFA Fair Play Trophy: Colombia

WORLD CUP STADIUMS

Belo Horizonte: Estádio Mineirão, capacity 58,170
Brasilia: Estádio Nacional de Brasília, capacity 69,349
Cuiabá: Arena Pantanal, capacity 41,112
Curitiba: Arena da Baixada, capacity 39,631
Fortaleza: Estádio Castelão, capacity 60,342
Manaus: Arena Amazônia, capacity 40,549
Natal: Arena das Dunas, capacity 39,971
Porto Alegre: Estádio Beira-Rio, capacity 43,394
Recife: Arena Pernambuco, capacity 42,610
Rio de Janeiro: Estádio do Maracanã, capacity 74,738
Salvador: Arena Fonte Nova, capacity 51,900
São Paulo: Arena de São Paulo, capacity 62,601